THE TEACHING FOR SOCIAL JUSTICE SERIES

William Ayers—*Series Editor*   Therese Quinn—*Associate Series Editor*

Humanizing Education for Immigrant and Refugee Youth: 20 Strategies for the Classroom and Beyond
MONISHA BAJAJ, DANIEL WALSH, LESLEY BARTLETT, & GABRIELA MARTÍNEZ

Child Care Justice: Transforming the System of Care for Young Children
MAURICE SYKES & KYRA OSTENDORF, EDS.

Rise for Racial Justice: How to Talk About Race With Schools and Communities
COLETTE N. CANN, KIMBERLY WILLIAMS BROWN, & MEREDITH MADDEN

Dignity-Affirming Education: Cultivating the Somebodiness of Students and Educators
DECOTEAU J. IRBY, CHARITY ANDERSON, & CHARLES M. PAYNE, EDS.

Where Is the Justice? Engaged Pedagogies in Schools and Communities
VALERIE KINLOCH, EMILY A. NEMETH, TAMARA T. BUTLER, & GRACE D. PLAYER

Teacher Educators as Critical Storytellers: Effective Teachers as Windows and Mirrors
ANTONIO L. ELLIS, NICHOLAS D. HARTLEP, GLORIA LADSON-BILLINGS, & DAVID O. STOVALL, EDS.

Surrendered: Why Progressives Are Losing the Biggest Battles in Education
KEVIN K. KUMASHIRO

Holler If You Hear Me, Comic Edition
GREGORY MICHIE & RYAN ALEXANDER-TANNER

Same as It Never Was: Notes on a Teacher's Return to the Classroom
GREGORY MICHIE

Spectacular Things Happen Along the Way: Lessons from an Urban Classroom, Second Edition
BRIAN D. SCHULTZ

Teaching with Conscience in an Imperfect World: An Invitation
WILLIAM AYERS

Worth Striking For: Why Education Policy Is Every Teacher's Concern (Lessons from Chicago)
ISABEL NUÑEZ, GREGORY MICHIE, & PAMELA KONKOL

Being Bad: My Baby Brother and the School-to-Prison Pipeline
CRYSTAL T. LAURA

Fear and Learning in America: Bad Data, Good Teachers, and the Attack on Public Education
JOHN KUHN

Deep Knowledge: Learning to Teach Science for Understanding and Equity
DOUGLAS B. LARKIN

Bad Teacher! How Blaming Teachers Distorts the Bigger Picture
KEVIN K. KUMASHIRO

Crossing Boundaries— Teaching and Learning with Urban Youth
VALERIE KINLOCH

The Assault on Public Education: Confronting the Politics of Corporate School Reform
WILLIAM H. WATKINS, ED.

Pedagogy of the Poor: Building the Movement to End Poverty
WILLIE BAPTIST & JAN REHMANN

Grow Your Own Teachers: Grassroots Change for Teacher Education
ELIZABETH A. SKINNER, MARIA TERESA GARRETÓN, & BRIAN D. SCHULTZ, EDS.

Girl Time: Literacy, Justice, and the School-to-Prison Pipeline
MAISHA T. WINN

Holler If You Hear Me: The Education of a Teacher and His Students, Second Edition
GREGORY MICHIE

Controversies in the Classroom: A Radical Teacher Reader
JOSEPH ENTIN, ROBERT C. ROSEN, & LEONARD VOGT, EDS.

The Seduction of Common Sense: How the Right Has Framed the Debate on America's Schools
KEVIN K. KUMASHIRO

Teach Freedom: Education for Liberation in the African-American Tradition
CHARLES M. PAYNE & CAROL SILLS STRICKLAND, EDS.

Social Studies for Social Justice: Teaching Strategies for the Elementary Classroom
RAHIMA C. WADE

THE TEACHING FOR SOCIAL JUSTICE SERIES, *continued*

Pledging Allegiance:
The Politics of Patriotism in America's Schools
JOEL WESTHEIMER, ED.

See You When We Get There:
Teaching for Change in Urban Schools
GREGORY MICHIE

Echoes of Brown: Youth Documenting and
Performing the Legacy of *Brown v. Board of
Education*
MICHELLE FINE

Writing in the Asylum: Student Poets in City
Schools
JENNIFER MCCORMICK

Teaching the Personal and the Political:
Essays on Hope and Justice
WILLIAM AYERS

Teaching Science for Social Justice
ANGELA CALABRESE BARTON ET AL.

Putting the Children First:
The Changing Face of Newark's Public Schools
JONATHAN G. SILIN & CAROL LIPPMAN, EDS.

Refusing Racism:
White Allies and the Struggle for Civil Rights
CYNTHIA STOKES BROWN

A School of Our Own: Parents, Power, and
Community at the East Harlem Block Schools
TOM RODERICK

The White Architects of Black Education:
Ideology and Power in America, 1865–1954
WILLIAM WATKINS

The Public Assault on America's Children:
Poverty, Violence, and Juvenile Injustice
VALERIE POLAKOW, ED.

Construction Sites: Excavating Race, Class, and
Gender Among Urban Youths
LOIS WEIS & MICHELLE FINE, EDS.

Walking the Color Line:
The Art and Practice of Anti-Racist Teaching
MARK PERRY

A Simple Justice:
The Challenge of Small Schools
WILLIAM AYERS, MICHAEL KLONSKY, &
GABRIELLE H. LYON, EDS.

Teaching for Social Justice:
A Democracy and Education Reader
WILLIAM AYERS, JEAN ANN HUNT, &
THERESE QUINN

Humanizing Education for Immigrant and Refugee Youth

20 Strategies for the Classroom and Beyond

Monisha Bajaj, Daniel Walsh, Lesley Bartlett,
and Gabriela Martínez

TEACHERS COLLEGE PRESS

TEACHERS COLLEGE | COLUMBIA UNIVERSITY
NEW YORK AND LONDON

Published by Teachers College Press®, 1234 Amsterdam Avenue, New York, NY 10027

Copyright © 2023 by Teachers College, Columbia University

Cover art by Favianna Rodriguez

Library of Congress Cataloging-in-Publication Data is available at loc.gov

ISBN 978-0-8077-6706-1 (paper)
ISBN 978-0-8077-6707-8 (hardcover)
ISBN 978-0-8077-8108-1 (ebook)

Printed on acid-free paper
Manufactured in the United States of America

Contents

Preface   ix

Acknowledgments   xiii

Introduction: Dimensions of Success for Immigrant
and Refugee Students   1

Profile of Ana   17
As Told to Gabriela Martínez

School Profile 1: Lincoln High School, Nebraska   19
Edmund T. Hamann With Lesley Bartlett

Profile of Ko   23
As Told to Gabriela Martínez

CATEGORY I: STRATEGIES FOR CLASSROOM AND INSTRUCTIONAL DESIGN

School Profile 2: The International High School at Prospect
Heights in Brooklyn, New York   26
Nedda de Castro and Daniel Walsh

Strategy 1: Utilize Translanguaging in English Language Development   31
Lesley Bartlett and Esther Bettney

Strategy 2: Honor Histories and Heritages   37
Monisha Bajaj

Strategy 3: Practice Purposeful Grouping   44
Lesley Bartlett

Strategy 4: Incorporate Differentiated Instruction and Universal Design for Learning   49
Lesley Bartlett and Monisha Bajaj

Strategy 5: Support Students With Limited and Interrupted Formal Education   55
Lisa Auslander With Daniel Walsh

Strategy 6: Undertake Holistic and Continuous Assessment   63
Monisha Bajaj

Strategy 7: Include Advisory Periods   70
Monisha Bajaj

Profile of Asmaa   76
As Told to Gabriela Martínez

CATEGORY II: STRATEGIES FOR SCHOOL DESIGN

School Profile 3: Wellstone International High School in Minneapolis, Minnesota   80
Laura Wangsness Willemsen and Lesley Bartlett

Strategy 8: Enact Democratic School Governance   85
Alexandra Anormaliza With Daniel Walsh

Strategy 9: Adopt Intentional Staffing   91
Daniel Walsh, Kathleen Rucker, Orubba Almansouri, and David Etienne

Strategy 10: Integrate Coaching for Culturally Responsive Teaching   97
Joanna Yip With Daniel Walsh

Strategy 11: Address School Language Policies   104
Esther Bettney and Lesley Bartlett

Strategy 12: Promote a Positive School Climate and Culture   111
Lesley Bartlett and Ariel Borns

Strategy 13: Emphasize Students' Health and Wellness   119
Monisha Bajaj and Sailaja Suresh

Strategy 14: Establish Dual Enrollment and Early College Programs   125
Daniel Walsh, Yvonne Ndiaye, and Asmaa Amadou

Profile of Miguel   132
As Told to Gabriela Martínez

CATEGORY III: STRATEGIES FOR EXTRACURRICULAR PROGRAMS, AND COMMUNITY AND ALUM PARTNERSHIPS

School Profile 4: Rudsdale Newcomer High School in Oakland, California   136
Monisha Bajaj and Emma Batten-Bowman

Strategy 15: Provide After-School and Summer Programming   141
Lesley Bartlett and Mary Mendenhall

Strategy 16: Involve Families   147
Monisha Bajaj

Strategy 17: Offer Legal Services   154
Monisha Bajaj

Strategy 18: Develop Community Partnerships for Social Support and Civic Engagement   160
Lesley Bartlett and Claudia M. Triana

Strategy 19: Implement Internships and Career Preparation Programs   167
Dariana Castro With Daniel Walsh

Strategy 20: Engage Alum in Schools and Community Building   174
Monisha Bajaj and Gabriela Martínez

Profile of Shaheen   179
As Told to Gabriela Martínez

Conclusion   181

Appendix: Additional Resources and Video Playlist   183

Glossary of Key Terms   184

Notes   188

References   190

Index   213

About the Authors and the Contributors   221

Preface

In the past few years, newcomer students, their families, and their teachers have witnessed three presidential administrations with different approaches (and corresponding rhetoric) toward immigration, deportation, asylum practices, and refugee admission and resettlement. These larger policies are reflected in the experiences of individuals we interviewed during our research. Our goal in this book is to highlight the vision, commitment, and resourcefulness of educators, students, and administrators in schools that find ways to foster achievement, agency, and engagement for immigrant and refugee youth, even within systems that are often labeled broken beyond repair, and amidst larger exclusionary discourses.

The lessons and examples included in this book are drawn from educators and schools that we authors have come into contact with either personally or through the literature, with heavy reliance on schools in California's Bay Area, New York City, and the Midwest, where our collective research and work has been focused over the past decades.

Monisha Bajaj and Lesley Bartlett met in the early 2000s, when both were faculty members at Teachers College, Columbia University. Monisha and Gabriela ("Gaby") Martínez met in 2015 at Oakland International High School (OIHS), a public high school for newcomer immigrant and refugee youth that is part of the Internationals Network for Public Schools (INPS).[1] In 2015, Gaby, who was an alum of OIHS, was working at the school part-time while in college, and Monisha was carrying out research at the school. Daniel ("Danny") Walsh was a teacher, team leader, and instructional coach at the International High School at Prospect Heights in Brooklyn, New York, and served as school leader of the International High School at Union Square in New York City. He also served as the director of multilingual learners for the borough of Manhattan with the New York City Department of Education before joining the teaching faculty at the University of Wisconsin–Madison. Monisha and Lesley both coauthored separate articles on their research with immigrant and refugee youth for a special issue of the *Theory Into Practice* journal in 2018 that Danny coedited, and the three have been connected as colleagues since then (Bajaj & Suresh, 2018; Jaffe-Walter et al., 2018; Mendenhall & Bartlett, 2018).

Gaby was born in 1992, the same year the 13-year civil war in El Salvador ended and in which an estimated 75,000 people were killed; the United States spent over $1 billion in aid during the war to support government and security forces that committed over 85% of the abuses, such as torture and killings of civilians (Samway et al., 2020). Gaby migrated to the United States in 2009 with her parents and brother, sponsored by her uncle who had lived in Oakland for many years. Her parents' primary motivation in migrating was to provide their children with better educational opportunities. Gaby spoke very little English when she arrived in the United States, and her cousin recommended OIHS as a good school for her. Arriving in April of the school year, she was placed in the 10th grade. She took intensive summer school and, with the support of teachers and through her own dedication, she graduated from OIHS in 2011 at the age of 18 with all of her statewide requirements—including, at that time, a statewide high school exit exam offered only in English. Gaby enrolled in San Francisco State University and completed her bachelor of arts degree in international relations in 2016. After graduation, she was hired to work full-time at Oakland International High School as the administrative assistant in the office.

Monisha—a child of immigrants from India and grandchild of refugees of the violent partition of India and Pakistan in 1947 that displaced some 15 million people and caused the death of at least 1 million (see Ansari, 2017)—grew up as a second-generation South Asian American in California's Bay Area. Her father migrated to the United States to pursue higher education in 1969—an opportunity afforded by the passage of historic immigration law in 1965 by then-President Lyndon B. Johnson, responding to demands from the civil rights movement, that reversed the racist immigration quota system. From 1965 to 1970, immigration to the United States from Asia quadrupled (Hing, 2004; E. Lee, 2019). Monisha, already familiar with the Internationals Schools model from her time as a professor in New York (and having previously worked as an after-school teacher in a newcomer school in the Bronx during graduate school), in 2014 began a multi-year research collaboration with OIHS along with two colleagues (Amy Argenal and Melissa Canlas) from the University of San Francisco. The action ethnography project included running an after-school human rights club at OIHS weekly for 2 years. Having spent more than 2 decades as an educator and education researcher in the United States and internationally, Monisha was inspired by the work of OIHS and other newcomer programs in the Bay Area that the project expanded to include (Bajaj, Argenal, & Canlas, 2017; Bajaj & Bartlett, 2017; Bajaj, Canlas, & Argenal, 2017; Bajaj & Suresh, 2018; Bajaj & Tow, 2021).

Lesley is an anthropologist of education whose work has focused on questions of migration, multilingualism, and educational equity. Born in a white working-class family in western North Carolina, as a student and later as a teacher and researcher in the state, Lesley was struck by the social and political tensions that accompanied the influx of immigrants, primarily from Mexico and Central America, many of whom accepted low-wage positions in agriculture, textile and furniture plants, and chicken and pig processing plants in the state beginning in the 1980s (Holland et al., 2007; Murillo, 2002; Villenas, 2002). While at university, she was inspired by the ideas and work of Paulo Freire, who revolutionized thinking about the purposes and possibilities of education. Later, she went to study how teachers in youth and adult literacy programs in Brazil understood, adapted, and implemented his political pedagogy (Bartlett, 2005). Subsequently, she moved to New York City. There, with renowned scholar Ofelia García, she conducted a 4-year study of a bilingual high school for newcomer immigrant youth (Bartlett & García, 2011). With Drs. Mary Mendenhall and Ameena Ghaffar-Kucher, Lesley later conducted a study with immigrant and refugee youth from schools across New York City, examining what the students identified as crucial supports (Bartlett et al., 2017; Mendenhall et al., 2017) and detailing the importance of a transnational lens on culture and curriculum (Bajaj & Bartlett, 2017; Bartlett et al., 2017).

Danny's teaching, research, and scholarship in immigrant and refugee education can be traced to his own connections to immigrant New York City. The great grandchild of European émigrés, Danny was born into a working-class family in Queens, New York, one of the most linguistically and culturally diverse counties in the United States. As part of the white flight from the city in the late 1970s, his family moved to a nearby Long Island suburb. Always interested in language, culture, power, and pedagogy, he studied teaching English to speakers of other languages and taught English in Ecuador while a master's student. He began teaching immigrant youth learning English in New York City in 2000 and shortly thereafter, both entered a doctoral program in urban education and became a founding English as a Second Language (ESL)/English teacher at the International High School at Prospect Heights. As a doctoral student, he employed participatory action research methodologies to explore how immigrant adolescents learning English make sense of the cultural, political, racial, linguistic, and economic landscape in a global city like New York (see Jaffe-Walter et al., 2018; S. Lee & Walsh, 2013, 2015, 2016, 2017; Walsh, 2018).

In 2019, discussions began among the authors about the need for a practical resource for educators, school leaders, and social service providers with sociopolitically/culturally congruent and humanizing practices for educating newcomer immigrant and refugee youth. Thus was born the idea for this book focused on 20 strategies through which newcomer immigrant and refugee students can thrive. This book draws on our perspectives collectively as immigrants or children of immigrants/refugees, educators, school leaders, and/or researchers.

We are also joined in this book by several colleagues who work as district officials, school leaders, educators, and/or were newcomer students themselves.[2] More information about these individuals, who form an integral part of the authorship team of this book, is provided at the back of the book in the About the Authors and the Contributors section. In this book, you will be introduced to students, alum educators, administrators, and school communities. We hope that you find insight, new ideas, and inspiration in these pages for the work of making schools sites of welcome, learning, and possibility for immigrant and refugee-origin students.

Acknowledgments

This book was truly a collaborative effort of so many individuals: those who contributed to the book; those who advised us on the content, approach, and process; and those who cheered us on along the way. We thank series coeditor Bill Ayers for encouraging and supporting this book, and Sarah Biondello, Rachel Banks, Emily Spangler, Sue Liddicoat, and Brian Ellerbeck at Teachers College Press for their support and bearing with us as this project's shape shifted many times during the pandemic. We express our gratitude to Tatyana Kleyn for helping us shape the manuscript to better reach its intended audience and to Favianna Rodriguez for permission to use the image that appears on the cover. Jazzmin Gota provided essential support in the formatting of the manuscript as well as in the creation of the companion website.

In California, Gaby and Monisha thank the following individuals who generously gave of their time and knowledge: Sailaja Suresh, Nate Dunstan, Lauren Markham, Madenh Ali Hassan, Raquel Franker, Jizabel Navarrete, Veronica García, Carmelita Reyes, Tom Felix, Nicole Knight, Emma Batten-Bowman, Nina Rabin, and Rocio Reyes. A small grant from the Spencer Foundation and funding from the University of San Francisco (a Jesuit Foundation Research Grant and Faculty Development Funds) supported much of the California-based research that is presented in the book.

Monisha: I thank the many folks who brainstormed with me about this project, particularly in its initial stages and as it morphed over the 5 years it took to complete it. I send a special shout-out to the Rockefeller Bellagio Thematic Residency (2017) participants who helped seed and nourish this idea, especially Anna Penido, John and Angela Rickford, Laurentien van Oranje-Nassau, Esra'a Al Shafei, Khary Lazarre-White, Henry De Sio, Aya Chebbi, Novuyo Tshuma, Ananya Kabir, and Kiran Gandhi. Members of my "brain trust" and writing groups also helped provide support, insights, and a listening ear throughout the process: Chitra Aiyar, Rajeev Bajaj, Colette Cann, Andrea Chandrasekher, Michele Hamilton, Maria Hantzopoulos, Brooke Harris-Garad, Malathi Iyengar, Nidhi Kohli, Sangita Kumar, Trisha Moquino, Kiruba Murugaiah, Genevieve Negrón-Gonzales, Mona Puri, Carolyn Sattin-Bajaj, Roozbeh Shirazi, Nisha Varia, Hakim Williams, Dana Wright, and Zeena Zakharia. I'm also grateful to my amazing collaborators on this project: Lesley Bartlett, Danny Walsh, Gaby Martínez, and all our wonderful coauthors of the school profiles and strategies. The supportive environment at the University of San Francisco contributed to this project, and I express particular thanks to Amy Argenal, Rick Ayers, Patrick Camangian, Melissa Canlas, Sarah Capitelli, David Donahue, Emma Fuentes, Rosa Jiménez, Susan Katz, Shabnam Koirala-Azad, Danfeng Koon, and Christine Yeh. I offer special thanks to my family (especially Bikku Kuruvila, our little one Kabir, and Asha and Dinesh Bajaj) for their support, encouragement, and understanding of the time this project required.

Danny: This project was a homecoming for me, and I'm indebted to Monisha Bajaj and Lesley Bartlett for their gracious invitation to join. After 20 years in New York City and working in its public schools, I took a leap of faith and joined the Education Policy Studies Department at the University of Wisconsin–Madison; I read Monisha and Lesley's invitation as a sign that the universe was caring for me. The project became a homecoming because it returned me to friends and colleagues I had met as many as 18 years ago, a number of whom were part of the team that initiated and developed the International High School at Prospect Heights, and others I met along my journey. I'm infinitely thankful for their enthusiasm to reveal their lives and memories for this project. Alexandra Anormaliza and Nedda de Castro were founding school leaders, and no one else could have provided the insight they do in the school profile and strategy that feature the school's governance and instructional practices. Dariana Castro conceived and supported the school's internship program while Joanna Yip was an English teacher, college advisor, and instructional coach; they possess incomparable insight into the complex lives of immigrant and refugee youth. Similarly, Kathleen Rucker, Orubba Almansouri, and David Etienne, educators at a sister school in New York City, deftly describe how they have instituted a program that purposely hires the school's graduates as cultural workers. Lisa Auslander and I became acquainted as we codeveloped professional learning as part of the implementation of state and federal education policies, and she's now a foremost authority on instructional matters for students with limited/interrupted formal education. And, finally, my former students and coresearchers Asmaa Amadou and Yvonne Ndiaye still awe and inspire me with what they have become and how they reflect upon our time together in a dual enrollment program. I thank them all for jumping in with me and reminding me of what it means to be both human and humanizing!

Lesley: Working on this project has provided a joyous opportunity to revisit previous projects; read the phenomenal work that has been published in the past decade on migration, education, language policy and pedagogy, and translanguaging; discuss new ideas with brilliant coauthors; and learn more about the amazing and inventive work being done by educators across the country to bend schools toward equity for multilingual immigrant students. I'm grateful to my colleagues in the School of Education and specifically the Department of Educational Policy Studies at University of Wisconsin–Madison for sharing readings and insights, and to the university for the gift of time in the form of a sabbatical.

Gaby: I am very grateful for having had the opportunity and the honor to participate in this incredible project alongside amazing people who are knowledgeable about the subject. I extend a special thanks to Monisha Bajaj for her unconditional support and guidance all throughout. Working on this project has helped me recognize and learn about the value and the importance of the support that many educators and institutions provide to newcomer students like myself. That is why I want to give a special thanks and recognize all of my teachers, colleagues, and friends at OIHS. I have witnessed your enormous commitment and love toward all of your students and the community. It is thanks to your dedication and unconditional support toward all of us that accomplishments like this one can be possible. I also recognize all of the alum that I had the opportunity to interview for this project. It was an honor to get to know and learn from each and every one of you. To my family and Juan Colin, I say thank you for your unconditional love and support.

Introduction
Dimensions of Success for Immigrant and Refugee Students

Across the world, there is general consensus that going to school is a basic human right of all children, including those who are immigrants and refugees. This was not always true historically, when in previous eras access to school was limited to members of certain genders; racial, ethnic, or religious groups; social classes; or those favored by a colonial or ruling power. However, access to school doesn't always mean that children are receiving anything of value once there. In fact, scholars have discussed how schools can be places where students learn to reject their own communities based on biases (hidden or explicit) in the curriculum and pedagogy (Anyon, 1980; Bourdieu & Passeron, 1977; Giroux & Penna, 1979).

At their best, schools can open up students to new worlds, new ideas, and new possibilities. And, especially for immigrant and refugee children, schools can help them dream beyond their past and present realities—oftentimes realities that have been traumatic enough to spur their migration—to envision a future that transcends current structures of inequality and exclusion.

In the United States, while unequal and disparate education has been a legacy, freedom schools during the civil rights movement and other community-based educational efforts (Kelley, 2002; Payne, 1995), alongside demands for integration and access to higher-quality education, have sought to offer students from marginalized groups possibilities for greater self-determination and socioeconomic mobility. While some of these efforts have been assimilationist, particularly toward new immigrants, and draw on deficit theories about the communities that students come from, others have emphasized "additive" and sociopolitically/culturally congruent, relevant, and sustaining approaches alongside high-quality education aimed at developing the whole child (Bajaj, Argenal, & Canlas, 2017; Bartlett & García, 2011; Gay, 2000; Ladson-Billings, 1995a, 1995b; Paris & Alim, 2017; Tate, 1995; Yosso, 2005).

One out of every four students in the United States is from an immigrant family (either immigrants themselves or the children of immigrants) (National Academies of Sciences, Engineering, & Medicine, 2015). Public schooling—often the first point of contact immigrant families have with a government institution after migrating—continues to be a site of contestation and debate. Questions about public schooling include the following:

1

- Who should run schools?
- What should be taught?
- How should teachers be prepared to work with immigrant and refugee students?
- How can educators best support students' language development?
- What forms of assessment and accountability ought to be utilized?

Inherent in the enterprise of public education in the United States is a foundational dilemma: While schooling is perhaps the only economic and social right that *all* children have access to (whether rich or poor, documented or not, and regardless of race, gender, sexuality, or religion), the model of school financing linked to property taxes results in a highly unequal and stratified system of education. For example, a 2019 report found that predominantly white school districts in the United States have received $23 billion more in public funding than districts that are comprised primarily of students of color (EdBuild, 2019).

Perhaps not unique to the United States but symptomatic of the inequalities in public education, where there is most need there are often the *fewest* resources and the most inexperienced teachers, particularly in schools with high numbers of students of color, newcomer immigrant and refugee students, and students living in poverty (Darling-Hammond, 2000). Indeed, immigrant students "are vastly more likely than their peers to live in poverty, . . . to attend under-resourced and ethnically segregated schools, and to experience other factors that have been associated with academic risk in U.S. schooling contexts" (Sadowski, 2013, p. 1).

Despite the many structural challenges teachers and schools face (see, e.g., Ayers et al., 2018; Fishman, 2021; Markham, 2017; Seilstad, 2021; Thorpe, 2017), educators and schools across the nation and globe are helping students transform their realities through innovative curricula, pedagogy, and school practices, as well as holistic and humanizing approaches. This book seeks to understand how this happens and to document what lessons emerge from a closer look at such efforts in the United States. Certain school districts are also innovating with staffing and districtwide programs to adequately meet the needs of newly arrived immigrant and refugee students (see, e.g., Santos et al., 2018; Umansky et al., 2018). By looking at these innovative efforts for newcomer students, we can derive strategies that can be tailored, adapted, and localized, as this book seeks to inspire.

CENTERING IMMIGRANT AND REFUGEE STUDENTS

In the United States, immigrants make up 14.4% of the population (Migration Policy Institute, 2020), and in some states such as New York and California, nearly 30% of the population is foreign-born. A quarter of the nation, some 78 million people, are immigrants or U.S.-born children of immigrants (National Academies of Sciences, Engineering, & Medicine, 2015). While the teaching force (some four million educators strong) is predominantly white (80%), the U.S. public school population is roughly 49% white (down from 61% white in the year 2000), 15% Black, 26% Latinx,[1] and 5% Asian American/Pacific Islander (the remaining 5% being Native

American or multiracial) (Loewus, 2017; National Center for Education Statistics, 2021). These demographic shifts impact who is in our schools and the widening mismatch between the backgrounds of educators and the students they serve.

Newcomer immigrant and refugee youth who are labeled as English learners (ELs) have some of the highest dropout rates of all students in the United States (up to 40%, compared to 20% for the general U.S. student population) given their higher poverty levels, developing English proficiency, and other obstacles to persistence in school through high school graduation (Sugarman, 2015, 2019). Among Latinx students, there exists a wide gap in the dropout rate for U.S.-born students (11% dropout rate) as compared to foreign-born Latinx students (34% dropout rate) (Lukes, 2015). Of course, the term *dropout* is often a misnomer; many students (disproportionately students of color) who are labeled "dropouts" are actually "pushed out" of systems that have failed them (Morris, 2018).

Few teachers—whether pre- or in-service—receive sufficient training on how to best meet the needs of immigrant and refugee students. Innovative approaches have been developed and must be shared and expanded in order to effectively educate students, particularly those who are migrants themselves or children of immigrants and refugees. Additionally, the forces of nativism and xenophobia in policy and public discourse require teachers to equip themselves and their students to critically understand the larger social context and determine how to collectively engage. One teacher we talked to for this research remarked that her school had had an influx of hundreds of newcomer students (mostly unaccompanied minors from Central America) over the past few years, yet not a single teacher on staff at her school spoke Spanish. Our education system is woefully underprepared to meet the needs of the students entering it. This book offers concrete strategies for educators, administrators, after-school providers, and researchers working with immigrant and refugee youth.

We present 20 humanizing strategies derived from public schools serving immigrant and refugee youth (with many strategies that could also be applied to immigrant-origin students and students of color broadly). These strategies look not just at achievement, but at how to cultivate the collective agency and academic and civic engagement of young people who are recent migrants. We also include case studies of schools that work with newcomer students, to offer an insider glimpse into the ways in which school and instructional design strategies come to life in practice; we also highlight the voices of several alum throughout the book. We focus on examples from the United States, though there are lessons in this book for many international contexts as well.

"Success" in the schools we examine is not based on quantitative test scores, but instead relies on a more holistic demonstration of mastery and competency of knowledge and skills that are useful, relevant, and foundational for students' future aspirations. We define success broadly in this book. Drawing from Michael Sadowski's (2013) research with adolescent immigrants, we believe it is important for students to

1. "form strong bonds with teachers and know when, where, and how to ask for help"; and

2. "draw upon their languages and cultures of origin as assets and complements to the learning of English (and to learning *in* English), using both cultures in ways that are 'additive' rather than 'subtractive'" (pp. 2–3).

Further, we add that humanizing education oriented toward holistic success can allow students to

3. develop proficiency in academic and life skills that facilitate postsecondary (post-high school) transitions to further education or into the labor market within the United States, in their country of origin, or elsewhere;
4. become equipped with the skills, tools, and opportunities to deal with past and current trauma in culturally congruent ways; and
5. have opportunities to cultivate and practice local and transnational civic engagement toward social justice, whether in pan-immigrant collectives, in their diasporic communities, or in cross-racial coalitions and social movements.

We see these five broad criteria as constituting holistic success for newcomer immigrant and refugee students, particularly in North America and Europe, where students must work to succeed amidst legacies of exclusion and historic and contemporary xenophobia fueled by anti-immigrant policy and rhetoric.

EDUCATIONAL HISTORIES IN THE UNITED STATES

In the United States and globally, education has been both an institution to dominate and assimilate and a site in and through which communities seek greater freedom and opportunity. During slavery in the United States, enslaved people subversively sought out education and literacy—both of which were outlawed. As a corrective to this disenfranchisement, in the early part of the Reconstruction era (1865–1877), the Freedmen's Bureau established more than 1,000 schools for Black children in the U.S. South (Goldberg, 2007). Amidst the backlash to the racial progress of Reconstruction, the 1896 *Plessy v. Ferguson* case upheld "separate but equal" schooling that—counter to its catchphrase—was far from equal. Not until the 1947 *Mendez v. Westminster* Supreme Court case fighting against the segregation of Latinx children in California, and the subsequent 1954 *Brown v. Board of Education* case seeking to dismantle the segregation of Black children, were schools legally required to integrate (though many sought alternative means to maintain segregation).

In the 1800s and 1900s, public education, particularly in the Northern states, sought to "Americanize" newly arrived immigrant children from Europe. While people tend to think the U.S. immigrant population has grown in recent years, the highest proportion of immigrants vis-à-vis the entire national population actually dates back to 1890, at 14.8% (current estimates are slightly lower, at 14.4%).

National efforts were undertaken to "assimilate" the millions of newly arriving European immigrant children (very few children from elsewhere arrived during these periods, given severely restrictive immigration laws for non-European countries). By 1918, every state required children to complete an elementary school education as part of these efforts (Tyack, 1976).

While immigration from Europe soared without restriction, the 1882 Chinese Exclusion Act barred the immigration and naturalization of Chinese migrants, followed in 1917 by the "Asiatic Barred Zone Act," which excluded entrants from as far west as Turkey and as far east as the Polynesian islands. The 1921 Immigration Act set up a quota system by national origin; unsurprisingly, given the xenophobia and nativism dominant in national policy at that time, 99.8% of visas to the United States were allotted to migrants from Northern, Western, Southern, and Eastern Europe in the years that followed (Samway et al., 2020). Not until the Luce-Celler Act of 1946 were Asian immigrants granted expanded, but still limited, access to immigration and the opportunity to become naturalized citizens. In 1965, Congress passed and President Lyndon B. Johnson signed the Immigration and Nationality Act—emerging from the demands of civil rights activists and reformers—which finally removed the racist quotas and restrictions that had long been in place for immigration from Asia, the Middle East, sub-Saharan Africa, and Latin America and the Caribbean (E. Lee, 2019).

Turning to the experiences of Native American children, from 1860 through the 1970s, many were forced into off-reservation boarding schools as a strategy of assimilation and domination, forbidding them from speaking their languages and engaging in their cultural practices, and often subjecting them to violence in these school settings (Lomawaima, 1993; Lomawaima & McCarty, 2006). In recent decades, efforts have sought to reclaim languages in part due to the violent erasure imposed by residential schools; for example, the Keres Children's Learning Center and the Indigenous Montessori Institute in New Mexico offer "culturally sustaining" forms of Indigenous education and language revitalization for children, youth, and educators (Moquino & Blum Martínez, 2017; Paris & Alim, 2017).

Decades past these discriminatory national policies and landmark Supreme Court decisions, there has been mixed progress in education vis-à-vis desegregation and equalization of resources and outcomes across diverse racial groups in the United States (Rooks, 2020). For example, high school completion rates vary across groups, with recent data showing a 74% high school completion rate for Native Americans as compared to 80% for Black Americans, 82% for Latinx Americans, 89% for white Americans, and 93% for Asian Americans and Pacific Islanders (National Center for Education Statistics, 2021). An additional obstacle to high school completion is that some schools deny immigrant and refugee students equal access to education because of their age at the time of arrival (Napolitano, 2021).

Earlier theories of immigration and education primarily focused on the experiences of European immigrants to the United States in the 1800s and 1900s as a template for all students, (falsely) emphasizing a linear path to assimilation for the creation, in part through schooling, of a "white, de-ethnicized American" (Fass, 1989; Tyack, 1967). More recently, scholars have challenged classical assimilation theories as conformist, racially biased, and limited (Alba & Nee,

2003; Glazer & Moynihan, 1963). Segmented assimilation theory (Portes & Zhou, 1993) posits that immigrants and their children may experience diverse trajectories depending on factors such as context of reception, family structure, education, and community support. According to this theory, immigrant-origin students may tend toward "successful assimilation," as per older models; negative forms of assimilation, such as through joining gangs; or "selective acculturation," where attitudes and practices of the home culture are maintained while the second generation slowly integrates (Portes & Zhou, 1993). Subsequent work has refined the theory, recognizing the structural barriers of racism, poverty, documentation status, segregation of racially diverse immigrants from the 1960s onward, and the underfunding of urban schools that many immigrant students face upon arrival to the United States (S. Rodriguez, 2020; Waters et al., 2010; Zhou, 1997; Zhou & Gonzalez, 2019).

It is clear that new models are required for understanding the realities and experiences of newcomer immigrant and refugee youth—many of whom come to the United States as unaccompanied minors, pursue work while also in school, and engage in various forms of transnational civic engagement via social media and diasporic community networks. Additionally, in the post–World War II period until the present, many immigrants to the United States have fled nations that have been ravaged by war and violence directly *caused* by U.S. foreign policy overseas: for example, U.S. aid to right-wing forces in El Salvador in the 1980s, U.S. support for the coup in Honduras in 2009, and U.S. and Saudi involvement in the Yemeni civil war—which together have claimed hundreds of thousands of lives. These complexities require new theories and understandings of how immigrant and refugee students and their families engage with institutions, such as schools, in the United States as well as how they continue to live their lives in local and transnational settings (Walia, 2021).

The intersection of migration and education produces a wide range of outcomes based on factors such as socioeconomic class, reasons for migration, race/ethnicity, language, authorization status, religion, gender and gender identity, sexual orientation, ability, type of schooling, levels of violence in the neighborhoods in which immigrants settle, debts owed for the migration journey, and more. Education continues to be sought out by immigrant and refugee families for the opportunity it can provide for social and economic mobility; unfortunately, too often, the education of immigrant and immigrant-origin students stresses assimilation and a "one-size-fits-all" approach to socialization into an "American way of life" (Saenz et al., 2007). Recent research has emphasized transnationalism and has documented more progressive approaches to responsive schooling for immigrants (Bajaj & Bartlett, 2017; Dyrness, 2021; Dyrness & Abu El-Haj, 2020; S. Lee & Walsh, 2017; Macleod, 2021; Oliveira, 2018; Turner & Mangual Figueroa, 2019). Education scholars have shown that the development of a critical consciousness and pride in their heritage can result in strong civic identities as well as academic achievement for immigrant and immigrant-origin students (Bajaj, Canlas, & Argenal, 2017; Dyrness & Abu El-Haj, 2020; Ginwright & Cammarota, 2007; Quinn & Nguyen, 2017; Rubin, 2007). Building from these perspectives, schools can serve as safe spaces for immigrant and refugee students (and their families) to seek out information, receive support, expand opportunity, and navigate their new society (Patel, 2013; S. Rodriguez, Monreal, & Howard, 2020).

INSIGHTS FROM SCHOLARSHIP ON
IMMIGRATION AND EDUCATION

Make Schooling Relevant

To be sure, education is a political project of the nation-state, and situated at the intersection of schools and communities lies a contested space in which social movements have long sought equity and justice. When unable to secure it within the system, communities have found ways to offer culturally sustaining and affirming education to their communities outside of the formal education system (e.g., the citizenship schools run during the civil rights movement in the U.S. South to politically empower Black communities). Communities of color in the United States have demanded what scholar Gloria Ladson-Billings (1995b) terms "culturally relevant pedagogy" as a "pedagogy of opposition . . . committed to collective, not merely individual, empowerment as well as academic success" (p. 160). Cultural relevance in schooling has also been explored for various ethnic groups in the United States. For example, studies highlight various forms of relevance for youth, including the incorporation of ethnic studies curricula (Otero & Cammarota, 2011), the integration of students' and families' funds of knowledge (Moll et al., 1992), and the recognition of "community cultural wealth" by schools (detailed later in this Introduction) (Yosso, 2005).

Further development of the tenets of culturally relevant pedagogy has led to other conceptualizations such as culturally responsive teaching (Gay, 2000), culturally sustaining pedagogies (Paris, 2012; Paris & Alim, 2017), and for immigrant youth particularly, what S. Lee and Walsh (2017) term "socially just, culturally sustaining pedagogy," as well as what Bajaj, Argenal, and Canlas (2017) have termed "socio-politically relevant pedagogy." These approaches encourage educators to offer newcomer youth tools to analyze their own social location and experiences, as well as the distinctions between school requirements and authentic learning vis-à-vis their future aspirations. Such strategic learning provides students a chance to "understand inequalities on a global scale—both in their positioning in their home countries in addition to being recent migrants living oftentimes in under-resourced communities in the United States—and to historicize their realities in ways that suggest opportunities for solidarity with other immigrants and communities of color" (Bajaj, Argenal, & Canlas, 2017, p. 260).

Acknowledge Transnational Connections and Futures

Immigrant students and families have long been seen in scholarship and policy, and by service-providers, as being on a linear trajectory that ends with resettlement and assimilation into the United States (e.g., Fass, 1989). What we know, particularly with those whose authorization to be in the United States may be impermanent and tenuous, is that the lived realities of transnational youth and families are often much more complex. Migration, return migration, family separation, and ethnic networks that span multiple countries shape how youth imagine and prepare for their futures (Kleyn, 2017, 2021; Oliveira, 2018). Recent scholarship has emphasized how youth consider their educational trajectories and the ways in which schools and educators need to help prepare them for their multidirectional possible futures (Bajaj & Bartlett, 2017; Bartlett & Oliveira, 2018; Dyrness & Abu El-Haj, 2020).

The opportunity to cultivate home languages can serve as one factor in preparing students for multiple pathways during and after high school. Through translanguaging and efforts to continue to develop their home language practices (García & Kleyn, 2016), alongside learning English, students maintain opportunities to pursue, in the future, professional opportunities as well as personal relationships in their countries of origin. Another way that educators can support students who may have diverse future pathways (such as full-time or part-time tertiary education, or paid work in the United States or elsewhere) is by enriching the curriculum with a focus on issues and competencies beyond the United States (e.g., Bartlett & García, 2011). For example, in the Gregorio Luperón High School for newcomer Latinx students in New York City, teachers develop curricula that link issues in the home country to standards and content in the United States for completing high school requirements:

> In a Luperón social studies class, after discussing the civil rights movement in the U.S., students were asked to critically discuss the treatment of people of Haitian descent in their hometowns in the Dominican Republic, which led to contrasting experiences of those at the border to those in resort areas and those in bigger cities. Teachers were careful not to assume that students' lack of knowledge of American history meant the students didn't know history. Instead, they encouraged students to draw upon and compare what they had learned in their previous educational experiences, and they incorporated specific students' life stories when discussing contemporary events. (Bajaj & Bartlett, 2017, p. 32)

By drawing parallels between issues across borders, educators can help build a sense of critical global and transnational citizenship that allows immigrant students to feel connected to what they are learning, and to find relevance and meaning in their studies (Dyrness & Abu El-Haj, 2020).

College and guidance counselors often direct students toward traditional professional pathways, encouraging 2- or 4-year colleges based on grades, test scores, and other perceptions of the student being counseled. Recent literature on immigrant youth has documented what has been a long-recognized practice of guidance counselors to dampen students' aspirations. For example, a Muslim participant in Shapiro's (2018) study reported that her teachers "assumed she was not likely to attend college, because she is the oldest female in a large family. 'You're just going to get married,' one teacher chided. Madina said that this message was given to 'a lot of students from my culture'" (p. 335). While some assumptions could be based on experiences with previous students (e.g., girls who may not pursue higher education because of getting married in their teens) and perhaps unfairly generalized to others from that group, other studies show that such assumptions undermine students' agency, dehumanize them, and disregard the complexity of their lives. In her study of adolescent newcomer girls from West Africa in New York, Bangura (2014) finds that marriage during or after high school actually *enabled* young women's pursuit of higher education, because it often provided a stable income source for them and allayed parents' fears about girls being "corrupted" by U.S. culture and norms if they were unmarried and off at college on their own. Other pathways to opportunities in the labor market in the United States, in home countries, or in other countries may also be in store for newcomer students—all of which necessitate good listening skills on the part of school staff and appropriate and open-minded advice for the multiple postsecondary pathways students may embark upon.

Foster Strong Relationships

The ultimate aim of caring educators and schools is to foster strong relationships within a school between students and educators, and among students themselves. In fact, scholars of immigration and education have found that strong relationships are essential for student success. In their foundational book detailing the findings from a longitudinal study with more than 600 newcomer immigrant adolescents, Carola Suárez-Orozco, Marcelo Suárez-Orozco, and Irina Todorova (2008) report that

> Positive relationships with peers and caring adults at school are associated with many positive outcomes for students: they become more social, motivated, academically competent, and high achieving; they are more likely to attend school regularly; and they become more academically engaged. (pp. 44–45)

The authors term this aspect of their findings "relational engagement," or "the extent to which students feel connected to their teachers, peers, and others in their schools" (p. 43). Their study found that the strength of relationships directly correlated to students' academic achievement.

Teachers also serve as important role models, mentors, and translators of different cultural and professional norms for students; in fact, the relationship with a teacher can be the closest and most trusting relationship a student has with someone from their new country of residence. Families often hold deep respect for teachers, and educators can offer assistance to students navigating decisions and pathways academically, personally, and professionally. Suárez-Orozco et al. (2008) recommend more comprehensive approaches to place newcomer students with mentors in their schools and communities to foster the relationships that can help them navigate postsecondary pathways effectively.

Recognize "Community Cultural Wealth"

Extending Bourdieu's traditional conceptions of "cultural capital"—or the ways that middle- and upper-class status is valorized and reproduced through public schooling—sociologist Tara Yosso (2005) developed a framework of "community cultural wealth" for students of color. Yosso defines community cultural wealth as "an array of knowledge, skills, abilities and contacts possessed and utilized by Communities of Color to survive and resist macro and micro-forms of oppression" (p. 77). She posits that students of color bring six different forms of capital to the educational process; however, and critically, she stresses that these have been neglected and underutilized by educators and schools. Yosso offers the following conceptualization of the forms of community cultural wealth that students of color, including immigrant-origin students of color, possess:

1. *Aspirational capital* "refers to the ability to maintain hopes and dreams for the future, even in the face of real and perceived barriers."
2. *Linguistic capital* "includes the intellectual and social skills attained through communication experiences in more than one language and/or style."
3. *Familial capital* "refers to those cultural knowledges nurtured among *familia* (kin) that carry a sense of community history, memory and cultural intuition."
4. *Social capital* "can be understood as networks of people and community resources. These peer and other social contacts can provide both instrumental and emotional support to navigate through society's institutions."
5. *Navigational capital* "refers to skills of maneuvering through social institutions. Historically, this infers the ability to maneuver through institutions not created with Communities of Color in mind."
6. *Resistant capital* "refers to those knowledges and skills fostered through oppositional behavior that challenges inequality. This form of cultural wealth is grounded in the legacy of resistance to subordination exhibited by Communities of Color." (pp. 77–78)

Taken together, these forms of community cultural wealth reframe deficit perspectives about communities of color and immigrant-origin families and their relationship to schooling.

While Yosso does not refer to newcomer youth specifically in this foundational article, scholars such as Shapiro and Jiménez have drawn on, applied, and extended Yosso's framework to tailor it specifically to immigrant, refugee, and immigrant-origin students (Jiménez, 2020; Shapiro, 2018). Shapiro (2018) examines the role of familial capital in postsecondary transitions for refugee students in New England. The author offers an account of "specific strategies—both discursive and non-discursive—used within the family to motivate, support, and prepare students for educational success" (p. 334). Acknowledging the paradox that refugee-background students are "told at home they should be high educational achievers," yet "encounter a culture of low expectations at school," Shapiro shares students' narratives of agency in discussing their families' contributions to their educational success (pp. 334–335). Shapiro finds that family contributions in students' narratives were related to nurturing their aspirations, seeking out the best schools, and cultivating a sense of collective responsibility; the author concludes that familial capital was seen as a clear resource for refugee-background students.

Further extending Yosso's (2005) framework, Rosa Jiménez (2020) examines "community cultural wealth counter-stories" in a 6th-grade classroom comprised primarily of immigrant English learners (ELs) in California's Central Valley. Through a unit codesigned by the teacher and the researcher rooted in Yosso's community cultural wealth model, the educators' and students' migration experiences were normalized in the classroom context and shared through the production of counterstories. Through this collaborative and participatory ethnographic research, Jiménez adds a seventh category of "migration capital" to Yosso's six forms of community cultural wealth,

> defining it as the knowledges, sensibilities, and skills cultivated through the array of migration/immigration experiences to the United States or its borderlands. Topics about immigration are often taboo, hidden, or cause shame or fear, particularly around issues of ethnicity/race, poverty, legality/illegality, documentation, and everyday life as migrants. Yet when teachers are equipped to see, connect with, sustain, and expand on students' lived experiences as immigrant youth, it generates pedagogical spaces of possibility. (p. 780)

Providing examples of student- and teacher-generated forms of migration capital through family interviews and oral histories, Jiménez further posits that this form of community cultural wealth can be an important pedagogical tool to destigmatize issues such as unauthorized immigration, undocumented status, and deportation. The concept of migration capital—drawing on the knowledge, insights, and strengths generated through migration to the United States—offers a significant addition to Yosso's framework when examining the educational strategies that contribute to the academic success and well-being of newcomer immigrant and refugee youth.

In this book, we start from an assets-based perspective that honors the cultural "wealth" that immigrant and refugee students and their families bring to the schools and communities they arrive in. In this context, we have selected practices that best facilitate this definition of holistic academic success and provide immigrant and refugee students with humanizing educational environments that can foster achievement, well-being, resilience, and hope.

THE 20 STRATEGIES

Some of the schools we examined refer to themselves as "community schools," defined as "both a place and a set of partnerships between the school and other community resources. [Their] integrated focus on academics, health and social services, youth and community development and community engagement leads to improved student learning, stronger families and healthier communities" (Coalition for Community Schools, 2020). Certainly, educators may find it easier to introduce some of the ideas in this book if the entire school has an explicit focus on going beyond conventional approaches with an espoused commitment to a larger vision to being a community resource. Yet there are also ways that individual teachers can create change and efforts can build from one classroom to impact students in positive ways and have ripple effects on the entire school and community.

Newcomer students enter into different types of educational settings in the United States. Many are placed in their local schools with support for English language learning in special classes or pull-outs with specialized teachers (see School Profile 1). Some schools are exclusively oriented to newcomers, and students spend their 4 (or more) years of high school together with others who have similar needs and realities; schools in the Internationals Network for Public Schools exemplify this approach (see School Profiles 2 and 3). Newcomer students face specific challenges: they may "age out" of the system, or they may have specific work obligations. In response, some districts have opened "alternative" settings to meet students' needs (see School Profile 4). Finally, some school districts have stand-alone newcomer programs, where recently arrived students with very limited English proficiency receive targeted, wrap-around support in short-term newcomer programs for a year or longer before being "mainstreamed" to another location. For example, the Doris Henderson Newcomers School in Greensboro, North Carolina, serves recently arrived immigrant and refugee students in grades 3–12 who are emergent bilinguals. The school provides focused instruction in English as a second language, with integrated content area instruction. Newcomer programs help students acquire basic oral and written English and introduce them to schooling in the United States; they often offer flexible scheduling of courses, content instruction, extended time to provide extra support, and opportunities to connect with social services (Short & Boyson, 2012).

The strategies we highlight in this book center on high school programs (grades 9–12) from all of the aforementioned types of educational settings, with a few added examples from kindergarten through grade 8 (K–8). For a more comprehensive examination of K–8 education, we recommend the book *Supporting Newcomer Students: Advocacy and Instruction for English Learners* (Samway et al., 2020) as an exemplary text focused on English language learning and community building strategies for newcomer students, particularly in the elementary and middle grades.

In this book, we focus on curricular, extracurricular, schoolwide, and community engagement approaches that can support newcomer integration and success. In deciding what strategies to include, we sought practices that do the following:

- address the distinct realities (cognitive, linguistic, cultural, sociopolitical) of newcomer students in their academic pursuits
- foster a school climate in which immigrant and refugee students can persist and thrive
- address the needs (material, emotional, legal, etc.) and realities of students and their families, and increase the students' ability to deal with past, present, and potentially future trauma

- transcend the boundaries between schools and communities to create trust and belonging for immigrant and refugee families
- prepare students for postsecondary transitions and future life trajectories

Further, we chose to select approaches—sometimes unconventional ones—that have yielded positive outcomes for student achievement and agency; that use innovative and humanizing ways of engaging families and communities in the life and work of schools; and that advance newcomer students' well-being (in and outside the classroom).

Taken together, these strategies offer ways that educators and school leaders can better serve immigrant, refugee, and otherwise marginalized youth. Of course, not every strategy will work for each student or in each context; however, reading through these strategies may inspire new thinking, adaptations, and innovations for the setting that you work in. The 20 strategies we offer are grouped into three categories, as follows:

Category I: Strategies for Classroom and Instructional Design

Strategy 1: Utilize Translanguaging in English Language Development
Strategy 2: Honor Histories and Heritages
Strategy 3: Practice Purposeful Grouping
Strategy 4: Incorporate Differentiated Instruction and Universal Design for Learning
Strategy 5: Support Students With Limited and Interrupted Formal Education
Strategy 6: Undertake Holistic and Continuous Assessment
Strategy 7: Include Advisory Periods

Category II: Strategies for School Design

Strategy 8: Enact Democratic School Governance
Strategy 9: Adopt Intentional Staffing
Strategy 10: Integrate Coaching for Culturally Responsive Teaching
Strategy 11: Address School Language Policies
Strategy 12: Promote a Positive School Climate and Culture
Strategy 13: Emphasize Students' Health and Wellness
Strategy 14: Establish Dual Enrollment and Early College Programs

Category III: Strategies for Extracurricular Programs, and Community and Alum Partnerships

Strategy 15: Provide After-School and Summer Programming
Strategy 16: Involve Families
Strategy 17: Offer Legal Services

Strategy 18: Develop Community Partnerships for Social Support and Civic
    Engagement
Strategy 19: Implement Internships and Career Preparation Programs
Strategy 20: Engage Alum in Schools and Community Building

In this book, we explain and discuss each of the 20 strategies, with insights
from students, teachers, school staff, and parents. To exemplify the strategies, we
provide profiles of four schools and five former students. We begin with a profile
of a large, comprehensive high school in the Midwest (Lincoln High School in
Nebraska) to give a sense of the general challenges faced by newcomer students.
Each subsequent school profile is located at the beginning of each of the three
categories. To highlight the impact of the recommended strategies, we also interviewed several youth who had been newcomers to the U.S. education system between grades 6 and 12. Five profiles, with information about these individuals'
backgrounds and advice they have for educators, are interspersed throughout the
book; the first, highlighting Ana, follows this Introduction.

The book also has a companion website with all the additional resources
listed in each chapter, as well as a video playlist (accessible at www.bit.ly/Immig
RefugeeEd; see also Appendix A for a scannable QR code that leads to the website).
Following the Appendix is a Glossary in which key terms utilized throughout this
book are defined and explained.

TOWARD HUMANIZING AND CARING SCHOOL COMMUNITIES

Humanizing pedagogies draw originally from the writings of Brazilian scholar
Paulo Freire (1970), and from many others who have built upon his foundational ideas, to center students' realities and needs in the educational process.
Humanizing pedagogies exhort educators to cultivate deep care for students
rooted in "trust, relations of reciprocity, active listening, mentoring, compassion,
high expectations, and interest in students' overall well-being" (Salazar, 2013,
p. 129). By acknowledging the linguistic and cultural heritage of students in the
classroom, educators are able to "validate and value students' interests, experiences, and emotions and localize curriculum to reflect the realities of students'
lives" (p. 134). These pedagogies rely on several key principles:

> Educators orienting toward a humanizing pedagogy build trusting and caring rela-
> tionships with students [and] engage in the following: listen to students' interests,
> needs, and concerns; know students on a personal level and attempt to understand
> students' home experiences; acknowledge the challenges associated with the develop-
> ment of bilingualism and biculturalism; model kindness, patience, and respect; tend
> to students' overall well-being, including their emotional, social, and academic needs;
> create a support network for students inside and outside of school; build on the values
> and contributions of parents; create a safe learning environment where risk-taking
> and active engagement are valued; allow for native language support; and facilitate
> student connections to their communities (Bahruth, 2007; Fránquiz & Salazar, 2004;

Huerta, 2011; [A.] Rodriguez, 2008; Salazar, 2008). Caring relationships are founded on mutual respect between students, families, and teachers, thus humanizing the context of schooling (Bartolomé, 1994). (Salazar, 2013, p. 140)

Given the high dropout rate for newcomer students mentioned earlier, it is essential to create humanizing and caring school communities where their distinct needs are met. Schools can also serve as hubs for newcomer students and families, connecting them with information, services, and resources in their new country.

Through the 20 strategies that follow, we offer a vision for creating humanizing school communities that, first and foremost, exhibit deep and authentic care for students (Antrop-González & De Jesús, 2006; García et al., 2013; Noddings, 1984, 1988; Thompson, 1998; Valenzuela, 1999). We further define CARING schools for immigrant and refugee youth as humanizing educational environments that exhibit the following traits:

Compassionate: Many immigrant and refugee youth have experienced unspeakable violence (or the threat of it) that has forced them to migrate. In working with immigrant and refugee youth, educators and staff must be compassionate and understanding of such circumstances, which includes being patient, empathetic, and trauma-informed. An educator may never know all the details of a student's past, but care and compassion can offer students the space to learn and thrive in a school community.

Achievement-Oriented: Being compassionate may result in the pendulum sometimes swinging toward pity and low expectations (Antrop-González & De Jesús, 2006). We argue instead that educators and school staff must also focus on achievement, particularly in ways that are culturally congruent, holistic, and informed by student aspirations, rather than purely measuring achievement through high-stakes standardized tests that research has argued are culturally biased (Strauss, 2017). Holding high standards while acknowledging and valuing students' backgrounds is what scholars have termed "critical caring" (Antrop-González & De Jesús, 2006) and is what we advocate for as well in our call for humanizing and caring school communities.

Relationships-Focused: At the core of what we know about immigrant and refugee youth's success is that relationships matter: relationships among students and teachers; between families/communities and schools; and among students themselves. Schools that foster the development of strong, reciprocal, and supportive bonds can encourage help-seeking behaviors that improve achievement, and best prepare youth for postsecondary transitions whether to the labor market or to higher education (Suárez-Orozco et al., 2008).

Inclusive: Refugee and immigrant youth do not all have the same experiences; there are hierarchies, differences, and tensions within and across groups. Schools must accommodate diversity in all its forms: ethnicity, race, language, national origin, caste/class, religion, gender identity and expression, sexual orientation, documentation status, dis/ability, and other forms of difference. Inclusion doesn't mean there won't be conflict, but it means that a school environment is created where conflict can be managed in constructive and productive (rather than destructive) ways.

Nurturing: In educational scholarship and in our own research, we find that the best schools are often those that students describe as places that feel "like family" (Antrop-González & De Jesús, 2006; Bajaj, 2009; Bajaj, Argenal & Canlas, 2017; Bartlett & García, 2011; Hantzopoulos, 2016; S. Lee & Hawkins, 2008). A nurturing environment consists of teachers and staff who care for the whole student—not just their mastery of academic content and preparation for exams—and transcend boundaries between the school and families/communities. Nurturing school communities can also serve as a refuge and a place to gain support for students when dynamics in their own households or communities may be difficult (as exemplified in the profile of Miguel later in this book).

Genuine: A school where authentic learning can flourish requires a commitment to developing relationships, continual learning, betterment through adaptive approaches, and engaging partners that can strengthen the experiences of students and families. Educators, school leaders, and staff must be willing to accept feedback and continually grow in ways that reflect cultural humility (Tervalon & Murray-García, 1998) and a genuine commitment to the students they serve. Practices must be developed and implemented to ensure ongoing, critical self-reflection on the part of educators, staff, and school leaders to continually meet the needs of their often-changing student population.

In the framework of CARING schools we have developed, these six components manifest through specific practices and strategies. We assert that incorporating the strategies detailed throughout this book can foster a CARING and humanizing community in which immigrant and refugee youth can thrive and succeed.

The strategies presented in this book seek to catalyze the potential of and encourage innovations in schools to better serve immigrant and refugee youth. By adjusting how we as educators approach youth who statistically are the least likely to succeed, we can offer them the information, supports, and skills for smoother post–high school transitions and for their holistic well-being.

Despite their challenges in many places, public schools have tremendous promise as sites of learning, opportunity, and critical thinking. By highlighting educators and schools that are "doing the work"—however imperfect and challenged—and inspiring others with their unique approaches to serving immigrant and refugee youth, this book seeks to amplify these counterstories to dominant discourses of deficit in education, offering pragmatic optimism (Noguera, 2003), critical hope (Duncan-Andrade, 2009), and concrete strategies for educators and scholars in the field.

Profile of Ana
As told to Gabriela Martínez

Ana was 16 when she left El Salvador for the United States. The gang violence had gotten intense in her neighborhood and her family was being threatened—especially Ana and her brother, who was 15 at the time. Her dad was in the United States, and Ana, her brother, and her cousin set off on the journey north in search of a better, and safer, life. Along the way, she fell, was badly hurt, and was nearly apprehended in Guatemala by Mexican migration officials. Her cousin didn't make it across the border with them. After crossing the U.S. border, Ana and her brother were placed in the *hielera*—what migrants call the overcrowded detention facilities in South Texas that are known as the "ice boxes" for their freezing temperatures. As unaccompanied minors to the United States, Ana and her brother were assigned lawyers who found them a home to stay in while their cases were pending. They were very scared in an unknown place, especially because authorities at one point told them that, even if they were allowed to stay in the United States, they would be placed into adoption because their father was not a legal resident of the United States and had been previously deported. Eventually, however, the family was reunited in Oakland.

The violence in El Salvador and the migration/detention process had interrupted Ana's schooling (see also Strategy 5), and she entered 9th grade at Oakland International High School. At age 19, Ana gave birth to a daughter. She transferred to Rudsdale Newcomer High School in 11th grade; Rudsdale is a continuation school that has more flexible block schedules and allows for leaves of absence (see School Profile 4). Rudsdale proved more manageable for Ana's new dual role as both a mother and a high school student. At age 21, Ana received her high school diploma from Rudsdale.

Ana noted,

> I had a beautiful experience at both schools. I liked in-person learning better than online during the pandemic because sometimes the signal was weak and it was hard to learn, but my teachers were very understanding even if my daughter would interrupt. They would always help me with my work.
>
> I had really good relationships with my teachers and I enjoyed my time with them in both schools. The teachers I had were so friendly and I liked getting to talk to them. And I really enjoyed advisory periods—they would get us together for icebreakers and activities.

     I also felt supported by the school counselors. Sometimes you feel sad being in a new country, a new environment, with different things happening all the time and different people around. The counselors help with that. They talk with you and make you feel better. Sometimes my teachers and counselors still text and check in on me.

Ana's advice for educators of newcomers is to have patience, especially as newcomer students are trying to learn English, because it's a new language and it can be really difficult to learn. Her advice for schools based on her own positive experiences at the schools she attended is to make newcomer students and their families feel included and welcome (see also Strategies 12 and 16). And her advice to newcomer students is *"que sigan adelante,"* to keep moving forward by studying hard and working toward their goals of learning English, graduating, and fulfilling their dreams.

School Profile 1

Lincoln High School, Nebraska

Edmund T. Hamann With Lesley Bartlett

Founded in 1871, Lincoln High School (LHS) is the oldest public comprehensive high school in Lincoln, Nebraska. With the highest poverty rate (56%) of the six comprehensive high schools in Nebraska's second largest district, LHS is Lincoln's only high school that is not majority white. In 2020–2021, LHS's enrollment was 11% African American, 10% Asian American, 22% Latinx, 1% Native American, 11% "Two or More Races" and 44% white (Nebraska Department of Education, 2021). That same year, of the nearly 2,400 students, approximately 10% were classified as English learners (a drop of almost 25% compared to each of the previous four years). Collectively they spoke more than 30 languages at home, including Spanish, Arabic, Kurdish, Vietnamese, and Karen as the most common ones. LHS was one of the three high schools in the district with an English as a second language (ESL) program. In 2017, Lincoln High School was selected by the National Education Policy Center (NEPC) at the University of Colorado–Boulder as an exemplary "School of Opportunity" (Schools of Opportunity, n.d.), wherein it was deemed exemplary in several areas, including efforts to "broaden and enrich learning opportunities," "create and maintain healthy school culture," "support teachers as professionals, and "sustain equitable and meaningful parent and community engagement."

Lincoln High School emphasizes providing support and services for *all* students in its highly diverse student body. Educators maintain a school culture premised upon recognizing and building on the assets, or "funds of knowledge" (Moll et al., 1992), that students bring with them to school. LHS leaders hire new talent with an eye toward sustaining this view: during job interviews, candidates are asked about their attitudes toward cultural and linguistic diversity, and only those who see home language(s) and cultural background as assets are offered positions.

EDUCATIONAL APPROACHES FOR NEWCOMERS

ESL Program, With Gradual and Supported Mainstreaming

In LHS's ESL program, emergent bilinguals (EBs) are grouped into five levels based on English proficiency. Students at Level 1 spend most of the day in ESL classes with other EBs in content courses in literacy, writing, and math. But once they are ready for still heavily supported Level 2, they add content learning in science and civics (in English). At Levels 3 and 4, EBs take one daily ESL course but also enroll in language arts and other content courses (with non-ESL students) that count toward graduation. At Level 5, after students exit ESL classes but before they pass the state's English Language Proficiency Assessment (ELPA), they take an entirely non-ESL load while the English Language Learner (ELL) Department continues to track their success and guide student placement. It should be noted that, unlike in some districts and states, courses taken by higher-level EBs can count toward graduation credit, so students do not need to take, let alone formally pass, the ELPA to graduate. This helps explain the ELL program's success earning a disproportionate percentage of LHS's annual totals of Susie Buffett Scholarships (for 4-year college) and Learn to Dream scholarships (for community college). Unlike in many communities, where Spanish is the first language of a substantial majority of EBs and where monolingual English instruction would be ignoring an obvious asset shared by most students, at LHS, because no one additional language dominates, EBs use English as the lingua franca to communicate with other EBs, even as their peer-to-peer use of first languages to support their comprehension is both welcome and common.

Heritage Language Program

As further evidence of how LHS frames multilingualism as an asset, in 2014, educators developed Spanish for Heritage Learners (SHL) coursework to support students with prior familial and community backgrounds with Spanish (Eckerson, 2015). This orientation acknowledges that students with some background but little academic experience in Spanish approach Spanish class differently than do peers who encounter Spanish as a foreign language. SHL classes still build toward the Spanish Advanced Placement test, like the Spanish as a foreign language pathway, but heritage learners study Spanish with an emphasis on building upon what they know, and their course sequence more overtly recognizes the multiple "Spanishes" found around the world (and in Lincoln).

ADDITIONAL SERVICES AND SUPPORTS

LHS provides EBs and all students with additional services and supports beyond academic classes. In 2016, with support from a nonprofit community organization called The Lighthouse, LHS extended its media center hours into the evening and also opened for 3 hours on Saturdays. (The pandemic reduced but did not eliminate these after-school hours.) Access to the media center has made it easier for low-income students to use the Internet and technology necessary for them to complete their schoolwork. During these extended hours, volunteer community members are usually available to tutor students; students who have fallen behind due to attendance issues, athletic or theater involvement, or other factors can also work on missing and late work with the help of teachers and administrators on campus.

More recently, the after-school program was split into two parts: quiet hour studying and tutor opportunities in the library and a community-learning-center (CLC) partnership with Civic Nebraska that offers more than 30 after-school clubs. The school features clubs that affirm students' backgrounds, identities, and languages (such as Las Razas Unidas and the Karen/Zomi/Karenni Club) and that offer opportunities for social connection. Our point here is not to exhaustively document each club, nor would we claim that each are as dynamic and active as the next. Rather the point is that LHS endeavors to help all students find multiple and various points to engage and connect.

LHS also supports students, including EBs, by offering curriculum-specific support through its Academic Resource Center (ARC). ARC ensures teachers for each curricular area are available Monday through Friday after school. Students can be assigned to ARC, or they can voluntarily walk in to talk to and work with a teacher in the curricular area in which they need support.

Cultural Ambassadors

Further situating multilingualism as an asset, LHS runs a program called Cultural Ambassadors, through which students serve as multilingual liaisons to help families and other visitors new to English negotiate the school when there are public events. Students are not interpreters for high-stakes and private communication (about an IEP, for example)—the school district relies on paid community liaisons for that—but the ambassadors help parents and visitors find out where to go to get from Point A to Point B and otherwise negotiate the school. Most of the ambassadors act as interpreters between English and their home languages and include many current and former identified EBs.

Communication With Family and Community

Since 2016, LHS teachers and staff have participated in a professional development workshop on how to effectively call students' homes. In many instances those calls (and written communication) need to be in languages other than English. LHS staff work closely with district-level liaisons for the largest language groups in the district (Spanish, Karen, Kurdish, Vietnamese, Arabic, Ukrainian, and Russian) as well as six more languages (including Farsi and Kurmanji, the language spoken by Yazidis, an ethnic group from Iraq). While the bilingual liaisons and a related districtwide Welcome Center are not, strictly speaking, LHS programs, they do have a substantial impact on LHS and the school's commitments to welcome, support, and include EB students and their families. LHS does employ a full-time Parent and Community Engagement Specialist who has both direct and coordinating roles, including assuring the operation of an EB Parent Advisory Committee (see also Strategy 16).

CONNECTIONS TO POSTSECONDARY OPTIONS

LHS educators carefully prepare EBs for postsecondary opportunities. Language faculty also help students prepare to pass the English reading proficiency test used by Southeast Community College; once they pass that test, students may compete for a "Learn to Dream" scholarship that fully funds pursuit of an associate degree. The community college option is particularly valuable for students with limited or interrupted formal education (SLIFE), who may be older (see also Strategy 5). Nebraska allows enrollment in high school up to age 21; some SLIFE students "time out" before they can earn a high school diploma, and thus they need to pursue a GED. Southeast Community College (like other Nebraska community colleges) offers GED test prep, which includes both content and logistic support for the exam. ELL Department faculty help overage SLIFE students to continue with GED prep at community college.

EBs are also supported in planning for 4-year degrees and institutions. One of the most generous scholarships available for public higher education in Nebraska is called the Susie Buffett Scholarship. Typically identified EBs earn a fifth to a third of all Buffett scholarships that LHS graduates obtain each year.

As a final signal of its commitment to multilingualism as an asset, the LHS Bilingual Career and Education Fair brings employers, educational institutions, and government and community organizations together to showcase for students and families the opportunities available in Lincoln and across the state for multilingual students. From scholarship opportunities to on-the-spot interviews, the fair connects EBs and their families with recruiters and representatives of community institutions that value multilingualism (see also Strategy 19). The event, hosted annually in LHS's cafeteria since 2015, now boasts dozens of diverse exhibitors and is visited by hundreds of students and parents from across the city. Students in SHL courses help to organize the event. The fair is so successful in bringing families of minority-language students to the building that LHS counselors began to offer other services, such as college financial planning presentations, in conjunction with the fair.

CONCLUSION

Considering this book's list of 20 strategies that together humanize education and welcome refugee and immigrant students (among others), we have described how LHS honors student histories and heritages, supports translanguaging, and engages in purposeful grouping allowing differentiated instruction with common rigor and supported high expectations. SLIFE students are overtly supported. The school makes explicit efforts to hear and attend to the voices of the multiple student constituencies that call LHS home. The school is noisy, in multiple languages and accents, with the energy, bustle, and engagement of students tracing backgrounds to every settled continent on the planet.

Profile of Ko

As Told to Gabriela Martínez

When Ko was 6 years old, she and her family had to flee their home in Burma in the middle of the night. Ko shared that the Burmese military dictatorship's goal "was to eliminate us [the Karen ethnic community] through ethnic cleansing," including mass violence, land seizures, burning down houses, and raping women. Ko's family fled to a refugee camp on the Thailand–Burma border, where other Karen-speaking families had gone for "a better hope for our family." Ko's family spent 8 years in the refugee camp. She remembers having friends there, being able to practice her culture and religion freely in the camp, and attending schools that had been set up for the refugee children.

Through an agreement between the United States government and the United Nations High Commission for Refugees (UNHCR) that operated the camps that Ko lived in, her family applied for and were granted political asylum in 2011. With her parents and six siblings, Ko arrived in the United States at age 13 and first entered a middle school that had no program for newcomer students; she recalled that "when I first came to the U.S., every day was a culture shock."

Ko started 9th grade at age 15 at Oakland International High School, which is a school exclusively for newcomers from over 35 different countries. Ko discussed how she formed strong relationships with her high school teachers, some of whom she still maintains contact with as a senior now at the University of California (UC)–Davis majoring in political science.

Ko shared that she was struggling to write in English in high school, and she decided to first write essays and assignments in her home language of Karen (see also Strategies 1 and 11). She shared,

> I would start writing my essay in my own language because it would give me a lot of thoughts and ideas, and then I would translate it into English. When I would start first in English, I would just freeze when I didn't know a word. When I started in my own language, there were a lot of details that would come to mind in my own language and then after, I'd translate it to English; then I'd say to myself "Oh, wow, this is a very good essay!"

Ko discussed how participating in afterschool programs like the GSA (Gay–Straight Alliance) and the human rights club, as well as participating in the school's annual May Day March for immigrant rights, helped her find her identity and voice as a leader and as an activist both in her Karen ethnic community and at college, serving as the first former refugee student ever elected as a student senator at the University (see also Strategy 15).

Ko's advice to educators is to get to know their students, since many students come from cultures where they are taught to be afraid of teachers and not to ask questions for fear of being disrespectful, which may hinder their academic success (see also Strategy 2). By reaching out, teachers "show that you care about students, that you want them to succeed."

Ko further shared that the transition from high school to college was difficult especially with regard to writing assignments, and that applying the same techniques of attending office hours and building strong relationships with her professors helped her adjust to the expectations after having been admitted to one of the state's top 4-year universities. Ko is now 23, is on track to graduate from UC Davis, and is applying to law school to further pursue her goal of advancing justice and human rights, especially for marginalized communities, in the United States and worldwide.

STRATEGIES FOR CLASSROOM AND INSTRUCTIONAL DESIGN

School Profile 2

The International High School at Prospect Heights in Brooklyn, New York

Nedda de Castro and Daniel Walsh

> In a grades 9 and 10 biology course, students collaboratively create posters that explore various aspects of climate change's impact on reproductive health. Students are grouped according to home language; they clearly possess varying degrees of fluency in English. The translation of "climate change and reproductive health" into Russian, French, Spanish, and Arabic appears on the board. Students also use these languages orally as they collaborate around their posters. Also on the board, in English, are a number of sample sentences connecting global temperatures and human fertility. One reads: "It has been observed that this global [overheating] is impacting fertility and reproduction."
>
> —Observation notes, January 6, 2022,
> The International High School at Prospect Heights

The International High School at Prospect Heights (IHSPH) first opened its doors in September 2004 to approximately 100 immigrant and refugee youth, all English learners, who had been in the United States for fewer than four years. Located in the Prospect Heights/Crown Heights neighborhood in Brooklyn, across the street from the Brooklyn Museum, the school has consistently attracted the diversity represented in New York City's immigrant communities.

According to coauthor and Principal Nedda de Castro, the student demographics at IHSPH are as follows:

Latin America and the Caribbean, 64%
    Dominican Republic, 25%
    Central and South America (Ecuador, Honduras, Guatemala, El Salvador), 31%
    Haiti, 8%
Yemen, 14%
West Africa (Guinea, Senegal, Mauritania, Mali, Togo), 12%
Other (Uzbekistan, Bangladesh, Pakistan, China), 10%

In addition to this linguistic, cultural, and national origin diversity, 60% of the students are beginning English learners and 27% of the students have experienced limited or interrupted formal education (see also Strategy 5).

The IHSPH is part of the Internationals Network for Public Schools (INPS), which creates schools and academies within larger schools that serve the unique needs of newcomer immigrant and refugee youth. Such models first emerged in the 1980s in New York, and the network now includes some 30 schools in five states plus Washington, DC. Like other schools in the Internationals Network, IHSPH is committed to heterogeneous classrooms, collaborative structures, experiential learning, integration of language and content learning, localized autonomy and responsibility at all levels within a learning community, and a model in which both students and educators learn continuously (Internationals Network for Public Schools, 2022). The schools also work to center student assets and attend to multilingual immigrant students' socioemotional needs.

This profile's authors have known one another since 2004, the founding year of IHSPH. Nedda first served as the school's social worker, became assistant principal in the second year, and has been the school's principal for the past 11 years. Danny served as English teacher, interdisciplinary team leader, union chapter leader, and instructional coach at various points during his 5.5-year tenure at the school. Together, Nedda and Danny have over 40 years of experience in New York City public schools, primarily serving immigrant and refugee youth who are English learners.

As the opening vignette suggests, our intention in this profile is to provide readers with a window into instructional practices that have guided the school's staff since inception. To frame these practices, we rely on the theoretical constructs of scaffolding and asset-based pedagogies such as translanguaging (García & Kleyn, 2016; García & Wei, 2014; García et al., 2017; Walqui, 2006; Walqui & Van Lier, 2010; see also Strategy 1). To illustrate such constructs, we highlight the following strategies, which we find to be emblematic of the school's ideological and pedagogical commitments: (1) use of home languages and cultures as resources (see also Strategy 2), (2) heterogeneous grouping and peers as resources (see also Strategy 3), and (3) differentiated instruction (see also Strategy 4). These strategies are combined with consistent/familiar instructional routines and practices across various subject areas within a grade level.

HOME LANGUAGES AND CULTURES AS RESOURCES

Students bring linguistic and cultural resources to every learning activity; they build upon their home language and prior knowledge as they develop new language and content knowledge. Through strategic peer grouping, students build conceptual knowledge of content while growing in the target language. As shown in the observation at the beginning of the profile, students grouped by language build their understanding of the science content through interactions in their home language, and then they produce an artifact and present it in English to a linguistically heterogeneous small group of peers. Because collaboration among heterogeneous groups of peers is central to scaffolding for multilingual learners, groupings are purposeful both upon formation of an entire grade level and within each class in that grade. In other words, all classes are socially engineered so that they are heterogeneous by language and ability. Within the class, teachers will group students depending on the purpose and the task within a lesson or unit. In the case above, the teacher grouped students by language group in the first part of the lesson, so students could more deeply build their conceptual understanding of the science content by engaging in discussion in their home language with peers. This activity was then followed by a regrouping of students, where the common language for all students was English.

Creating a culturally and linguistically sustaining and affirming environment is central to the vision and mission of the school and is reflected in its instructional practices. As stated earlier, home language and culture are assumed assets. It is understood and expected that students will use the language of their choosing to make meaning and generate understanding within the classroom, among their peers, and with their teachers, as they build knowledge in content and in the target language. Students are encouraged to tap into the entirety of their linguistic repertoire in home languages and English. In the classroom scenario, students can be heard alternating between speaking in home languages and English while engaging in their work. Students use technological resources to translate primary sources, access classroom materials, and conduct research.

Moreover, students at all levels of abilities are active members in student-centered classrooms that prominently display their work products, which serve as evidence of learning and continuous scaffolding in the classroom. For example, in this classroom, the essential questions displayed were generated by the students. Students added to the growing Word Wall of vocabulary throughout the unit. The daily classroom questions and objectives were written on the board in English and translated by the students into their home languages.

A final schoolwide practice evidenced in this classroom is the use of outcomes-based grading and assessment. For this group task, learning outcomes, as part of student-friendly rubrics, were distributed to each group, clearly articulating expectations and allowing for student and group self-assessment. Such practices place the students at the center of their learning and reflect to them the teacher's belief that students can learn deeply and share their learning long before "mastering" English. This asset-based approach is central to promoting equity for multilingual learners and is directly opposed to the deficit-based approaches that assume the level of target language literacy is an indicator of content knowledge and/or cognitive ability.

HETEROGENEOUS GROUPING AND PEERS AS RESOURCES

According to Walqui (2006), scaffolding is both structure and process, entails intersubjectivity, and incorporates collaboration that moves beyond the expert–novice context. In other words, with intersubjectivity, we witness the establishment of mutual engagement and rapport and "there is encouragement and nonthreatening participation in a shared community of practice" (p. 165). Within this shared community of practice, we observe students in purposefully constituted groups and processes that optimize the "zone of proximal development" (Vygotsky, 1978) by creating a synergistic space in which the learning and development surpass what would happen if students were left to their own devices. Additionally, such grouping creates the circumstances where students construct knowledge with both more and less advanced peers (in both English language development and content background knowledge), as well as with the teacher. In essence, such structures and processes acknowledge the hope and promise of what is not yet realized.

In the classroom scenario briefly described above, the teacher planned and implemented various instructional moves to shape how the students engaged with the content. Students were purposefully grouped by language as well as other attributes so that they would grapple with the content, develop a conceptual understanding of the material, and produce a poster so that each member of the group would be able to present and explain what they learned to members of the class in English. Purposeful grouping is the central structure through which learning takes place.

DIFFERENTIATED INSTRUCTION AND PREDICTABLE INSTRUCTIONAL ROUTINES

Observations conducted in other IHSPH classrooms demonstrated a critical combination of differentiated instruction and predictable pedagogical routines. Teachers use intake tools to learn about their students' language abilities and previous schooling (see also Strategy 2); they also use continuous assessment to carefully track student development (see also Strategy 6). Using that information, depending on the learning objective, they may place students in homogeneous or heterogeneous groups, in terms of language and/or content.

By employing predictable pedagogical routines or tools across classrooms, teachers ensure that students do not simultaneously face high content, language, and process demands. Having familiar structures or processes across the content areas for each grade level is one way that teachers can reduce the cognitive load for students when they are learning new and complex content. This predictability ensures that students can focus on what matters most, whether that be learning a new concept, developing a linguistic feature, or participating in a new instructional routine.

IHSPH instructors integrate language and content teaching, so it is important to use predictable pedagogical tools in these situations. One example of a common tool utilized across content areas is the graphic organizer called the Frayer model, which asks students to define, identify characteristics, and give examples that both fall within as well as outside the category. In a unit where students were learning about literary elements in linguistically homogeneous but heterogeneous background knowledge groups, they developed Frayer models to explore literary devices such as alliteration, metaphor, and simile. In their groups, students defined the term, translated the term, explained it in their own words and gave examples. Later, in English, they shared their work with other groups in the class, and their Frayer model graphic organizer was posted in the classroom. This process—working in the home language first, and translating jointly to present in English—and this graphic organizer are utilized in content areas across the teacher team for the cohort of students. Sharing routines and tools reduces the attention students must pay to the instructional strategy and frees it up for conceptual and then language learning.

At IHSPH, teachers are trained in a range of research-based strategies for multilingual learners; this shared preparation makes it easier to collaboratively plan common structures across the teacher team. For example, the teachers learned about using a model called "Writing Is Thinking through strategic inquiry" (aka WITsi)[1] for addressing literacy skills, and they decided to jointly implement three approaches in all of their classes across teams and grade levels. Portfolios are also used across the school: students in every grade engage in portfolio-based assessments in which they research and prepare a project, present it, and engage in a discussion of their learning with a panel (see also Strategy 6). This process is repeated from the 9th through 12th grades.

What we describe here reflects a pedagogy of hope and promise that exists within the realm of what is possible. As shown in the opening vignette, while expanding their knowledge of English, students engage in science content around climate change and reproductive health, as well as sophisticated literary terminology, by employing their ever-developing multilingualism to make sense of the world around them.

Strategy 1

Utilize Translanguaging in English Language Development

Lesley Bartlett and Esther Bettney

As School Profile 2 of the International High School at Prospect Heights shows, schools that successfully teach immigrant and refugee youth allow them to engage their home languages in the classroom, thus deepening their learning. Allowing students to build content knowledge with peers first in their home language or multilingually ensures better content learning. Students then work collaboratively to translate the content into English, giving them lots of opportunities for supported practice. This strategy, used in schools like IHSPH, is called translanguaging.

WHAT IS TRANSLANGUAGING?

The term *translanguaging* signals the effort to move across and beyond language boundaries (García & Wei, 2014). A translanguaging lens refuses to separate language practices into artificially constructed, static categories, like "Spanish" and "English." Instead, it emphasizes how multilinguals draw across their linguistic repertoire, selecting "features *strategically* to communicate effectively" (García, 2012, p. 1). This stance directly challenges the widespread monoglossic language hierarchies that position English as most valuable and the ideologies that frame bilingual children as deficient. Instead, translanguaging indicates a stance of respect for and cultivation of students' full linguistic and cultural repertoires (García & Kleyn, 2016).

Drawing on this concept, García and colleagues have developed a translanguaging pedagogy, which "build[s] on bilingual students' language practices flexibly in order to develop new understandings and new language practices, including those deemed 'academic standard' practices" (García & Wei, 2014, p. 92). Translanguaging as a pedagogical method creates space for a multilingual ecology that allows students to access texts, visual resources, and collaborative tasks that require communication using different types of language and skills. García et al. (2017) outline three goals of translanguaging as a pedagogical practice:

- to allow space for students to draw on the totality of their linguistic repertoires and their bilingual ways of knowing
- to provide students with opportunities to build off of their current languaging practices to incorporate new languaging practices that are associated with academic contexts
- to support students as they develop their bilingual identities

These authors call for teachers to plan for instruction through a translanguaging lens by including objectives that reflect appropriate content, as well as objectives for general-linguistic performance, language-specific performance, and translanguaging. Translanguaging allows emergent bilinguals to language freely and to determine when to use (or suppress) which language features. It also provides them with the space and support to draw across their linguistic repertoire throughout their thinking process.

Translanguaging pedagogies also make space for a more fluid understanding of linguistic identities. Recognizing diverse linguistic identities is particularly important for students who have experienced linguistic prejudice and discrimination. By moving away from "standardized" or monoglossic views of language, translanguaging pedagogies allow for more diverse identities and languaging practices, which are often excluded from other classroom spaces.

Schools that are responsive to the linguistic needs of immigrant and refugee students may engage in translanguaging in different ways. For example, Gregorio Luperón High School in New York City is a fully bilingual high school. In their first two years, students (who all speak Spanish at home) learn English even as they continue to develop their Spanish academic fluency not only in a language class but also in content classes taught primarily in Spanish, with lots of opportunities to translate texts and learn content-specific vocabulary in English. In their last two years of high school, students transition to classes that are taught primarily in English, but with frequent translanguaging. For example, students might read a text in English, summarize in Spanish, and then write responses in either (or both) language(s); they might make a presentation in Spanish while their peers write English definitions for key terms (Bartlett & García, 2011). The language approach in this bilingual high school is made possible in part because, in New York state, students can elect to take their content-area state exams (outside of English Language Arts) in English or Spanish (as well as other languages, such as Arabic, Haitian Creole, Russian, or Mandarin). This multilingual approach to assessment policy means that exams are less of a barrier to graduation for immigrant students.

In contrast, schools in the Internationals Network, such as Brooklyn and Oakland International High Schools, receive students from all parts of the world, and classes are all taught in English. However, English language development is not segregated to one classroom; rather, all teachers are both content and English teachers simultaneously. Further, teachers often draw on students' home languages as part of their teaching practice. For example, at Brooklyn International High School, one teacher provided students opportunities to participate in projects in which the students translated from their home language into English. Another teacher had students translate key concepts into their home language. She said: "If they don't want to explain DNA in English to me, they can explain it in French or Spanish to one of their peers who understands their language and then that peer will explain what they said" (interview, June 3, 2015). The former director of the Internationals Network for Public Schools explained that, in developing their performance assessments, they encourage students to include in their graduation portfolios "an original piece in their home language or one that has a bilingual component to it" (interview, as cited in Bajaj & Bartlett, 2017, p. 30). In this way, educators demonstrated the value of the students' language resources, and encouraged them to draw across languages in their conceptual development.

SCHOOL AND CLASSROOM STRATEGIES

Though translanguaging occurs naturally in the presence of multilingual students, teachers may benefit from learning how to cultivate and best leverage it (Barros et al., 2021). In the following sections, we offer a set of recommendations for utilizing a translanguaging approach that respects students' home languages while helping them develop English proficiency.

Cultivate a Multilingual Ecology

Schools can create a multilingual ecology in which the languages and language practices of all children and families are heard and seen (García & Menken, 2015). This entails key multilingual signage around the school, using students' languages in announcements and school publications, multilingual welcome packets and notes home, multilingual resources in school libraries, and after-school language learning clubs. Creating a multilingual ecology indicates to students that all aspects of their identities, including their diverse multilingual identities, are welcome and seen as beneficial in the classroom.

Promote Multilingual Approaches to Meet Content Standards

Like all students, newcomer students are expected to be working toward particular content standards. Yet, often students can demonstrate their mastery of content standards when they are encouraged to draw on their entire linguistic repertoire. For example, in an English class for newcomers at La Follette High School in Madison, Wisconsin, students worked with the classroom teacher to develop a project around the content standard of writing a narrative. Students were encouraged to write a narrative about their immigration story using whichever language(s) they needed to develop their own story. The teachers provided a variety of multilingual supports, including the use of an online platform in which students could express parts of their stories through images. Once they had written their narratives, the teachers drew on the expertise of other students, staff, and community members to help translate the stories into English (interview with Lisa Valverde, November 11, 2021).

Expand the Use of Multilingual and Multimodal Texts

In order to create a multilingual classroom, students need access to texts in languages other than English. Yet, it can be extremely difficult to find these resources, particularly for languages that are less common in the U.S. context. By moving beyond traditional definitions of texts, though, teachers can expand the possibilities. As well, in our tech-dependent world, language users communicate through many different modes, not just through written text. In addition to the traditional domains of reading, writing, speaking, and listening, students can engage with and create multimodal texts, which incorporate images, videos, symbols, charts, tables, audio, and so forth, as "the use of multimodalities increases the flexibility with which students can interpret and create meaning" (WIDA, 2020, p. 357). By expanding beyond a traditional definition of academic texts, students are provided with more opportunities to use and strengthen all of their communicative repertoires. As an example of incorporating multilingual and multimodal texts, newcomer students at La Follette High School were asked which type of texts they engaged with outside of school. Many students cited songs they listened to in different languages. The students brought in the lyrics of the songs, and teachers and students collaboratively translated them into English while engaging in a variety of language arts skills with the lyrics. Students were positioned as language experts who were provided with the opportunity to share relevant texts in their home languages while engaging in metalinguistic comparisons through translation and English language arts content standards. Teachers could provide further opportunities through having students read thematically in multiple languages from books that incorporate translanguaging or other multimodal resources (see, e.g., the guide to Latinx literature produced by Rosario & Cao, 2015). Teachers might also develop a listening library that contains summaries or translations of class texts in students' languages.

Position Every Teacher as a Language Teacher

To meet the needs of immigrant and refugee students, schools must adopt the stance that every teacher is a language teacher. Pull-out or push-in/coteaching English as a second language services will not be sufficient to help students develop English. All teachers need extensive professional development so that they can learn to integrate language development throughout the curriculum (National Academies of Sciences, Engineering, & Medicine, 2017). Lessons should include content and language learning objectives, with the language objectives carefully planned and scaffolded. Instruction should build on student experiences while developing the necessary background knowledge. Lessons should be well-organized and engaging, including "clear goals and objectives; appropriate and challenging material; well-designed instruction; clear input and modeling; informative feedback . . . ; application of new learning . . . ; practice and periodic review; structured interactions with other students; frequent assessments, with reteaching as needed; [and] well-established classroom routines and behavior norms" (Goldenberg, 2013, p. 5).

It is often beneficial to incorporate pictures and realia (or real, everyday objects), to incorporate visual cues and gestures, and to provide hands-on learning activities (Echevarria et al., 2008). While these strategies are essential to support newcomers across all of their content, all students benefit from an explicit attention to language within content classes.

Provide Peers With Multiple Opportunities to Interact Using English and Home Languages

Even within contexts in which all instruction must be provided in English, teachers can provide opportunities for students to draw on their home languages as learning resources. For example, de Mejía et al. (2012) describe how a high school science teacher provided instructions for an oral presentation in English and expected the final product in English, but students were encouraged to draw on all of their languages as together they brainstormed, researched and discussed their topic, and wrote initial drafts (see also Strategy 2 for examples). Teachers can draw on students' home languages as resources through exploring cognates, providing brief explanations in home languages, and previewing or reviewing a lesson in students' home languages (Calderón, 2008; Goldenberg, 2013). When teachers are not proficient in students' home languages, the students themselves can be encouraged to partner with a classmate with a shared language or to use online multilingual tools and resources. In a study about translanguaging conducted with adolescent newcomers, Stewart and Hansen-Thomas (2020) found that students expanded their understanding of English texts through peer discussions in home languages. Maximizing opportunities for students to describe their learning to others, in English or home languages, is a valuable learning tool.

Provide Opportunities to Develop Metalinguistic Awareness

Translanguaging recognizes the fluid and dynamic language practices of multilingual learners while providing explicit and intentional opportunities for students to expand their linguistic repertoires. For example, students should be encouraged to summarize and predict in English and/or home languages. One way to expand students' repertoires is through highlighting the relationship between languages (Cenoz & Gorter, 2011; Jiménez et al., 2015). Prasad et al. (in press) developed content-based projects in which teachers and students engaged together in various multilingual activities, such as comparing the front covers of books translated into multiple languages and creating charts to compare vocabulary across different languages. Regardless of their own linguistic background, students creatively and strategically accessed and strengthened their linguistic repertoires by making connections across languages. Intentional translating opportunities, where students consider word choice and sentence order across different languages, can further enhance students' metalinguistic awareness, which is shown to improve their reading comprehension (Celic, 2009; Jiménez et al., 2015).

SUMMARY

- Translanguaging pedagogies allow students to draw on their multilingual resources to expand their repertoire, including the expansion of their English language skills, as they also learn content.
- Teachers can meet their goal of helping students develop their English while respecting students' other languages by cultivating a multilingual ecology, promoting multilingual approaches to meet content standards, expanding the use of multilingual and multimodal texts, positioning every teacher as a language teacher, providing peers with multiple opportunities to interact using English and home languages, and providing students with opportunities to develop metalinguistic awareness.

ADDITIONAL RESOURCES

All resources are linked at the book's companion website: www.bit.ly/Immig RefugeeEd

- The website of the City University of New York–New York State Initiative on Emergent Bilinguals (CUNY-NYSIEB) has many resources for educators. See https://www.cuny-nysieb.org
- National Academies of Sciences, Engineering, & Medicine. (2017). *Promoting the educational success of children and youth learning English: Promising futures.* The National Academies Press. https://doi .org/10.17226/24677

Strategy 2
Honor Histories and Heritages

Monisha Bajaj

During one class, the topic of child soldiers came up while referencing a photograph of a young boy holding a gun in Uganda seen on a field trip to a local exhibit. Zau (pseudonym), a 19-year-old senior from the Chin region of Burma who was often quiet in class, spoke at length. "Seeing that photo, I learned that it's not just us, our country, our families facing problems. It's not us alone. That photo is like my story. The government had taken our farms over and the military forced us off our land; we had to leave and find work. I was forced to work in the mines when I was 11 years old. We had to dig holes 20 feet down, and then go inside to see if there was gold. It was so quiet when I would go inside there. The mine owners hire children because we have more energy and we are small so we can go inside the holes and go way down into the mines. Plus, if something falls as we dig, we can move quickly to escape. It was really scary, but I didn't really have a choice but to do it.

—Observation notes, October 2014

Acknowledging and bringing the histories, experiences, and heritages of students into the classroom is an essential way to humanize the educational process and engage learners in it (Salazar, 2013). Whether it be the linguistic or cultural heritage of students or bringing in issues related to their communities in the United States, scholars have found that the more students are engaged in the curricular material, the more likely they are to persist in school (Bartlett & García, 2011; Suárez-Orozco et al., 2009). And, incorporating students' backgrounds and present realities into the curriculum in diverse ways can allow them to see themselves in school, making learning more meaningful and connected to their realities, as Zau's comments indicate in the strategy's opening vignette. Doing this in ways that are enriching—and not traumatizing or essentializing—is key.

In discussing curricular approaches in multicultural education, educational scholar Christine Sleeter draws on Style's (1996) window–mirror metaphor, arguing that "both mirrors into [a student's] own world and windows into someone else's have value" (Sleeter, 2005, p. 149). Other scholars have also extended this metaphor from windows and mirrors to sliding doors, which offer entry points to new worlds and realities beyond the reader's or learner's experiences (Sims Bishop, 1990). In research with immigrant and refugee newcomers exploring human rights issues, Bajaj, Canlas, and Argenal (2017) found that relevant curricular materials that honored students' histories and heritages "offered (1) a *window* into past and present realities; (2) a *mirror* for reflecting on students' own experiences of rights violations; and (3) a *prism* for heightening their critical awareness of [differential] access to rights and resources" (p. 125). The prism builds upon Style's metaphor, adding a lens that can offer students complexity in understanding social justice issues as well as global and local inequalities that shape their lives, and can enrich the recognition of themselves in the curriculum through critical engagement.

CURRICULAR RELEVANCE

The ways that students' backgrounds can find a home in the classroom are multiple: through a multilingual ecology such as welcome signs in different languages and bulletin boards where students can post images that are meaningful to them; through lessons that bridge migration histories and home cultures to the curriculum; and through projects that allow students to delve deeper into their own histories, languages, and cultures. Assignments can be structured to utilize rather than stigmatize the home language, thus scaffolding students' emerging multilingualism (as discussed in Strategy 1). These types of projects allow students to see their linguistic capital as valued and built upon in the school context.

Gathering Student Background Information

Getting to know students and their backgrounds when they first arrive is an important first step in developing curriculum and school events that honor students' histories and backgrounds. In the interview form utilized in many newcomer schools and programs, as shown in Figure 2.1, questions are asked of each new student (ideally in their home language) when they join the school. This interview may take up to 45–60 minutes and may require the presence of someone to interpret and/or read aloud, depending on the situation.

Many newcomer programs also hire staff with linguistic and cultural competency for their student population who can assist in communication with families (see also Strategies 9 and 20).

Developing Interdisciplinary Projects

Teachers play an important role in advancing sociopolitically relevant, culturally sustaining, and humanizing pedagogies at their schools (Bajaj, Argenal, & Canlas, 2017; S. Lee & Walsh, 2017; Paris & Alim, 2017; Salazar, 2013). For newcomers, classrooms are where they learn English, master curricular content, and make connections from the learning to their own lives. The following collaborative unit

Figure 2.1. Sample Student Intake Interview Form

Personal History:
1. What language(s) do you speak at home?
2. Where were you born? (city/country)
3. When did you arrive in the United States? (month/year)
4. Where did you live before entering the United States?
5. Did you live anywhere else before you came to [current town/city]?
6. When did you arrive in [current town/city]?
7. With whom do you live?

Schooling and Academic History:
1. In what language(s) do you feel most comfortable speaking, reading, and/or writing?
2. Did you go to school in your home country?
3. How old were you when you began the 1st grade/primary school?
4. What language(s) did teachers use with you when you were going to school in your country?
5. How did you get to school? How long did it take you to get to school each time you went to school?
6. How many days a week did you go to school?
7. How many students were in each of your classes?
8. How long were your classes? How many minutes?
9. What subjects did you study in school?
10. Did you go to school every day or did you miss days? Why did you miss school days?
11. Did you like going to school in your home country? What did you like best?
12. Have you ever been in a special needs program or have you received special needs services? Please indicate types of programs or services.
13. What are your interests? (e.g., music, arts, sports, hobbies, etc.)
14. How do you feel about going to school here?
15. What would help you feel good/better about going to school here?

Future Goals:
1. What are your future goals?

Note: Modified from Boston International High School and Newcomers Academy, as cited in Castellón et al. (2015) and Samway et al. (2020, p. 36).

from Oakland International High School exemplifies how educators sought to meet state standards and curricular goals while also making the content relevant and engaging for their newcomer students from dozens of different countries.

In the summer of 2015, two teachers from the 9th- and 10th-grade classes at OIHS (on the value of multigrade classes, see also Strategy 3) developed an interdisciplinary unit across science and history related to issues of water use and scarcity. Rather than focusing solely on the statewide issues of drought and water use in California, the teachers together decided to develop a multiweek unit that would have students also research water collection, use, and management in their home countries. After compiling their research, students first developed a presentation in their home language directed at someone in their families; as the teachers instructed, "imagine you are presenting this information to your grandmother." The students brought in photos of the people their presentations were tailored to; these photos of cousins, parents, or grandparents were assembled into a collage on a bulletin board. After developing their presentations in their home languages, they then, as a last step, translated their work into English in language groups and with the teachers' help, and delivered these presentations to the class. In their presentations, students discussed how they collected water in their home countries, analyzed inequalities in terms of access to water in rural and urban areas, and examined differences between water use in their home countries and in the United States.

In a classroom with dozens of nationalities, and diverse ethnicities and languages even among those groups, achieving "culturally" relevant pedagogy to match each "culture" may be difficult. By highlighting the role of knowledge production linked to their own realities (e.g., teachers' instructions to "develop the presentation for your grandmother"), teachers were able to engage the class in discussions of local environmental issues from vastly diverse places around the globe. Also, by having students first develop presentations in their home language and then translate their work into English, the project built fluency and skills in students' home languages and in English, stressing the importance of both languages, while also focusing on English language instruction.

Another example of a project—initiated by students rather than the teacher—was in the government class at OIHS immediately following the 2016 U.S. presidential election. Many students and their families—especially those with Latinx and Muslim heritage—were extremely worried about changes to immigration policy that could affect their ability to stay in the United States. Students asked the teacher to carve out time in class, and the teacher agreed, to discuss the complexities of federal and state laws. Together, the students, with support from their teacher, created "Know Your Rights" posters in multiple languages based on what they had learned in class (see Figure 2.2). Students posted the information around the school, especially for students in younger grades who hadn't been in the country as long and were extremely fearful about potential impending changes; students were also later asked to share these posters with community groups to display and distribute.

FAMILY HISTORIES

Another way for students to engage in projects that relate to their own backgrounds is through oral history and family interviews. These can take place through class assignments or school events that explore the experiences of families and communities. For example, at Oakland International High School, students have a multimedia lab and annually make videos about their migration stories and/or family experiences. Assignments, whether utilizing video or writing, can also include comparisons of something that is different in home countries

Figure 2.2. Sample Bilingual (Arabic-English) "Know Your Rights Poster" Made by OIHS Students (2016)

Note: Provided by Sailaja Suresh, then coprincipal of Oakland International High School. It also appears in Bajaj and Suresh (2018, p. 96).

versus in students' new country. Educators must take care with such an assignment, given that students and family members may have experienced trauma during migration.

Another such approach to gathering more information about families' backgrounds is what Munter et al. (2007) have documented in the Oral History Nights held annually at Canyon Valley School, where the majority of students were immigrants from Mexico and Honduras. The authors explain,

> Oral History Night events have provided a platform for lively and enriching exchanges of family history, "funds of knowledge," and cultural exchanges. Parents, grandparents, and all extended family members are invited to the school/community center, and as part of the event, these community members bring photographs that can help them

to tell the unique story of their own family's journey, accomplishments, sacrifices, and experiences. With their own children in the storytelling circle, . . . these conversations can be guided with questions such as:

- "Tell me about the place in which you were born."
- "What was it like growing up in [name of town or city]?"
- "How did you (or relatives) come to the decision to leave your home to travel to this country?" (p. 124)

Students can be involved in such Oral History Nights as participants or as interviewers—recording, transcribing, and translating the interviews as a literacy practice, as well as illustrating such stories into comics or short graphic novels (e.g., Bui, 2012). Students can also interview family members as a homework assignment rather than gathering all the families together, as in the example provided by Munter et al. (2007).

Schools with large numbers of immigrant and refugee students may use their life stories as part of the curriculum to facilitate learning from one another in the classroom. This allows the students to draw on their histories and heritages, and highlights the strengths and resilience of diverse students. The organization Reimagining Migration has a Moving Stories Educational Guide that offers prompts to facilitate peer conversations and interviews (Suárez-Orozco & Strom, 2021). At Gregorio Luperón High School in New York City, students were often asked to draw upon their personal experiences to write essays. In one class, students were to write about and then contrast their school experiences back home. It soon became apparent that these students, who hailed from across Latin America, but primarily from the Dominican Republic, had differential access to and quality of education in their home countries, depending on factors like location and family income (Bajaj & Bartlett, 2017).

Educators at comprehensive high schools can also use this approach. For example, to meet the Language Arts content objective of writing a narrative, teachers in a sheltered English class at La Follette High School in Madison, Wisconsin, invited students to tell their immigration story. First, the students used an online platform to tag on a map where they had lived and added images and text (using multiple languages) to visually tell their story. Then, the students could share and record the story in whatever language they felt was most accessible for them. Finally, the educators found teachers and community members who could help translate the narratives into English, so the students' stories could be widely shared with their classmates. In some cases, the narrative was translated orally. For example, a student from Laos told the story in Laotian to a bilingual peer, who then translated it out loud, and it was written down in English. These efforts also pushed the teachers to identify linguistic resources in the broader community and draw on them to get to know their students and help them engage with each other (interview, Lisa Valverde, December 2021).

The opportunity to explore one's own story and put it into conversation with others can also provide greater understanding for students of the complex dynamics that spur migration (aligned with the "prismatic" approach discussed earlier). Such explorations can trigger pain, trauma, and distress, and trained counselors should be available to provide students support if such emotions arise (see also Strategy 13). However, the potential for healing and greater engagement in learning through such activities makes them worth considering as a strategy for educating immigrant and refugee youth. In an alum focus group at Oakland International High School, a former student who was in college at the time of the interview remembered the video she made about her family and community as one of the highlights of her time in high school. Ultimately, honoring in one's classroom who the students are and where they have come from can be a powerful way to connect the classroom experience with students' lives and stories.

SUMMARY

- Spaces in the classroom can be created to center elements of students' lives: for example, a bulletin board in a classroom with family pictures, a unit that has them explore issues in their home countries as compared to the United States, and/or multilingual posters and projects.
- Educators should give students multiple options and agency over how much to disclose about their families and communities, as recounting difficult stories may be traumatizing.
- Students from the same country or region may have different cultures, languages, and histories due to the forces of marginalization and other complex histories. Take time to get to know students and their unique backgrounds and avoid essentializing.

ADDITIONAL RESOURCES

All resources are linked at the book's companion website: www.bit.ly/Immig RefugeeEd

- The article on "Culture in the Classroom" from Learning for Justice (formerly Teaching Tolerance) offers videos, self-assessments, worksheets, and links to further resources for educators. See https://www .learningforjustice.org/professional-development/culture-in-the-classroom
- The article from Colorín Colorado entitled "Learning About Your Students' Backgrounds" offers tips for exploring students' languages, cultures, attitudes toward schooling, and forms of parental engagement, especially for students with family origins in Latin America. See https://www.colorincolorado.org/article/learning-about-your-students -backgrounds
- Modules and videos from the City University of New York's Initiative on Immigration and Education (CUNY-IIE) offer helpful resources for educators of newcomers. See https://www.cuny-iie.org/

Strategy 3
Practice Purposeful Grouping

Lesley Bartlett

You have to think about when you're grouping, how you're grouping, why you're grouping.

—Sara, Math Teacher, 2013

Schools that successfully serve immigrant and refugee youth frame diversity as a learning opportunity. Rather than automatically dividing students based on academic ability, linguistic ability, race, ethnicity, grade level, age, gender, or membership in an ELL subgroup, students are purposefully grouped based on factors such as choice, interests, available resources, and the overall learning goal.

Scholars have argued that tracking and ability grouping have few academic benefits and serve to further class-based social stigmatization and alienation from schooling (Boaler & Staples, 2008; Burris et al., 2006; Oakes, 1985), although Figlio and Page (2002) urge caution in overgeneralizing findings. Tracking is often framed as a strategy that supports meritocracy or efficiency. However, as critic Jeannie Oakes (1985) states, "Tracking does not equalize educational opportunity for diverse groups of students. It does not increase the efficiency of schools by maximizing learning opportunities for everyone" (p. 40). Tracking students into different classes, and ability grouping within classrooms, provides access to high-status knowledge to some and denies it to others. Tracking has been shown to be deleterious to the academic achievement of students categorized as English learners (Callahan, 2005; Swail et al., 2005). In addition, it socially stigmatizes students in a way that increases as they move toward secondary school.

NEWCOMER PROGRAMS

However, there are school models that strategically separate immigrant and refugee students for a period of time. Newcomer programs are small, tight-knit programs for students who have been in the country for a limited time (often 6 months or less). They are specifically tailored to the needs of newcomer students,

44

providing emergent bilinguals with intensive English language instruction while supporting content area instruction (Short & Boyson, 2012). Typically, enrollment in a newcomer program is short term—usually 1–2 years, depending on the program—giving students time to develop their English skills before being mainstreamed. Programs may be full- or part-day; they can be established for any grade level; they may be programs within a school, at separate sites, or encompassing full schools.[1] Based on a national survey of secondary school newcomer programs and case studies of 10 of them, Short and Boyson (2012) identified several key aspects of successful newcomer programs:

- flexible scheduling of courses and students
- careful staffing plus targeted professional development
- basic literacy development materials for adolescents and reading interventions adapted for English language learners
- content area instruction to fill gaps in educational backgrounds
- extended time for instruction and support (e.g., after school, Saturday, and summer programs)
- connections with families and social services
- diagnostics and monitoring of student data
- transition measures to ease newcomers into the regular school programs or beyond high school (p. 2)

Thus, at the school and program levels, educators need to think through the goals and available resources, and develop programs accordingly.

GROUPING WITHIN CLASSES

Comparing Diverse Forms

Similarly, within classrooms, educators may need to pursue purposeful grouping. There are occasions and tasks that call for grouping by shared language (De Jong & Commins, 2006): for example, teachers might on occasion use "homogeneous grouping to promote language development, target literacy needs, or focus on specific academic skills" (Kessler et al., 2018, p. 18). Students who share a home language can work collaboratively on content area learning tasks, engaging their full linguistic repertoire. However, this approach should not be the default option.

In contrast, heterogeneous groups allow students to learn from and interact with people with diverse perspectives. Students working below grade-level can learn from peer explanations and work; those who have a firm grasp of the material can learn a great deal from explaining it to peers. According to Glass (n.d.), in heterogeneous groups, "less able pupils are at reduced risk of being stigmatized and exposed to a 'dumbed-down' curriculum" and "teachers' expectations for all pupils are maintained at higher levels" (p. 1). Heterogeneous grouping may also foster positive relationships among students with different backgrounds and improve attitudes toward school.

Many schools serving immigrant and refugee students embrace heterogeneous, multigrade grouping. In fact, the Internationals Network for Public Schools (2017) has declared heterogeneity and collaboration as one of its five core tenets, along with experiential learning, language and content integration, localized autonomy and responsibility, and promoting learning for students and adults alike (see also García & Sylvan, 2011). As reported by Bajaj and Bartlett (2017), Internationals Network schools such as Brooklyn International High School and Oakland International High School support heterogeneous and collaborative learning environments. Classes are small, and each group works with the same team of teachers for the first two years, during 9th and 10th grades. For example, students work on group projects and complete different aspects of a task according to either their skill level, their linguistic level, or personal preference, allowing all to experience success and contribute to the project. When necessary, they engage peer translators or use Google Translate to communicate. Several schools in the Internationals Network combine 9th and 10th grades, allowing for some intergenerational support and extra time to learn the pedagogical model in a small-team environment. As explained by Roshan, a student who had previously lived in Lebanon and Turkey, "Teachers know that students just got to New York, [that we] don't speak that much English, and [we] don't have a lot of participation. So, the thing about 9th and 10th grade is to get ready for 11th grade. That's what the teachers try their best [to do]" (as cited in Bajaj & Bartlett, 2017, p. 28).

Further, students who are less familiar with the emphasis on inquiry-based learning and critical thinking may need more time to adapt to the pedagogical model. Bajaj and Bartlett (2017) report that some Internationals Network students noted that their previous schools had emphasized memorization. For example, Aboubakar attended private school from grades 1 to 8 in Guinea. There, he said, "you have to like, memorize the lessons, without knowing like what you're studying. . . . And here, you have to like—they show you what you are studying and everything. You don't have to memorize, you just have to, like, know what you are studying" (p. 29). Pedagogies are deeply cultural; they encapsulate ideas about how young people learn (e.g., Schweisfurth, 2013). Students may find such a pedagogical shift challenging, and multigrade settings provide peer models to draw on and time to adapt.

Thus, in forming groups, educators may consider a range of factors. They may intentionally separate students with the same home language, in order to force a focus on English, or they may, when possible, pair newcomers with a peer who shares their language and can explain tasks. Heterogeneous groupings often incorporate students with various levels of English proficiency. Teachers might consider academic background and ability. They might intentionally spread out the students who demonstrate leadership skills and/or a talent for collaboration (Kessler et al., 2018). Educators should revisit groupings frequently, considering learning activities and social goals.

Utilizing Heterogeneous Grouping

Heterogeneous grouping requires careful planning of engaging tasks. Teachers must structure learning activities so that students are interacting with and learning from each other. As noted in School Profile 2 about the International High School at Prospect Heights, it helps if teachers can team together and coplan, so they all draw on the same pedagogical routines, thus reducing the cognitive burden as students are trying to learn English and content knowledge.

Heterogeneous learning involves mixing students with different levels of English proficiency, background knowledge, and/or content knowledge. It pairs well with translanguaging pedagogy. As shown in School Profile 2, teachers often group students with others who share their home language to research and write content before working together to translate it into English and present it to peers. In heterogeneous groupings, it is important to remember that students have different levels of literacy proficiency in the language spoken by their families, as well. At Manhattan Bridges High School in New York City, where most students share a Spanish-speaking background, students in heterogeneous groups in a social studies class worked on a bilingual text about the Mayan civilization:

> Students were reading the text independently while the teacher moved from student to student quietly asking questions and then asking if students had any questions. Since the text was in both Spanish and English, the teacher showed the students how to use one text to help facilitate comprehension in the other. . . . A student whose home language was English had difficulty with some of the Spanish text. Ms. Y. suggested that the student read the same section in English first, and then try the Spanish. She also suggested the student look for similar words in both languages, known as cognates. The teacher in this case recognized that the Spanish text was challenging for the student, and she used instructional strategies to help her access it. These instructional strategies involved developing metalinguistic awareness about features that were similar in both languages, and about how reading the text in the dominant language and comparing it to the target language version can assist understanding of it in the target language. (Castellón et al., 2015, p. 103)

Heterogeneity may entail mixing students with different language backgrounds, as well. In another example, this time from an 11th-grade history class from the High School for Dual Language and Asian Studies in New York City, "heterogeneous small groups and the whole class could be seen doing a close reading and analysis of a Supreme Court case (*Korematsu v. U.S.*, 1944) and a Presidential Executive Order (9066, February 19, 1942), both related to how the U.S. government justified the Japanese-American internment during the 1940s" (Castellón et al., 2015, p. 50). During this lesson, "ELLs, former ELLs, and fully English proficient students who have never been ELLs worked together to develop metacognitive strategies for understanding these complex historical texts, deepening their historical perspectives and knowledge as to how these arguments have been made in U.S. history" (Castellón et al., 2015, p. 50).

Heterogeneous grouping facilitates a translanguaging pedagogy (see also Strategy 1) and an asset-based stance toward students that honors students' histories and heritages (see also Strategy 2), while requiring differentiated instruction (see also Strategy 5).

SUMMARY

- Schools serving immigrant and refugee students need to think carefully about the pros and cons of different models for grouping students by newcomer status, grade level, home language, or English language ability. At the same time, they should make sure the groupings are flexible, so as to allow students to pursue more challenging educational settings when they are ready to do so.
- Grouping students by home language in the early stage of a learning task allows them to engage their home language resources while dedicating attention to learning new and challenging content. It can also be valuable at other moments in time.
- Heterogeneous grouping uses diversity as an educational resource. It entails mixing students with different home languages, different levels of fluency or literacy in the home language, and different levels of English proficiency.

ADDITIONAL RESOURCES

All resources are linked at the book's companion website: www.bit.ly/Immig RefugeeEd

Both of these reports discuss strategies for grouping with newcomer students:

- Short, D. J., & Boyson, B. A. (2012). *Helping newcomer students succeed in secondary schools and beyond.* Center for Applied Linguistics. https://www.cal.org/resource-center/publications/helpingnewcomer -students
- Kessler, J., Wentworth, L., & Darling-Hammond, L. (2018). *The Internationals Network for Public Schools: Educating our immigrant English language learners well.* Stanford Center for Opportunity Policy in Education. https://edpolicy.stanford.edu/sites/default/files/ International%20Network%20v2.pdf

Strategy 4

Incorporate Differentiated Instruction and Universal Design for Learning

Lesley Bartlett and Monisha Bajaj

> I have a few main goals in differentiating instruction: 1) Activating prior knowledge; 2) Lowering the cognitive burden for my students; and 3) Giving opportunities for students to leverage collaboration and reading/writing/speaking/listening in order to develop new skills and strengthen language and content.
>
> —Rita, a high school teacher from Brooklyn, August 8, 2021

DIFFERENTIATED INSTRUCTION

When they differentiate instruction, educators modify content and processes to meet the needs of different students. In addition, teachers may provide "flexibility in the assignments and ways students demonstrate what they have learned" (CAST, 2013). Differentiated instruction (DI) seeks to strike a balance between the academic content or curriculum and students' individualized needs (Tomlinson, 2016; Tomlinson & Imbeau, 2010). As Irujo (2004) notes,

> Differentiated instruction is not the same as individualized instruction. Every student is not learning something different; they are all learning the same thing, but in different ways. And every student does not need to be taught individually; differentiating instruction is a matter of presenting the same task in different ways and at different levels, so that all students can approach it in their own ways. (para. 13)

Differentiated instruction provides multiple avenues to arrive at the same destination. Teachers may find it easier to differentiate if they can establish small groups for specific purposes. For example, at South High School in Denver, Colorado, the teacher worked with Goodwill Industries to recruit volunteers who helped facilitate small-group instructional time (Thorpe, 2017).

Students may well have special needs that require modifications: According to 2014–2015 data from the U.S. Department of Education, 13% of students have a diagnosed disability, and 95% of them are educated in general education

49

classrooms (National Center for Education Statistics, 2017). Teachers must be well versed in pedagogical strategies to address their specific needs (Florian & Linklater, 2010; Jordan et al., 2009).

At the same time, teachers of emergent bilinguals—especially those with limited and interrupted formal education—must differentiate and scaffold for language and content learning (see also Strategy 5). It's important that educators understand how students learn new languages for oracy and literacy while also connecting to their background experiences and prior knowledge (Herrera et al., 2013; Samway, 2006; Samway et al., 2020; Tellez & Waxman, 2006; Walqui & Van Lier, 2010).

UNIVERSAL DESIGN FOR LEARNING

In comparison to DI, universal design for learning (UDL) is an approach that seeks to create educational settings, content, and processes that are accessible to the greatest possible range of learners with different needs, backgrounds, interests, and abilities (CAST, 2018). In other words, rather than designing courses with typical students in mind and then modifying for specific learners, educators who are guided by the principles of UDL design teaching and learning materials to be accessible to all, from the start. The idea is to build in supports that can benefit a range of needs. For example, using video materials with closed captions makes visual content accessible to people who have hearing loss, while also benefiting language learners who are working to improve their reading or listening skills. UDL is about planning for diversity and variability by providing multiple means of engagement, representation, and action and expression (see Figure 4.1).

The elements of UDL are particularly important for immigrant and refugee students. Teachers need to know and honor their students' histories (see also Strategy 2) and goals in order to recruit their interest and heighten the salience of goals. Translanguaging (see also Strategy 1) offers multiple means of representation, one of the core tenets of UDL. Teachers can provide multiple options for perception by pairing text with auditory information (e.g., through an audio-taped book at a listening station) or visual information (e.g., through a subtitled video clip). Content can be illustrated through multiple media and using different means—for example, by incorporating objects or realia, still images, and videos.

UDL and DI differ in some ways. For example, proponents of UDL see it as a necessary shift from "fixing the student" to "fixing the curriculum" (CAST, 2013). While DI entails tailoring content for different students, the UDL teacher offers a "buffet" of options, and students pick the one(s) they find most appealing. However, a similar goal informs both approaches. In fact, recognizing a need to differentiate instruction can provide critical insights regarding how the curriculum is excluding some students; changes suggested by a DI lens may well benefit a range of students. For example, teaching vocabulary benefits all students who have not yet learned certain academic terms. In this way, UDL is essentially DI done at an earlier stage (during curriculum design) and at a broader scale. Universal design and differentiated instruction can work in tandem to align the

Figure 4.1. Universal Design for Learning Guidelines

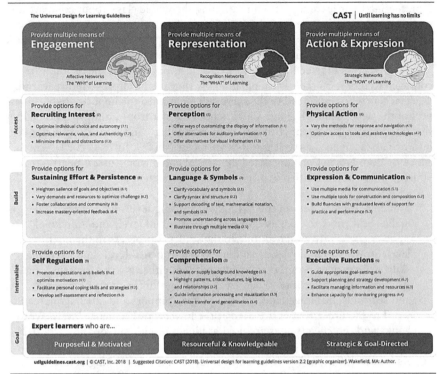

Note: From *Universal Design for Learning Guidelines Version 2.2,* by CAST, 2018 (http://udlguidelines.cast.org).

content of what students learn, the process of how students learn, the demonstrable outcomes of the learning, and the affective dimensions of student learning (Tomlinson & Imbeau, 2010).

DI AND UDL AS PATHWAYS TO LEARNING FOR NEWCOMERS

For newcomer immigrant and refugee students, particularly those who are labeled as English learners, differentiated instruction and universal design provide pathways to ensure the greatest possible engagement and accessibility with the curriculum. In an online survey we carried out in 2021 with educators of newcomer students that included approximately 40 open-ended questions about different educational approaches, teachers shared some of the strategies they use for differentiating instruction. A reading and English teacher in North Carolina noted, "During their guided instruction, I try to push them towards the next level by modeling through an 'I do, we do, you do' strategy. I also differentiate the process by providing sentence frames, word banks, picture support, etc. to different groups based on student need." She offered students different options for representing their learning: "If I am teaching the whole class about compare and contrast, some students might show understanding through a graphic organizer while another student writes a paragraph." Further, she allows students to "pick their projects based on interest" (survey, July 29, 2021).

Finally, students need to receive frequent feedback, and they should be encouraged to reflect on their learning and how they might improve future learning. The teachers who responded to the survey all mentioned the importance of this aspect of the work. Anjali Kamat, a high school teacher from California, noted that she incorporates "frequent checks for understanding" and "one-on-one frequent informal assessments," as well as self-assessments (survey, July 31, 2021). Another educator from North Carolina noted that initial and ongoing assessments (see also Strategy 6) are key for differentiating instruction effectively:

> Students are assessed on their [English] reading levels when they arrive. Students are each assigned an instructional level, and individual "power goals" are assigned to help the students progress to the next level. Strategies employed depend upon the students' levels and particular skills necessary to progress. Students work at either a word, sentence, or paragraph/discourse level. Each level involves a different set of supports and scaffolds, but in general, a lot of picture support and labeling/matching word to picture activities are used at the lower word/sentence levels. Word banks and sentence frames are used at higher levels. (survey, July 29, 2021)

As Novak (2018) suggested, "since students master speaking before writing, educators may provide English learners the option to audio record their learning, supplement with visuals, or use voice-recognition software to scaffold the language process as they continue to develop into writers" (para. 17). California educator Anjali Kamat further noted that her strategies for differentiating instruction for newcomers include "individual scaffolds such as word banks, formulaic expressions, explicit models and gradual release." She offers "many opportunities for peer collaboration" and "authentic learning experiences such as writing letters to the principal or preparing for a poetry reading" (survey, July 31, 2021).

Drawing from our survey of newcomer educators as well as scholars and practitioners who have explored effective approaches for newcomer students (Ford, 2012; Irujo, 2004), we suggest the following actions that are necessary to effectively differentiate instruction:

- *Garner a Deep Knowledge of Students.* Educators should draw on the initial intake survey about students' educational backgrounds and interests (see Figure 2.1 in Strategy 2), as well as their sense of students' background knowledge and readiness. In addition, teachers should utilize regular check-ins and continuous assessment (see also Strategy 6), documenting (in a central location) student development over time.
- *Consider Grouping and Accessibility.* As discussed in Strategy 3, small-group instruction and/or peer collaboration can be effective ways for students

to learn, especially in a new language. These groups could be collectively drawing on a text written in their home language, then translating it into English or utilizing a more simplified text than other students, as a means of differentiating the content and ensuring that all are making progress. It is essential that teachers provide emergent bilinguals with multiple avenues to access key content, including text in the home language and/or simplified text in English (Echevarria et al., 2008).

- *Have a Repertoire of Instructional Approaches.* Educators should have a repertoire of activities, strategies, and approaches to engage students. As mentioned by the educators in the survey responses above, these can include word banks, matching activities, graphic organizers, and so forth. Teachers holding high expectations for all students enable them to continually "level up" to new activities as they gain mastery. Further, having predictable pedagogical routines across classrooms can help reduce the cognitive load for newcomer students (see School Profile 2).

- *Differentiate Assessments and Homework.* Assessment and homework assignments that are aligned to the needs of each student maintain student engagement and ensure gradual mastery of the content with adequate opportunities to demonstrate their knowledge. The high dropout rate for emergent bilinguals has been attributed by some scholars in part to the inability of students to access the content and learning at school, resulting in frustration at what seems like a futile exercise (Callahan, 2013; D. Rodriguez, Carrasquillo, et al., 2020).

Drawing on the principles and practices of UDL and DI can help educators meet the distinct needs of newcomers in their classrooms.

SUMMARY

- Universal design and differentiated instruction are classroom-based strategies that can help students with varied educational backgrounds and English proficiency levels access the curriculum.
- UDL and DI can offer students different pathways to progress and mastery within a single classroom.

ADDITIONAL RESOURCES

All resources are linked at the book's companion website: www.bit.ly/Immig RefugeeEd

- EdWeek offers suggestions for differentiating instruction in general and for emergent bilinguals in particular. See https://www.edweek.org/ teaching-learning/differentiated-instruction

- CAST's website has many resources on universal design for learning. See https://www.cast.org/impact/universal-design-for-learning-udl
- Ferlazzo, L. & K. Hull Sypnieski. (2018). *The ELL Teacher's Toolbox: Hundreds of Practical Ideas to Support Your Students.* John Wiley and Sons.

Strategy 5

Support Students With Limited and Interrupted Formal Education

Lisa Auslander With Daniel Walsh

Students with limited and interrupted formal education (SLIFE, also sometimes called simply SIFE) are a unique group of newcomer English learners. Some have large gaps in their formal education due to political unrest, trauma, violence, or financial constraints in their home countries (Custodio & O'Loughlin, 2017; Hos, 2016). SLIFE students are truly heterogeneous; even among students from the same country, there can be great linguistic and cultural diversity. Given their limited or interrupted education, upon arrival in secondary schools in the United States they face an urgent need to learn academic content and English before they exceed the legal age limit for remaining in secondary school and "age out" of the system (Umansky et al., 2018). While all of the strategies in this book apply to SLIFE students, they may need additional or alternative supports; thus, this strategy is provided to offer ways to further center their distinct needs.

Data on SLIFE students are not systematically collected or reported, meaning districts and states often don't know the size or needs of the population. Too often, schools don't identify SLIFE students, leading to improper placement in classes. States and districts should set up systems for identifying, placing, and monitoring the progress of SLIFE students. In addition, scholars recommend specific professional development for and strategic planning by principals and teachers around the challenges faced by SLIFE students (Bigelow & Watson, 2013). Responsibility for meeting the needs of SLIFE students should be shared schoolwide, and not limited to ESL teachers.

RESPONDING TO THE NEEDS OF SIFE/SLIFE STUDENTS

Secondary schools may respond to the needs of SLIFE students in different ways. At New World High School in the Bronx, New York, teachers "receive a file to notify them of the SIFE in their classes. Furthermore, an English as Second Language (ESL) teacher spends three days a week after school working with these students. . . . This extra class in the afternoons allows students to develop skills that they missed. Peer tutors are also assigned to students for individual assistance" (Castellón et al., 2015, p. 199). Schools with larger populations of SLIFE students may set up separate classrooms for them. For example, Boston's Newcomer Academy (NA) accepts newcomer students, and most spend 1 year there before transferring to the colocated Boston International High School; SLIFE students have the option to stay for 2 years. In 2015, 53 SIFE students enrolled at NA (Castellón et al., 2015, p. 7). NA allows educators to dedicate more time to the specific needs of SLIFE students and a SLIFE student at NA takes "four [content] classes in her native language—Spanish, Haitian Creole, or Cape Verdean Creole—and two ESL classes. . . . The classes are typically small, which allows for a great deal of individualized attention from the teacher" (p. 7.)

Regardless of the setting, SLIFE students benefit from "an explicit focus on language development, with contextualized pronunciation work, vocabulary and sentence development, and discourse structure woven into lessons," in classrooms with sufficient "modeling and scaffolding" through, for example, "images, concept maps, and sentence frames" (Castellón et al., 2015, p. 7). "Learning is seen as a collaborative endeavor" and students interact "to assist in each other's learning, clarify meaning, and produce improved and greater sophistication in their discourse" (p. 7). In these classes, hands-on activities that activate prior knowledge and "value students' experiences and perspectives" are "designed to encourage purposeful communication using cognitively challenging and discipline-specific language and complex texts," and they "encourage the externalization of student learning so that teachers can formatively assess and monitor student comprehension of content" (p. 7).

SLIFE students have specific language, literacy, academic, socioemotional, and cultural needs. These students need learning programs that

- address their acculturation to the U.S. school system;
- attend to their socioemotional needs (poverty, posttraumatic stress disorder [PTSD], family separation or reunification, etc.);
- provide focused initial literacy instruction appropriate for adolescents;
- provide focused academic skill instruction to bridge gaps in knowledge; and
- provide integration of content and language instruction. (WIDA, 2020, p. 2)

BUILDING BRIDGES TO ACADEMIC SUCCESS

One program that provides useful guidance regarding how to address the needs of SLIFE students is Bridges to Academic Success, a project of the Graduate Center at the City University of New York (CUNY). In collaboration with the New York State Department of Education, Bridges includes an interdisciplinary team of researchers, curriculum developers, and instructional coaches that developed curricular materials for SLIFE students, including English language arts (ELA), English as a new language (ENL), home language arts in Spanish

(HLA), and math. These curricular resources were designed to meet the following needs:

- provide the necessary scaffolding of content and language development
- facilitate and foster translanguaging between the home language and English as the new language (Cioè-Peña & Snell, 2015; García & Kleyn, 2016)
- provide the necessary foundational literacy supports for those students who need them to access content in the classroom (Gibbons, 2014)

Bridges materials support teachers in creating a welcoming environment, with activities that develop students' social–emotional learning (SEL) and self-awareness through the lens of identity (see CASEL, 2020). Students begin the school year with activities that prompt self-reflection, drawing upon their cultural identities and life experiences (see also Strategy 2). The curricula also emphasize relationship building, teamwork, problem solving, and seeking or offering support when needed. Finally, the materials build toward critical consciousness.

To illustrate the value of such a program, the remainder of this section describes how one teacher utilizes the integrated ENL/ELA curricula with a group of students in scaffolding their social–emotional learning and their language and literacy skills.

Introducing the School Partnership and Teacher Collaborator

Bridges partners with schools across New York state to implement the curricula as a way to mentor students and provide a more meaningful pathway to success when they enter middle or high school. One such partnership is with the International Community High School (ICHS), a newcomer high school in the South Bronx, New York. ICHS is a small school with students and staff from all over the world. In 2021–2022, the home language of 80% of students was Spanish, followed by French (11%) and Arabic (4%). In terms of home country, 37% of the youth came from the Dominican Republic; 10% from Honduras; 4% each from Guatemala, Mexico, and Ecuador; and 3% each from El Salvador, Senegal, and Yemen (ICHS student demographics, 2021). Moreover, in 2019, 98% of students were considered to have low economic status by city metrics (*U.S. News*, 2019).

Drawing on Lisa's observations in classrooms and work with teachers, this strategy showcases Ivonne Mora, a teacher who has been working with immigrant and refugee youth at ICHS since 2012. She teaches English Language Arts integrated with English as a New Language, and a Spanish Drama class to promote and improve Spanish language literacy. She serves as the literacy department leader and has taught the Bridges program for SLIFE students since 2016. For language and literacy support, Ivonne's students spend approximately 4 hours per day exclusively in her classroom, but they join their peers for a science core content class and electives such as physical education, art, and music. Additionally, students may leave Bridges once they are deemed ready, but they continue to receive support in other ways.

Creating a Welcoming Community

Ivonne began the 2021–2022 academic year as an ENL teacher with a class of 14 students who read at or below the 3rd-grade level in their home language (based on home language assessment scores) and were quite new to English. Ivonne started the year by having students prepare presentations about their home country; with her guidance, the students developed slides with pictures about their home country and added short bilingual paragraphs. Students described their country's location, currency, traditional food, dance, languages spoken, holidays, and more. For example, one student gave a presentation about her home country of Ecuador, where, in addition to sharing food and the physical features of her country, she described traditional artistic culture (translated from Spanish): "In Ecuador we dance traditional music, we dance with *polleras* (full skirts) and a white shirt adorned with flowers."

After each presentation, the rest of the class gave respectful feedback, highlighting what the presenters did well and posing questions. The audience, with the help of Ivonne and peers, provided their feedback in English. This specific practice promoted appreciation and respect for all students' home languages while modeling English learning, risk-taking, and trust-building. One student said about this work, "I liked the presentation of countries because it makes you lose a little of the fear of presenting in the classroom."

Moving from descriptive presentations, Ivonne helped students create individual written profiles where they reflected on deeper aspects of their background, culture, identity, and individual interests and values. The Ecuadorian student talked about her dreams of being a doctor, her interests in social media and learning language, and the value she places on family, neighbors, and classmates. Through these activities early in the year, students began to develop social awareness and relationships with one another. One student described working together in the classroom (translated from Spanish): "Sometimes we ask classmates what it means here and they help us. It is good to work in a group."

Differentiating Classroom Instruction Through Language and Content Scaffolds

In addition to building on existing social–emotional learning skills, the Bridges ELA Unit 1 entitled "Identity & Connections" helps teachers scaffold language and literacy skills required to express complex ideas. The unit is based on principles of scaffolding; macro-scaffolds support students in making connections to central ideas (Walqui, 2006). In this case, throughout the unit, students explore complex questions about identity. Ivonne worked with the students to develop ways to describe and identify the essential question "How are we the same and different?" The students initially responded to the essential question in conversation and discussion in small groups based on the class presentations. In this activity, using a graphic organizer, students practiced the language of compare and contrast, noting similarities and differences in where different people are from, what they eat, what they wear, and what they like to do.

To extend their learning, students read a central text in English about a young African woman from Guinea describing her home, goals, interests, and values. Students worked in home language groups or pairs wherever possible to translate and annotate vocabulary using a glossary with visuals. They then read independently at their own pace. Afterward, students retold a chunk of the text: The partners took turns reading and retelling to make meaning from the text, first negotiating the text in their home language and then in English. In performing this activity, translanguaging was actively encouraged (see also Strategy 1). Students drew from their entire language repertoire to make meaning and explore their language skills in a way that centered understanding. After working together to make meaningful connections to the text, students completed a graphic organizer about the character's life. They wrote sentences about the character that included vocabulary related to the reading and writing assignment. Ivonne referred students to tools around the classroom such as word walls, student-created glossaries translating adjectives commonly used in writing, and common sentence stems. Later in the unit, they wrote compare-and-contrast paragraphs and short essays about the character's experiences.

This initial unit helped students learn how to talk and write about identity and community. In describing themselves and learning about their peers and characters from central texts, the students learned vocabulary, sentence patterns, and communication strategies in English. Students reflected on their own goals, values, and interests; in grappling with similarities and differences, students connected their own experiences to those of others. Ivonne described partner learning in her classroom: "Peers often model for one another, and it is here where students who are not learning at the same pace can see that learning is possible."

The Bridges curriculum specifically promotes the use of context or image clues to help students make meaning. Students gain confidence in using visuals as they build their language and academic skills. Over the course of the unit, Ivonne noticed that students were able to decode more words in English and use translanguaging strategies to understand what they were reading. In terms of writing, students were presented with various opportunities to learn how English works, including foundational skills and sentence writing instructions for students who needed that level of support. Ivonne said, "After students learn and acquire language within specific parameters in Unit 1, they are able to experiment with more language to explain their thoughts or ideas."

Developing Increasingly Complex Writing to Build on Ideas

In later units, students worked at their own pace to write more robust sentences and, as they were ready, paragraphs. The essential question in Unit 3 was "How does water impact people?" The unit helped students express more complex thinking about resources and the environment. For example, as shown in Figure 5.1, one student wrote simple sentences in response to the prompt in the preassessment and the essential question. Using the sentence stem "We use water for," he wrote, "People use water to drink and cook." Throughout the unit, the teacher provided sentence stems and transition words such as "for example" and "so."

Figure 5.1. Student Preassessment From Unit 3

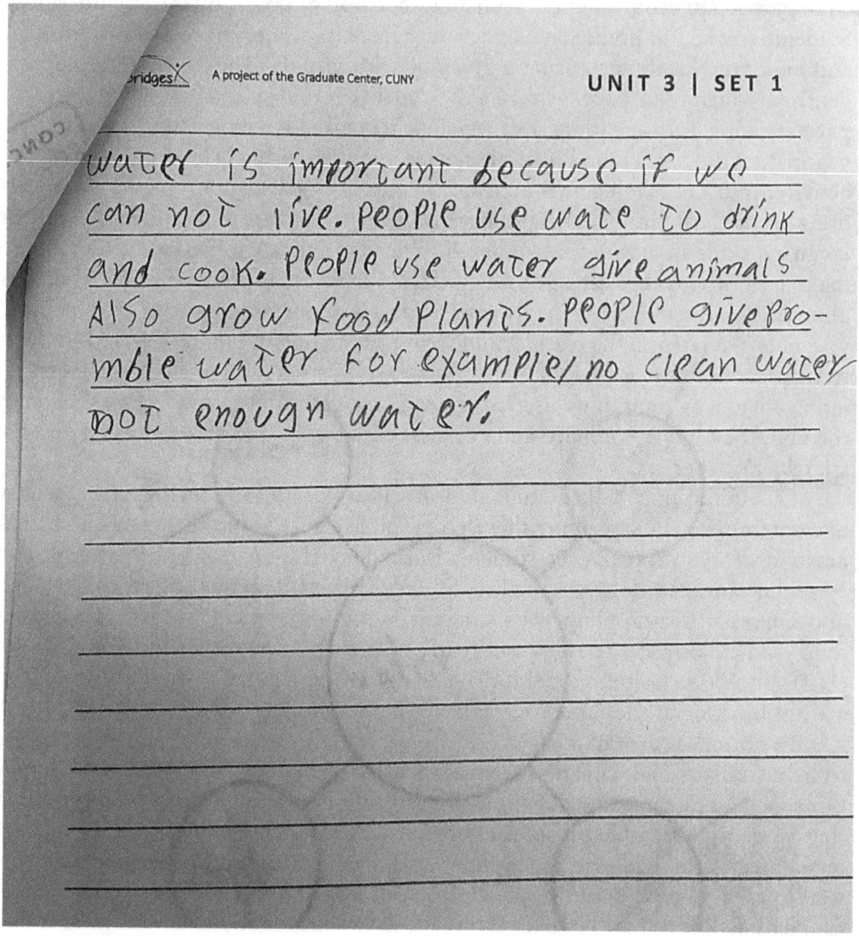

bridges. A project of the Graduate Center, CUNY   UNIT 3 | SET 1

water is important because if we can not live. People use wate to drink and cook. People use water give animals Also grow food Plants. People give promble water for example/ no clean water not enough water.

Note: Photo by Lisa Auslander, 2018.

As the unit progressed, students experienced scaffolding around sentence expansion and use of transitions. As a result, this student was able to write much more complex sentences that reflected his ideas and arguments. An excerpt of what he wrote follows (see also Figure 5.2):

> When people don't have enough clean water they can not drink water so people drink dirty water [and] get sick. For example water crisis in Flint. The government changes Flints [sic] water source to save money. So the drinking water was brow [sic] and smelled. As a result people in the community did not have enough money to purchase water.

Figure 5.2. Student Postassessment From Unit 3

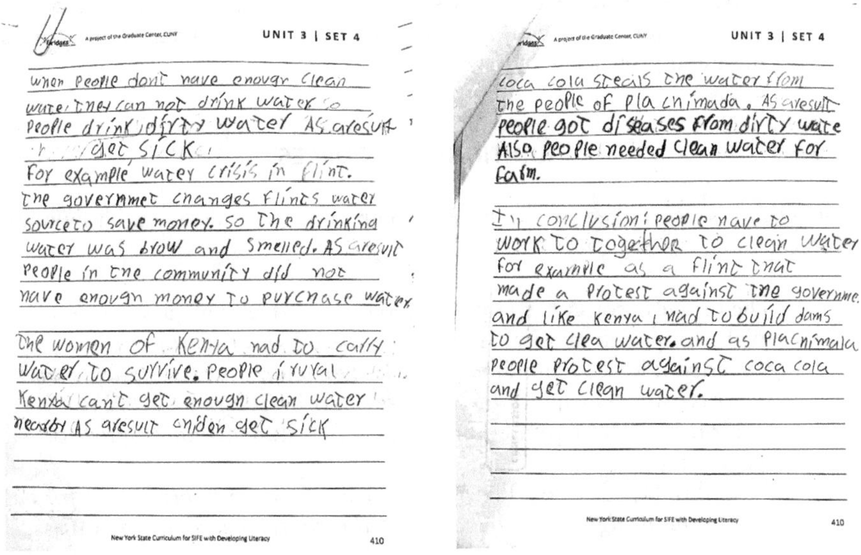

Note: Photo by Lisa Auslander, 2018.

Students demonstrated remarkable growth in their writing production and complexity over the course of the unit.

Designing Responsive Curriculum and Instruction

As exemplified in Ivonne's classroom and the additional writing samples, the Bridges curriculum helps teachers differentiate instruction for students with lower levels of literacy in their home language who have experienced interrupted or limited schooling (see also Strategy 4). Immigrant and refugee youth come to the United States from vastly different education systems, and secondary classrooms can leave them feeling unsuccessful if the right supports are not in place. Skilled teachers like Ivonne can use strategies from the Bridges curriculum and elsewhere to meet SLIFE students where they are while scaffolding language and content to build the knowledge and skills necessary to succeed in U.S. classrooms.

SUMMARY

- Teachers can use the curricular resources situated in thoughtfully designed classrooms to integrate students' language and home culture in ways that value student interests and backgrounds.

- Teachers using varied strategies such as oral practice, vocabulary instruction, sentence frames, visual supports, group activities, and peer collaboration enable SLIFE students to draw on their linguistic resources and build proficiency in English.

ADDITIONAL RESOURCES

All resources are linked at the book's companion website: www.bit.ly/Immig RefugeeEd

- The Bridges project has useful materials featuring strategies that teachers might adopt and modify. See https://www.bridges-sifeproject.com
- Robertson, K., & Lafond, S. (n.d.). *How to support ELL students with interrupted formal education (SIFEs)*. Colorín Colorado. https://www .colorincolorado.org/article/how-support-ell-students-interrupted-formal -education-sifes
- Custodio, B., & O'Loughlin, J. (2017). *Students with interrupted formal education: Bridging where they are and what they need.* Corwin Press.

Strategy 6
Undertake Holistic and Continuous Assessment

Monisha Bajaj

High-stakes assessments—often available only in English and shaped by cultural biases (Rosales & Walker, 2021)—frequently prove to be obstacles to the educational achievement of many newcomer students. Developing the specific variety of English academic language skills needed for such tests is a challenge. In their collaborative and participatory research with newcomer students, Bajaj, Canlas, and Argenal (2017) had newcomer high school students do an activity where they drew what was on their mind, in their hearts, and what they were working toward (represented by the head, heart, and hands, respectively, of a silhouette drawing). As Figure 6.1 shows, the high-stakes California High School Exit Examination (CAHSEE) weighed heavily on some students' minds and hearts. This image shows one of the student's silhouettes with words that multiple students wrote during the check-in. Notably, as Menken (2008) has argued, any content assessment that is in English assesses a student's facility with the language first and foremost.

Furthermore, some systems impose age limits and/or penalize schools for not graduating students within 4 years. These combined policies significantly constrain the education of newcomer youth. As a result, some programs have narrowed their academic focus. For example, responding to the needs of overage newcomer students with interrupted formal education (SIFE) who had insufficient credits, one program in Ohio dedicated half of its instructional time to English and the other half to career preparation, hoping it could help students land a job and possibly get a diploma equivalency (Seilstad, 2021, p. 48).

In the field of education, assessments and their politicization have been a topic of great debate, particularly when they have been tied to school funding and teacher salaries in punitive ways rather than utilized as a source of information about student progress toward mastery of new topics and skills. Well-crafted assessments can be an extremely useful tool for educators, especially those working with newcomer youth whose educational backgrounds are extremely varied due to conditions in their countries of origin and have often been interrupted through the migration process (see also Strategy 5). Not all newcomers are English language learners, but for those who are, research on schools serving ELLs

Figure 6.1. Refugee High School Students' Visual Check-In

Note: Photo by Melissa Canlas, 2014.

has shown that assessment is most effective (1) when it is done with a continuous-improvement mindset, (2) when it is varied, and (3) when it is utilized to improve learning approaches and student supports. Ongoing and intentional forms of assessment, with follow-through, comprise a core design element of strength for newcomer programs and schools (Castellón et al., 2015).

Within classrooms, teachers guide the academic assessment process through diagnostic or formative assessment practices, or ways to monitor student learning in real time while learning is still taking place and to give feedback immediately. Such forms of assessment are usually low stakes and allow educators to incorporate them easily into their classes. Larger-scale portfolio-based assessments—often rooted in project-based learning that offers students the opportunity to dive deep into topics—facilitate comprehensive learning. Many newcomer programs and schools use portfolios alongside statewide assessments or have exemptions from statewide exams for their students (Hantzopoulos et al., 2021).

CONTINUOUS AND FORMATIVE ASSESSMENT

Ongoing and formative assessments are regular ways that educators can attend to the academic, social, and emotional lives and progress of their students, identifying where any interventions may be needed. There are many activities that can be utilized at the start or end of class to gauge students' progress individually and collectively, such as the following:

- *Do-Now.* A quick warm-up activity (usually 5–10 minutes) at the start of a class, a Do-Now can also assess learning from the previous class session. One way to construct a Do-Now is to write or display a quote or question on the board and ask students to spend 5–10 minutes responding to it in writing or visually.
- *Pair-Share.* Putting students in pairs usually at the end of class for 5–10 minutes with a question such as "What are one or two learnings you are taking away from class today?" can be a way to assess what they've learned. Students can discuss with their partner, write their responses, and submit them to the teacher.
- *Entry and Exit Slips.* These quick activities can be used at the start or end of class. Similar to a Do-Now, they can be a question or a series of questions that students answer on a Post-It and place on chart paper at the front of the class, or answer on sheets of paper they submit, to demonstrate their learning from the previous or the same day's class session. Technology such as Poll Everywhere or Google Forms can also be utilized.
- *Free Write.* A free write for 5–10 minutes can allow students to respond to a prompt such as "What are three things you learned, two things you're still curious about, and one thing you don't understand?" or "Right now I'm feeling . . ." (Thomas, 2019).
- *Colored Cups or Thumb Signals.* These strategies can be utilized during the class by a teacher asking students for feedback as to where they are in terms of their understanding. For example, with colored cups, students each get three cups on their desk, and when asked, they can display their (1) green cup indicating that they understand what's being explained, (2) yellow cup indicating that they are "working through some confusion," or (3) red cup indicating that they are confused and in need of assistance (Thomas, 2019). Hand signals can work the same way, with thumbs up to indicate understanding, thumbs to the side to indicate some confusion, and thumbs down to indicate that they are not understanding at all. For online learning, the emoji features on platforms such as Zoom can quickly gauge group responses.

Looking at the aggregate of student data procured through these formats allows an educator to see where the majority of students are in terms of mastery and to alter or adapt the current or next lesson accordingly. If a majority of students have not mastered the intended content, then new strategies may be required for reaching them.

PROJECT-BASED LEARNING AND ASSESSMENT

At Oakland International High School, we do this portfolio process which is actually a more authentic and rigorous assessment of what our students know and can do. And we want to continue to put our energy there as opposed to putting it towards the state exams which is a test that's not accessible. Our portfolio process starts at 9th grade and follows the student through 12th grade. The 12th-grade portfolio is a senior project that's interdisciplinary and there's a lot of work the students have to do for it.

—Sailaja Suresh, former coprincipal,
Oakland International High School (interview, October 2015)

The increasing reliance on high-stakes exams as the sole learning metric and indicator of school quality has resulted in skewed incentives for schools. Since the passage of the No Child Left Behind Act (2002), which tied school funding to performance on high-stakes exams, some scholars have noted adverse impacts for students of color, students with special needs, and English learners, including, in some cases, deliberate attempts to push out these populations so schools' average scores can appear higher (Advancement Project, 2010; Au, 2011; Hantzopoulos & Tyner-Mullings, 2012; Hantzopoulos et al., 2021). Such efforts undermine students' basic human right to an education (Hantzopoulos et al., 2021).

As a more holistic approach to summative assessment, several schools have implemented portfolios and project-based assessment tasks (PBATs) in tandem with high-stakes tests or, where allowed, in lieu of such exams (Hantzopoulos et al., 2021). Generally, portfolios, projects, and performance tasks are characterized by their focus on the application of knowledge and skills, not just memorization. They also are typically open-ended and offer opportunities for the demonstration of contextualized understanding. Portfolios include academic projects that demonstrate a depth of understanding and can include artwork, creative writing, and even some components in students' home language and/or bilingually.

In New York City, a group of educators and schools formed the New York Performance Standards Consortium in the 1990s, which incorporates PBATs to "preserve their form of assessment rooted in experimentation, writing, and presentation"; schools in the Consortium are exempted from all the statewide Regents exams except for English Language Arts. According to Hantzopoulos et al. (2021), the 28 "consortium schools [have] graduated 50% more students in special education than the larger NYC school system and 40% more English language learners" (p. 3). Some schools within the Consortium, such as Bronx International High School and Manhattan International High School, are made up entirely of newcomer immigrant and refugee students; other schools in the Consortium serve a broader population with newcomers a segment of their student bodies.

The Internationals Network for Public Schools, which includes some 30 schools nationwide tailored for newcomer students, also includes portfolios as part of its performance assessment guidelines for its schools, most of which are not exempted from statewide exams. Other schools that are designed for newcomers and many others that have a broader population also use portfolios. For example, at Marble Hill School for International Studies in the Bronx, New York—a school that has an equal mix (50%) of incoming 9th-graders whose home language is English and 50% who are English learners—portfolio assessments are an integral part of the grading structure for all four years of high school. The school deliberately incorporated portfolios from its inception in 2002 as a way to "make sure that our assessment system was rigorous and meaningful and allowed students to be able to show what they were learning and to use language. [Portfolios are] a way for students to get deeper into content and to have a more extended learning project," according to the school's founding principal (as cited in Castellón et al., 2015, p. 146). Portfolio presentations at Marble Hill occur two times a year from grades 9 through 12, and take approximately 2 weeks to complete. Other courses support the portfolio process, such as by including presentation skills in advisory classes and scaffolding lessons toward the completion of portfolios. Some schools assemble panels of community members as the audience/evaluators for their portfolio presentations; other schools have students do these presentations one-on-one with faculty.

The content of portfolios is directly linked to the subjects under study as well as state and Common Core standards. Opportunities are given for students to revise in an iterative and scaffolded process for demonstrating content mastery. For example, at another newcomer school in New York City, a portion of student portfolios focused on content from their project-based learning over 4 weeks in various courses:

> In a Global History class, for example, sophomores worked on a "Gandhi project" that required them to conduct research on India and produce a brochure with their findings.
>
> Tenth graders in a science course participated in a project that involved looking at DNA, and . . . produc[ing] articles and lab reports. . . . Students learned that 96% of everyone's DNA was exactly the same. Students then wrote their findings in reports . . . and, as a culminating task, students presented their findings in an oral defense to teachers, peers, and community members. That content knowledge was further examined in a question and answer period with the panelists, in which students were expected to be able to answer direct, unrehearsed questions about the work they did as well as speculative questions that were informed by that work. (Roc et al., 2019, p. 10)

While the topics vary based on the subject matter under study, the opportunity for building toward a larger project, delving deeply into a topic with a chance to revise and make the work stronger, offers students hands-on experience that prepares them for the world of work and higher education. At some schools, there is also the additional metacognitive component of reflecting on the portfolio process, especially when it is new for students in the 9th and 10th grades, and the chance to go even deeper through a months-long 12th-grade senior project. The sample questions below from Marble Hill School for International Studies offer one approach to leveraging both the *content* and the *process* of the portfolios as an opportunity for learning and reflection:

1. How did this project help you understand [the topic]?
2. Did this project help you improve your research skills? Explain.
3. Did this project help you improve your writing skills? Explain.
4. What specific steps did you take to complete this project?
5. How did writing this piece make you feel?
6. What was difficult about this project? What was easy?
7. If you did this project again, what would you do differently? Why?
   (Castellón et al., 2015, p. 147)

In their longitudinal study across 10 schools in New York City, Hantzopoulos et al. (2021) found that over 90% of educators surveyed felt that portfolios were a more rigorous form of assessment than statewide exams; additionally, more than 80% said that such forms of assessment allowed them to better evaluate both student needs and performance. Portfolios as a complement to statewide exams—or, where possible, in lieu of them—offer an opportunity for deepening the learning process and making it more engaging for students, especially newcomers, who can contextualize their learning in meaningful ways.

SUMMARY

- Incorporating ongoing and formative assessments of both content and language learning—with attention to when each or both are being assessed—throughout the school year is a way to direct and tailor instruction to best meet the needs of all students.
- Project-based learning, portfolios, and PBATs can offer students the opportunity to delve deeper into subjects and demonstrate holistic understandings of topics in ways that prepare them for higher education and the world of work.
- Twelfth-grade portfolios or senior projects can offer students the chance to explore their own interests as related to the curriculum and culminate their K–12 schooling with a demonstration of their mastery of skills, learnings, and English language. Providing the opportunity for the project to have a home language component can also offer students the chance to connect their senior project to their families and communities and showcase their multilingualism.

ADDITIONAL RESOURCES

All resources are linked at the book's companion website: www.bit.ly/Immig
RefugeeEd

- Darling-Hammond, L., & Adamson, F. (2013). *Developing assessments of deeper learning*. Stanford Center for Opportunity Policy in Education.
- Menken, K., Hudson, T., & Leung, C. (2014). Symposium article: Language assessment in standards-based education reform. *TESOL Quarterly, 48*(3), 586–614.

Strategy 7

Include Advisory Periods

Monisha Bajaj

In advisory period in 12th grade, everyone is given time to fill out and submit the community college application, and you can go to another classroom to work on a 4-year college application. At the time, I was thinking I would go to a community college and then transfer, so that's why I hadn't applied for any 4-year colleges or any scholarships. It was almost the deadline and I hadn't applied to any California State Universities (CSU) and my advisory teacher said, "You didn't apply? You have to apply!" I said, "Okay," and thought I would do it later. I didn't do it.

A couple days later, the college counselor called me to her office because my advisory teacher told her and then she explained that at that time my GPA was 3.9 which is good, and that I could even go to a University of California (UC) campus. And she really encouraged me. I applied to one CSU campus. Then my advisory teacher said, "Did you apply for the scholarship through the East Bay College Fund?" I said "No, Miss." She said, "Why didn't you apply for that?" There are two essays I had to write for the scholarship and I didn't have time because I'm always working after school. She gave me time in advisory period and helped me finish it. I got the scholarship and got into CSU. I never knew anything about college. In every advisory, what we learned was helpful for college.

—Seng, age 26, OIHS alum focus group, February 2020

In the opening quote, Seng (pseudonym), a graduate of Oakland International High School (2016) and California State University–East Bay (2020), describes her experience with the advisory period at OIHS. Having arrived in the United States at age 16 speaking very little English as a refugee from Burma, and being the oldest child in her family, Seng was not familiar with the requirements for high school and the college application process. This strategy highlights the importance of an "advisory" or "homeroom" period for all students, and especially for newcomer immigrant and refugee students.

STRUCTURE OF ADVISORIES OR HOMEROOM PERIODS

While advisory or homeroom periods may be structured differently across schools, generally an advisory period consists of a regularly scheduled period at least twice a week (of 30–45 minutes) in which a teacher follows a group of 10–20 students either for the school year or, in some schools, over their 4-year (or more) high school career, serving as an advocate and source of support. Advisory periods are a time for teachers to

- check in with students about grades, attendance, or other issues;
- identify any problems and offer support;
- engage in communication between the school and home;
- create a supportive peer group; and
- facilitate students' integration into the larger school community.

For example, at Marble Hill School for International Studies in the Bronx, "in the 9th grade, the focus of advisory is on socializing, adjusting to high school, learning study skills, and beginning to familiarize students with the college process. In later years, students are taken on college visits and their focus is more on postsecondary college and career success" (Castellón et al., 2015, p. 158). Similarly, at Oakland International High School, one teacher noted that educators collectively set the curriculum for advisory:

> In the 11th grade, advisory is by grade and occurs 4 times a week, on a set advisory calendar. On Mondays, we do a check-in circle to focus on socioemotional issues. Tuesdays are more of a study period where they can work on homework and get support. Thursdays, we go back and forth between a college readiness curriculum we have developed, and the other Thursdays we check in about academic progress, read progress reports, and discuss grades. Fridays is a follow up on anything from the week or reaching out to any other supports students might need. (interview, November 2015)

The literature on advisory programs defines them as "designed to focus on the social, emotional, physical, intellectual, psychological, and ethical development of students"; further, scholars have noted that a structured advisory period helps adolescents "find ways to fulfill their identified needs" as well as allows educators to "provide consistent, caring, and continuous adult guidance at school through the organization of a supportive and stable peer group that meets regularly under the guidance of a teacher serving as advisor" (Forte & Schurr, 1993, p. 117). Such programs were popularized in the 1990s after the Carnegie Corporation's Report "Turning Points" was released, calling for more intimate spaces within schools to "ensure every student is known well by at least one adult" (Schurr, 1992, p. 7).

Since the 1990s, educational entities have developed criteria for effective programs, such as the Educational Alliance report identifying five dimensions of success for advisory periods: (1) a stated purpose, (2) thoughtful organization,

(3) relevant advisory program content, (4) ongoing assessment, and (5) strong leadership (Osofsky et al., 2003). At one middle school in Maryland, educators reinvented their advisory periods to focus on social–emotional learning, lengthening them from 25 to 40 minutes, and adding an emphasis on the values of belonging, empathy, respect, and trust (Blad, 2019). Particularly with populations at high risk for dropping out or being pushed out, such as newcomers and English learners, the role of advisory as a space for educators to check in with and support students is essential.

ADVISORY DIMENSIONS FOR NEWCOMER STUDENTS

Many newcomer students have already experienced violence in their home countries, through migration, or in the United States, and may already be in adult roles as unaccompanied international migrants, wage-earners after school and on weekends, and as caregivers in their households. The six dimensions of advisory presented in Figure 7.1, along with sample activities, can help these periods meet the complex needs of immigrant and refugee students. The central transversal across the six dimensions is the importance of relationships, both teacher–student and peer–peer, as multiple research studies have shown the paramount role of these relationships in facilitating academic success, well-being, and meaningful integration for newcomers (Antrop-González & De Jesús, 2006; Suárez-Orozco et al., 2008, 2009).

Figure 7.1 discusses six dimensions that we have identified from existing literature (e.g., Osofsky et al., 2003), our own experience, and our own research that provide a holistic approach to best utilize the advisory or homeroom period, tailored to newcomer students' needs, in the areas of (1) academic progress; (2) advocacy; (3) socioemotional support; (4) connection; (5) information sharing; and (6) college/career preparation. Each of the six dimensions has its own objectives, as well as suggested activities that can help accomplish them. While some of these activities may also be held in schoolwide or classroom spaces, the advisory period is a chance to hone in and ensure that these objectives are being met. As illustrated in the opening vignette, Seng's erroneous beliefs about her ineligibility to attend a 4-year college and lack of time given her work schedule after school would have precluded her from attending a university and receiving a competitive scholarship had her advisory teacher not been closely tracking her progress on completing the applications, and enlisting the college counselor to support her as well. Advisory thus becomes a place for each student to be seen and for any issues to surface and be addressed.

The COVID-19 pandemic hit immigrant and refugee communities extremely hard. Reports have shown that many newcomer students did not return to schooling given the survival needs of their families and the push into greater economic precarity (Internationals Network for Public Schools, 2021). During the pandemic, the Richmond High School Internationals Academy in Richmond, California, a newcomer program within a larger comprehensive high school, extended their 25-minute homeroom period from twice a week to every day during distance

Figure 7.1. Advisory Dimensions for Newcomer Students

Dimension	Objectives	Sample activities
1. Academic progress	Ensure regular attendance and academic persistence, and that adequate academic progress is being made toward high school graduation/ completion of requirements	• Reviewing attendance, progress reports, and grades regularly • Addressing any obstacles to completing homework and assignments • Liaising with other teachers if needed
2. Advocacy	Advocate for additional services and supports within the school and/ or refer the student to out-of-school services if required	• One-on-one check-ins and monitoring of overall well-being • Referrals to school social worker, legal aid, health, or other services • Engage in school- or district-wide efforts to support students, such as advocating for sanctuary or safe haven policies
3. Socioemotional support	Utilize a trauma-informed approach to engage students and foster open communication with each student	• Regular check-ins with advisory students to identify any challenges • Activities in advisory such as journaling, art, or movement exercises that can address complex emotions
4. Connection	Build a sense of group identity and camaraderie within the advisory group to allow for a strong peer support network, especially for students who may not be part of an already-established peer social group at school	• Participate in a group activity as a collective (e.g., a field trip, create a group name, a collective bulletin board, shared playlist, etc.) • Celebrate each advisory student's birthday as a group • Rotate days on which students can share a talent, a story, a photo, music, or a recipe/food item

(continued)

Figure 7.1. Advisory Dimensions for Newcomer Students (*continued*)

Dimension	Objectives	• Sample activities
5. Information sharing	Allow time for advisor and students to share information with each other during the advisory period about, for example, community resources, internships, social services such as free Internet programs, etc.	• Have time for announcements and information sharing during advisory • Create an email list or a text/WhatsApp thread for advisory students to share information with one another
6. College/career preparation	Dedicate time during advisory for future-oriented planning to ensure all students are aware of deadlines and opportunities	• Structure time in the upper secondary grades to walk students through applications to 2- and 4-year colleges • Go on a field trip to a local college as an advisory group • Track scholarship, internship, and college application deadlines and have students work on applications during advisory period

learning. Given the difficulty of ensuring attendance (and students' sometimes irregular access to a stable device and the Internet), homeroom periods became a safe space for students and educators to connect, engage, and focus on social–emotional learning. School leader Rocio Reyes noted, "Homeroom is not graded so it takes the pressure off and brings a different vibe. Teachers are really focused on social–emotional learning; one of the teachers plays the guitar for the students to sing along, another one said they all did karaoke together. The teachers are really intentional about talking to the kids one-on-one and supporting them through the pandemic and the challenges they and their families may be facing. Our teachers really go out of their way to advocate for their students" (interview, October 2020).

Advisory periods are not a panacea for all the issues that may come up for newcomer students, but they are one important avenue for ensuring that issues are identified and addressed in a timely manner. They provide a space in which to create a sense of belonging and inclusion for students. Advisory or homeroom periods strike a balance between structure, by having some curriculum/ agendas as well as a designated time block, and room for spontaneity, through community-building activities, field trips, or student presentations/sharing and announcements. Anchoring newcomer students' educational experiences in a well-designed and thoughtful advisory program can support students' access to resources, opportunities, and successful postsecondary transitions as well as facilitate the creation of humanizing, caring, and reciprocal relationships within the school community.

SUMMARY

- An advisory period should be regularly scheduled for at least twice a week for 30–45 minutes. These can be led by one or two teachers and should have no more than 10–20 students in each advisory.
- Educators should collectively develop a curriculum for the advisory period in each grade that addresses different dimensions of newcomer students' educational needs.
- A trauma-informed approach should be utilized to engage students both one-on-one and as a group in order to identify and address any challenges, whether they be in school or in students' workplaces, homes, or communities. Connect and refer students to resources within and outside of school as needed.

ADDITIONAL RESOURCES

All resources are linked at the book's companion website: www.bit.ly/Immig RefugeeEd

- Blad, E. (2019). How schools can make advisories meaningful for students and teachers. *Education Week*. https://www.edweek.org/ leadership/how-schools-can-make-advisories-meaningful-for-students -and-teachers/2019/03
- The Education Alliance. (2003). *The power of advisories*. Brown University.

Profile of Asmaa
As Told to Gabriela Martínez

Asmaa was 13 years old when she, her siblings, and her mother came to the United States from Togo in West Africa in order to reunite with her father, who was already here. Her parents decided to migrate to give their children better education and opportunities in the United States. Asmaa started at a high school in the Bronx but later transferred to Brooklyn International High School, graduating in 2011. Asmaa discussed the challenges of being a newcomer student:

> Trying to navigate a whole different culture, being in a different country, having to take the subway to school, it was all hard. I also felt like it was a challenge to find my voice and feel comfortable here—it took a long time. It helped that I went to a school specifically for newcomers because the school is designed for people like me.

In 11th grade, Asmaa joined the dual enrollment course and internship led by Danny Walsh (see also Strategy 14); together the students and instructor engaged in a participatory action research project interviewing other newcomer students. As Asmaa said, "It was really awesome because it gave us a chance to learn how to do research and a space also to process our own experiences. All of us would sit in a circle and bounce ideas around."

When asked what advice she would offer schools that serve newcomers, Asmaa mentioned her wish to see the arts more integrated into the approaches used to teach different subjects:

> In an Internationals school where a lot of kids are coming from diverse cultures, from a lot of Indigenous cultures from around the world, it would be great to have more of an arts focus with different types of art. I wish I was told that art can be what you do and you can sustain yourself doing art. And also, art and science are very interrelated. We had all these different technical things, but I wish we could have had more opportunities to explore our imaginations.

Asmaa added that, especially with so many cultures and languages in her high school, the arts could provide an important connection between subjects, the English language focus, and students' diverse cultural backgrounds.

Asmaa slowly grew her passion for the arts and fashion in high school and, later, in college. She earned her Bachelor's degree from the State University of New York (SUNY)–New Paltz in Anthropology and French Literature in 2016. She mentioned (like Ko in an earlier profile) that writing proved challenging in her transition to college and that "you get to college and now you have to write at the same level as kids that grew up here and could speak and write English fluently, so it was hard. I studied anthropology, which required me to write a lot."

Asmaa is now a 27-year-old entrepreneur. She is the founder, designer, and creative director of Caméléon, a sustainable, transnational clothing brand. She travels between New York City, where her business is headquartered, and West Africa, where she works with communities to source materials. According to its website (cameleonstudios.com), Caméléon "aspires to thread the gap between transparent trade and local community empowerment/development and to intimately explore the nuances of Indigenous art and nature with a contemporary influence."

Asmaa's advice to newcomer students in high school is to take advantage of tutoring programs, to build strong relationships with teachers as well as seek their advice as mentors, and to "be yourself and absorb as much as you can from your classes and the opportunities both inside and outside of school."

STRATEGIES FOR SCHOOL DESIGN

School Profile 3

Wellstone International High School in Minneapolis, Minnesota

Laura Wangsness Willemsen and Lesley Bartlett

The school now known as Wellstone International High School started as the International Center for Accelerated Language Learning (ICALL) in 2001 in a repurposed factory. Coauthor Laura Wangsness Willemsen was one of the founding faculty members; interviews with Wellstone educators Carol Dallman, Ali Kofiro, Leigh Olmstead, and Daniel Hertz provided us with key information about Wellstone's past and present.

HISTORY

Wellstone was initially envisioned as a 1-year newcomer site for a cohort of approximately 40 English language learners aged 17–21. At the time, Minneapolis Public Schools were experiencing a significant influx of students from Somalia and Ethiopia, as well as students immigrating from Latin America and other locations. Many of these students had spent extended periods in refugee camps and had limited or interrupted formal education in their home countries (see also Strategy 5). As mainstream high schools were struggling to meet the needs of this growing population, district leaders advocated for the creation of a bridging program that would be a temporary, language-intensive stop for such students on their way to the district's larger, comprehensive high schools, where they would eventually graduate. With an eye toward supporting these students' transitions, district officials intentionally hired multilingual educators who had previously lived outside the United States (see also Strategy 9), and ICALL opened in September of 2001.

Two events occurred shortly after ICALL opened that quickly reshaped the school's trajectory, spurring its eventual metamorphosis into Wellstone International High School. First, ICALL opened its doors 1 week before September 11, 2001. Several months later, when the federal education law No Child Left Behind was passed, the state tied graduation to standardized tests (see also Strategy 6). Now Minneapolis high schools, already struggling, had even less incentive to receive students whose English proficiency was perceived as a threat to test score averages and graduation rates. At the same time, ICALL had become, for many students, a supportive and affirming haven of welcome against the backdrop of an increasingly Islamophobic national climate. Students who left ICALL for mainstream high schools frequently struggled; many returned to report regret at leaving. Responding to still-limited options for English learners in mainstream high schools, as well as student calls for a pathway to graduation at ICALL, educators worked to quickly transform ICALL into a fully accredited public high school.

Yet transforming the school into one that offered all graduation requirements was no simple task. ICALL's school counselor and teachers—notably there was no on-site administrator at the time—worked to overcome district skepticism, limited resources, and unique challenges, such as the complex issue of verifying overseas transcripts from conflict-affected areas. They lobbied district officials and school board members, advocated for additional hires, created new procedures, and proposed inventive solutions to many logistical challenges. Soon a newly hired physical education teacher, faced with no gym space, was bringing students to a nearby park to play soccer. To help students meet their fine arts requirements, an English teacher became credentialed to teach theater. Students took field trips, connected with community leaders and artists who would frequent the school, and organized student-led parties in which they would dance traditional dances for and with each other. By the time ICALL became officially certified to offer a diploma, it had become its own unique and celebrated learning community. When Minnesota Senator Paul Wellstone, esteemed for his support for immigrant communities and peace initiatives, died suddenly in 2002, ICALL students petitioned the school board to rename the school in his honor. In 2003, the first sizable class graduated with diplomas that bore the name Wellstone International High School.

Since then, the school has experienced major fluctuations in size, space, and student population. Wellstone has also experienced disruptive relocations and divestment, adding further complications. Yet through it all, educators have worked to refine, expand, and improve offerings to refugee and immigrant students in order to meet their specific needs, all with an asset-based framing. Their efforts include joining the Internationals Network for Public Schools in 2016, which gives educators professional development opportunities as well as access to a network of colleagues facing similar challenges and opportunities. As detailed below, Wellstone's staff continue to be just as committed and creative as the initial group of educators was when the school first opened.

SCHOOL STRUCTURE, STAFFING, AND VALUES

The structure, staffing, and values found at Wellstone are focused on responsively meeting the changing needs of its students. Although Wellstone currently has a licensed principal, for 8 years there was no licensed administrator on site. Rather, an English language teacher, Leigh Olmstead, served as the school's first on-site coordinator, resulting in a comparatively egalitarian school structure in which teachers shared decision-making and played an active role in leadership. Indeed, in the early years almost all school decisions were made by consensus of teachers and assistant educators (AEs)—at times a lengthy process, but one that resulted in a shared vision and robust ties (see also Strategy 8). This approach was further enabled by the school's small size and handpicked staff, which had expertise in serving and advocating for Wellstone's student population. The tradition of being fairly self-directed and of privileging educators' perspectives continues at Wellstone today, where teachers who facilitate collaborative grade-level meetings also serve on the school leadership team.

The egalitarian emphasis on connection and collaboration is further evident in the way that bilingual AEs, like teachers, contribute to the shared leadership at Wellstone. While the school's teaching staff has historically been multilingual, it is the AEs who specialize in providing the language support necessary to effectively connect with students, families, and communities (see also Strategy 11). This commitment to cultivate deep connections extends to AEs bringing parent–teacher conferences directly into the homes of students whose parents or guardians are unable to visit the school (see also Strategy 16). Although the school's official language of instruction is English, it's not uncommon for key ideas and terms to be explained in students' first languages to support comprehension and accelerate learning; AEs are frequently in classrooms supporting such efforts. AEs further connect communities to teachers and serve as sounding boards and coaches for teachers seeking to ensure that their pedagogical approaches and materials are culturally affirming (see also Strategy 10). Asset-based, celebratory, connected interculturalism rooted in multilingualism is cherished within Wellstone's staffing to the extent that the school has redefined several positions to require fluency in key languages (see also Strategies 9 and 12).

Students' communities and cultural backgrounds frequently take center stage in the classroom through intentional curricular and pedagogical choices (see also Strategy 2). These include an emphasis on hands-on learning, such as by offering an Advanced Placement Spanish class in an effort to affirm home languages, and providing students the opportunities to earn bilingual seals in Spanish, Somali, and Arabic.[1] Wellstone's schoolwide, additive, multilingual, intercultural approach allows for students to share their many assets while strengthening connections between communities. Educators helped students produce the essays and videos featured in *Green Card Youth Voices: Immigration Stories from a Minneapolis High School* (Wellstone International High School Studies, 2019), a unique collection of 30 personal essays (accompanied by 30 color portraits and some video pieces) written by Wellstone students from 13 different countries.

The school's approach also centers students' social and emotional needs, which are intentionally supported by Wellstone's curriculum and educators' pedagogies. Among the community resources with which AEs connect students and families are culturally and linguistically specific service providers and community organizations within the Twin Cities. Whether with health care providers visiting Wellstone's on-site clinic or the specialized services of the Center for Victims of Torture in the Twin Cities, the connections shepherded through Wellstone's network of partners are critical for newcomers navigating the challenges of creating a new home and community.

COLLEGE READINESS

In the earliest days of the school, in what former guidance counselor Daniel Hertz called "overdrive advocacy," several industrious educators at Wellstone leveraged personal and professional connections with leaders at Minneapolis Community and Technical College (MCTC) to establish a partnership that would allow Wellstone students to take dual enrollment courses (interview, December 8, 2021; see also Strategy 14). MCTC soon became a desired next step in students' educational trajectories, particularly fitting given Wellstone students' older ages. As a social studies teacher explained, "That's our mainstreaming. By the time they have the English to succeed in a mainstream high school, they don't want to be there. They're 20 or 21. So we mainstream them to MCTC" (interview, December 3, 2021). Although the early partnership faltered when the individuals who launched it moved elsewhere, faculty at Wellstone and MCTC later secured grant funding and have revived and systematized the partnership. Wellstone currently employs one staff member as a coordinator; that person spends several days a week at MCTC coaching and tutoring students to facilitate the transition to schooling in a new, postsecondary institution. Wellstone staff view the partnership with MCTC as holding further untapped promise, including creating a pathway to trades, such as plumbing and car repair.

CHALLENGES

Despite its many successes, Wellstone has contended with a number of recurring challenges, perhaps the most significant being frequent relocation. Since opening in the repurposed factory in 2001, the school has been relocated five times—to share premises with other high schools or to its own rented space. Aside from the upheaval of coordinating frequent relocations, additional challenges have arisen in various spaces. When Wellstone was located within a much larger school, maintaining a sense of cohesion and community was difficult. At one point, the district moved the school downtown so students would be closer to MCTC. Yet the location lacked space for a gym, science labs, a library, or a health and wellness room (see also Strategy 13). Moreover, many students drive to school because they need to quickly get to work at distant locations once classes end; downtown, they had to use their limited resources to pay for parking. Educators connect the inordinate amount of infrastructural instability in part to a district that they contend has a history of inattention to the school, as well as the fact that immigrant parents and caregivers are rarely well positioned to advocate for their teens. Teachers and others protested to the school board. In 2022, the school moved to the campus of MCTC, facilitating postsecondary opportunities.

Another key challenge, that of students needing to leave high school at age 21, has Wellstone's educators lobbying the Minnesota legislature. In Minnesota, schools receive funding for students only through the year they turn 21, after which the schools receive no state money. With a shortage of adult diploma or high school equivalency programs targeting emergent bilinguals, Wellstone's older students can find themselves in a race against the clock. Despite educators' continued advocacy, the law remains unchanged. As one teacher explained, Wellstone still finds a way to help students graduate who have surpassed the age limit of 21, at which point the school no longer receives any state funding to support the education of that student: "Each year Wellstone keeps a few students who are able to graduate with just one more year, but the 21 rule is discouraging for students who are not sure that they will have enough time to finish" (interview, December 15, 2021).

A final challenge is the fluctuating enrollment and differing backgrounds and needs of students coming into the school each year. In the early years, there were many East African students, the majority of whom were receiving forms of social assistance. Later, when a refugee camp in Thailand closed, the school "went from 1 to about 50 Hmong students in 3 weeks," according to a teacher (interview, November 14, 2021). More recently, the number of unaccompanied minors from Central America has grown rapidly; for many who are Indigenous, Spanish is their second language and English is their third. In addition to the demographic changes, the gross number of Wellstone students has fluctuated over time in accordance with the space affordances of the school's changing locations. These changes also require staffing shifts, particularly of AEs, in order to effectively communicate with students and families.

The unaccompanied minors, in particular, face severe economic constraints which, in turn, impact their education. As these students are typically undocumented, they receive no social or financial assistance. Therefore, despite the fact that they are school-aged youth, some work as many as 40 hours a week, leaving them with no time outside of school to learn or even rest. Teachers at Wellstone have worked to maximize learning in the classroom in response, knowing that many students will not be able to do any sort of homework. This challenge has resulted in some teachers calling for more flexible classes with variable pacing to accommodate those students who miss days of classroom instruction (see also School Profile 4), continuing the Wellstone tradition of creatively meeting students' evolving needs.

CONCLUSION

From the school's inception and continuing to the present, Wellstone educators have taken a committed, creative, asset-minded, community-oriented, student-centered, caring, and celebratory posture to their work with older high-school-aged newcomers. Despite setbacks, frequent moves, immigration fluctuations, district divestment and inattention, and state and federal policies that negatively impact newcomer youth, Wellstone remains a strong community of educators and learners that, working together, ensure all are welcome and able to thrive.

Strategy 8

Enact Democratic School Governance

Alexandra Anormaliza With Daniel Walsh

Jennifer (pseudonym) was a strong, smart classroom teacher with good ideas about how to improve the school during its second year. However, she found it difficult to take feedback from colleagues and school leaders, and she complained that her ideas were disregarded because the principal favored the founding team. She frequently wondered aloud why she could not participate in weekly Team Leader meetings with the principal. Over the course of the year, she became more and more frustrated. Her attitude affected how she collaborated with her colleagues on the instructional team.

School leadership and democratic school governance are essential to creating a school climate that welcomes and supports all students, including newcomer immigrant and refugee youth. New schools, of necessity, take time to develop and require vision, hope, and energy. Developing structures and processes to solve the constant organizational challenges that emerge in a school, with careful attention and alignment to a school's purpose, powerfully shapes the culture of an organization; in a great school, every staff member can explain the school's mission as well as the structures and processes instituted to achieve it.

Whether starting a new school or redesigning an existing one, developing a shared vision and mission is the first step in any school improvement effort. Then vision and mission must be translated into structures and processes. A school's stated objective, like that of the International High School at Prospect Heights in Brooklyn, New York, "to graduate change agents who were active and informed participants in our democracy," has important implications for what classroom instruction and routines look like, including the physical setup of the classrooms. At IHSPH, instead of individual desks, for example, the school purchased tables that were easily moved to create different groupings according to instructional needs. Classrooms at IHSPH have extensive libraries, with books varying by genre, topic, text complexity, and language. Students are given choices about their learning, and teachers explicitly teach them how to make good ones. The curriculum allows for student choice regarding projects and readings. Students sometimes also have choices in whom they work with and what roles they take within a group learning experience. The Professional Learning Committee and

85

the Content Area Teams ensure that the curriculum is aligned with the school's vision and mission (see also School Profile 2).

As they develop, strong schools rely on and cultivate teacher leaders who "lead within and beyond the classroom; identify with and contribute to a community of teacher learners and leaders; influence others toward improved educational practice; and accept responsibility for achieving the outcomes of that leadership" (Katzenmeyer & Moller, 2009, p. 6; see also York-Barr & Duke, 2004). Transformative democratic leadership is distributed and emergent, involving not only senior leaders but also, and importantly, teacher leaders. Teachers need to be not only consulted but truly included in developing, analyzing, and modifying governance structures. Teacher collaboration results in positive outcomes for immigrant and refugee students (Villavicencio et al., 2021). At the same time, collaborative school leadership contributes to language policies and practices favorable to multilingual students (Ascenzi-Moreno et al., 2016). Democratic leadership cultivates a sense of agency among staff and develops collaborative processes for decision-making. In addition, "democratic leadership grows from and is expressed through enabling structures, such as a culture that explicitly shows that inclusive participation is valued" (P. Woods, 2021, p. 1). In sum, "enabling structures and participative and empowering agency are essential features of democratic leadership" (p. 1). Finally, successful schools cultivate a "mindset of continuous improvement," in which all educators "reflect on their practices" and adapt their "teaching and course structures to how students learn. The continuous improvement stance extends into the classrooms where we see students taking charge of and reflecting on their own learning" (Castellón et al., 2015, p. 3).

In this strategy, we describe alternative school leadership and governance structures that facilitate democratic practices for both immigrant and refugee youth and the adults who support them, drawing in particular upon the authors' experiences as founding members of the International High School at Prospect Heights (School Profile 2). This particular school exemplifies strategies and approaches that can work in other schools and programs that include newcomers among their student population.

THE EVOLUTION OF DEMOCRATIC LEADERSHIP AT IHSPH

With the aim of graduating active and informed change agents who would forge a more equitable society, the founding educators of IHSPH developed a rich, interdisciplinary, project-based curriculum and an immersive approach to language learning that allowed students to develop fluency in speaking, reading, and writing English while valuing and engaging home languages. In tandem with the pedagogical development and practices presented in School Profile 2, the leaders of this school created and continuously refined structures and processes that elevated and integrated staff perspectives and were responsive to the day-to-day needs of our school (Apple & Beane, 2007), while aligning to five foundational principles: (1) heterogeneity and collaboration, (2) experiential learning, (3) language and content integration, (4) localized autonomy and responsibility, and (5) one learning model for all (Internationals Network for Public Schools, 2017).

There was a lot of energy and enthusiasm during the founding years, despite the myriad demands. The founding educators shared a sense of purpose, commitment to the young adults and their families, and a commitment to each other as members of the team. These values and sense of purpose allowed educators to relentlessly pursue the success of students while believing that these efforts made a difference (Edmondson, 2018). The learning of the collective mattered, even when it came from failure, because it made the team stronger. A stronger organization yielded better results, and those better results transformed lives.

As a member of the Internationals Network, IHSPH engaged that blueprint for leadership. At IHSPH, the Instructional Team was the main organizing structure for teachers and students. Upon hiring, every pedagogical staff member was assigned to an interdisciplinary team consisting of a social studies, ELA, math, and science teacher, as well as a social worker or guidance counselor and an elective (physical education/dance, music, art) teacher. At least one of the teachers was certified in teaching English as a second language. Some teams were also assigned teacher assistants or paraprofessionals, based upon the number of students with special needs on each team. Each Instructional Team was responsible for the academic and socioemotional support of a group of 75–80 students, who traveled together from class to class for most of the day. And the team remained together in grades 9 and 10 to facilitate acculturation into the school community. In addition to serving as content teachers, each teacher served as advisor to a group of 12–15 students (whom they also taught) (see also Strategy 7). Instructional Teams met once a week to discuss student academic and socioemotional needs and to raise operational challenges to bring to the school principal's attention.

Team Leadership

During the first year, as founding principal, coauthor Alexandra modeled team leadership by structuring agendas, facilitating conversations, and managing group decisions during formal and informal meetings with the staff. While she did this intentionally, she did not communicate that plan, which could have helped the founding teachers better develop this skill set in anticipation of the school's expansion. Much like a coach supports classroom teachers through demonstration lessons, it is crucial for school leaders to publicly and consistently open up their leadership practice for others to observe, slowly ceding leadership spaces to potential teacher leaders while providing supportive coaching and feedback to help shape and grow their practice (see also Strategy 10).

During its second year, the school doubled in size, from approximately 110 to 220 students; the number of educators doubled as well, from 7 to 14. To keep class sizes to about 25 students, IHSPH expanded from one Instructional Team (the founding staff) to 3. To ensure streamlined communication, participation in decision-making, and support for teachers new to the school, each team was required to have a Team Leader. The selection of a Team Leader was one of the most important decisions made each year. In the second year of the school, intending to spread institutional knowledge from the founding staff to the new staff, Alexandra selected three founding staff members to serve as Team Leaders and provided them with additional mentoring and support as their teams developed their own identities and cultures. At the weekly meeting, Team Leaders jointly developed agendas based upon examination of student data and any issues identified by the staff during Instructional Team meetings. Rapid growth and change meant that leaders spent time that second year creating policies for effectively running the school. For example, the Team refined and codified the grading policy created during the first year and developed written guidance for teachers for writing report card feedback to students and holding parent–teacher conferences.

By the third year, Instructional Teams selected their own leaders. This decision required that they formalize the position, write a job description, propose a budget to pay teachers for the additional work they were performing outside of their classroom teaching duties, and develop training processes. Weekly Team Leader meetings with the principal and two assistant principals brought about formal communication structures and protocols that previously did not exist. For example, to ensure transparency, weekly Team Leader meeting notes were published so that other staff members could understand what was being discussed and what decisions were being made.

As the school grew in size and complexity, needs were identified that could no longer be met via the Team Leader structure. Two committees were created to expand the breadth of teacher voice and decision-making—the Personnel and Professional Learning Committees. Each committee had a teacher leader serving as chair and also had the principal and assistant principals as members. By the end of the fourth year, when the school reached its full size, approximately half of the 33 teachers were serving in a leadership role. The Personnel Committee, created during the school's second year, was responsible for all full-time staff hires and peer observation processes, as well as reviewing yearly teacher course preference requests in anticipation of school programming for the upcoming school year. This group actually assigned teachers to teams based upon both these preferences and team needs. Additionally, the Professional Development Committee was responsible for schoolwide professional learning endeavors, including the scope and sequence and agendas for All-Staff Meetings. Content area leaders were also selected by the end of this year to develop scope and sequence documents and support Content Area Meetings. Membership in these committees was voluntary but had to include a teacher from each of the instructional teams.

In parallel, teachers needed to be able to make decisions about matters that impacted them most closely. The structures described above (Team Leaders Meeting, All-Staff Meeting, Professional Learning and Personnel Committees, Content Area Teams, Grade Level Teams) allowed for this. In addition to recommending the cadence of these meetings, teachers could choose what team to join from year to year, what their curriculum looked like within a defined scope, how they brought learning to life, and what committees they joined. A teacher with an idea for how to do something better was typically allowed to implement that idea, as long as it did not contradict the school's mission, and then share their learning with others for potential schoolwide adoption. As Ancess (2003) explains, schools should not simply "lecture students about the values and principles of our democracy" but rather "operationalize them so they can find meaning in them" (p. 121). IHSPH, and many other schools like it, work arduously each day to embody this suggestion.

Peer Observation

The development of a peer observation process further illustrates how teacher collaboration and leadership can strengthen democratic practice and organizational learning. As principal, Alexandra was deeply interested in continuous improvement. During the school's first year, she instituted a group observation process where the founding team collectively observed each member of the team informally. The group debriefed observations together. This practice was essentially in response to teachers' inclination "to close their doors" and operate in isolation, in part to protect themselves from a myriad of distractions, and in part to reduce personal and professional vulnerability. To further institute democratizing teaching practice, in the second year, the Team Leaders decided that it would make sense for the Personnel Committee to develop peer observation policies and lead this aspect of school improvement. Educators moved to interdisciplinary team and content area observations aligned to team improvement goals, followed by a group write-up documenting the entire experience. The teachers refined this process in the third and fourth years, aligning the peer observation experience to individual teacher improvement goals, changing the number of people doing the observations and the specificity of the debrief and write-up each time. In the fifth year, the school instituted peer observation triads; teachers chose with whom to group. Alexandra and the assistant principals each worked with three or four triads to engage in a more formal observation process together. One of them joined each observation conducted by the triads, participated in the debrief conversation for each teacher, and supported the resulting individual write-up. This process modeled how to give critical feedback that would lead to lasting improvement. Who better to help a teacher improve than another teacher? And why not make the process as structured as possible so that results could be analyzed and further improvements made? More important, why shouldn't teachers define how they set about improving their craft?

Democratic leadership, paired with a strong culture of engagement and ample opportunities for educational professionals to analyze and improve governance structures, strengthens organizational learning, even when disagreement emerges. To return to Jennifer, her frustration eventually became productive engagement after some difficult conversations that allowed for the deepening of collective leadership and shared decision-making:

It was the end of a particularly difficult second year. One of the teachers had committed an academic infraction by providing students with answers on a state exam that would have repercussions for the entire school. The principal communicated all relevant details to the district. All that was left was deciding what to tell the families and the students. Jennifer started the conversation by insisting that families had to be told who was at fault so that everyone else could be cleared from suspicion. The ensuing debate among members of the staff encompassed different points of view. There were tears. Eventually, calling the group back to core values, one staff member declared, "We are a team. We rise together, we fall together." The decision was made. Parents would know what happened and how it would be remedied, but the staff would take collective responsibility for the infraction and pledge to do better in the future. Jennifer agreed and apologized to the group. She was elected Team Leader the following school year.

SUMMARY

- Democratic leadership develops over time, in relationship with teacher-leaders.
- School leaders must build a strong culture around a shared sense of purpose, commitment to students and their families, and commitment to fellow educators. In addition, they must involve teacher leaders in the work of developing democratic structures and processes, aligned with the school's mission, to address the constant organizational challenges that emerge.

ADDITIONAL RESOURCES

All resources are linked at the book's companion website: www.bit.ly/Immig RefugeeEd

- Apple, M. W., & Beane, J. A. (Eds.). (2007). *Democratic schools: Lessons in powerful education.* Heinemann.
- Bond, Nathan (Ed.). (2015). *The power of teacher leaders: Their roles, influence, and impact.* Routledge.
- National Education Association. (2020). *The teacher leader model standards.* https://www.nea.org/resource-library/teacher-leader-model -standards

Strategy 9

Adopt Intentional Staffing

Daniel Walsh, Kathleen Rucker,
Orubba Almansouri, and David Etienne

Our description of this strategy is intended to illustrate the transformative power of intentional staffing. We show how recruiting multilingual teachers and employing alum and other community members humanize schools and make them more responsive to the needs of immigrant and refugee youth in ways that challenge the conventional logics of what schools can and should do.

THE NEED FOR DIVERSE STAFF

Research demonstrates the power of a diverse educational staff. Students need to see themselves and their community represented among the teaching staff. Teachers of color "improve social and emotional development, as well as learning," for students of color (Bristol & Martin-Fernandez, 2019, p. 147). Black students who study with Black teachers are more likely to graduate high school, and are less likely to experience negative disciplinary events that may derail them (Gershenson et al., 2021). Students of color report that teachers of the same race hold higher expectations for them (Cherng & Halpin, 2016).

The need for linguistically and culturally responsive instructors is pronounced among multilingual students. English learners constitute nearly 10% of K–12 enrollment in the United States. But there is a dearth of bilingual educators to help meet their needs: According to federal data, before the pandemic, 31 states and the District of Columbia reported a shortage of teachers (Mitchell, 2019), and the pandemic undoubtedly exacerbated those figures. The value of bilingual education is well established (Collier & Thomas, 2017). But, even (or perhaps especially) in monolingual programs, educators who are bilingual play a crucial role as instructor, interpreter, curriculum developer, and advisor. Their linguistic abilities and cultural background knowledge benefit their students, and they help raise and affirm the status of a language other than English (Ellis, 2013).

Consequently, it is imperative to recruit diverse, multilingual educators, as Wellstone and other schools profiled in this book have done. In one interview, a teacher at Gregorio Luperón High School in New York City explained why he thought it was valuable to have teachers from the same cultural and linguistic background: "We see [the students] from another point of view. The [English speaking teachers] see them more romantically, especially the motivated ones. . . . We know them more deeply, see them more fully. . . . We have a more realistic point of view. We know them. We see their virtues and their deficiencies, in order to be able to help them" (interview, 14 March 2008).

Another promising avenue is a "grow your own" program. These programs recruit educators from the community who are invested in staying local. Such programs must address the financial barriers and lack of support that teacher education candidates sometimes face (Gist & Bristol, 2022; Gist et al., 2021). Programs that are "designed to recruit Teachers of Color should create opportunities for students to engage in curricular and pedagogical approaches that are community centered and provide avenues to challenge educational inequities," even as they "provide a variety of support structures" (Gist et al., 2021, p. 9).

Schools serving immigrant youth may also hire support staff from the communities they serve and encourage them to complete advanced degrees in fields that will allow them to continue to work with the school. For example, Rudsdale Newcomer High School (see School Profile 4) uses the AmeriCorps program to hire alums to work with students on accessing social and legal services. Oakland International High School deliberately recruits alum for open positions, such as for administrative, after-school, and instructional assistants. Wellstone International High School (see School Profile 3) hires bilingual assistant educators from the community; these staff members provide essential language support for students and families. In the early days of the school, Ali Kofiro worked there as an assistant educator, using his fluency in Somali and Arabic to connect with students while completing a bachelor's degree at the University of Minnesota–Twin Cities. His fellow teachers noticed his talents and encouraged him to pursue a master's degree in counseling. Upon completing the degree, Ali joined the Wellstone staff as a school counselor.

THE CONTRIBUTIONS OF COMMUNITY ASSOCIATES AT BROOKLYN INTERNATIONAL HIGH SCHOOL

In this section, we draw examples of the power of intentional staffing from Brooklyn International High School (BIHS) in Brooklyn, New York. Three of the authors of this strategy—Kathleen, Orubba, and David—work together at BIHS. Kathleen was a teacher and then assistant principal; she is currently the principal. Orubba and David are both alums of BIHS who currently work as community associates (CAs). In the New York City Department of Education, CAs work in a variety of capacities supporting students, staff, and families; in schools serving multilingual learners, CAs also tend to provide essential translation and interpretation services.

Advice From Alum

The critical importance of turning to alum can be illustrated by a story Kathleen relayed. As a first-year principal, Kathleen said, "I would often encounter Jean in the hallway, sitting on the slop sink while classes were in session, not sure about whether to go late to class or wait for the next class to start." With his inconsistent attendance, open interest in neighborhood gangs, and lack of engagement in classes, Jean had been referred to school counselors, met with his team of teachers, and regularly met with Kathleen and the school's assistant principal. His guardian was beyond exhausted. Caring for multiple children and working long hours as a home health aide, she grew increasingly distant with each phone call home.

One afternoon, as Kathleen walked through the hallway and wondered what she could do to reach Jean, she bumped into Nesken, one of the school's alums, who had stopped by for his regular chat with the school's computer technician, who was also an alum and an informal mentor to many students. Kathleen asked Nesken to accompany her to her office, and she shared her struggles reaching Jean. Like Jean, Nesken was a recent immigrant from Haiti. Based on his lived experience, Nesken brainstormed some possible suggestions: How might the school involve Jean's family in Haiti to leverage those relationships and possibly renew his interest in and commitment to school? What about Jean's interest in becoming a rap artist? A quick Internet search revealed a young people's music recording studio not far from the school. This chance encounter left Kathleen not only with possible next steps to support Jean but also with a heightened awareness for the value of consultation and dialogue with alums (see also Strategy 20).

Alum as Staff

Alums may serve as role models and advocates, and they may more easily anticipate obstacles or barriers faced by students (see also Strategy 20). The power of hiring alums as educators can be illustrated by Orubba's experiences working at BIHS in spring 2019. Orubba is a Muslim, Arabic-speaking immigrant who wears the hijab, as did some of the students with whom she worked. She helped the students fundraise to attend a summer program at Harvard University. Orubba noted, "For almost all of my students, this was the first time they were leaving home on a journey of their own without their families. The process took months of preparation, including long meetings and discussions with families to explain why this opportunity would be of great benefit for their children."

The cost of the program was prohibitive, but the school used social networks to help fundraise through GoFundMe. Orubba explained, "Seeing these students, and seeing myself in them, I was reminded it is not just culturally relevant curriculum that is needed in schools, it is systems that advocate for immigrant students to have an equitable education that includes a supportive community and access to opportunities."

However, given their shared background, Orubba was aware that she also needed to prepare the students for the situation they would encounter in the Harvard program. She recalled that students would be interacting with students from all different states and with "different economic and cultural backgrounds." While Orubba had discussions about engaging across difference, she noted, "hearing about it and living it is a different experience." In response to the program, a student participant reflected, "I know we talked about the differences in student demographics, but I thought there was going to be at least some people that looked like us. You know even when we went on the tour, we only saw one Black teacher in all the places we visited. [Another student] and I were the only people [student participants] wearing hijab." Because Orubba had been a student herself, she could more easily anticipate challenges that might emerge and prepare the students for those. Hiring alums allowed BIHS to support students in class as paraprofessionals and teaching assistants, and outside the classroom as mentors, role models, and advocates.

Finally, alums who have shared in the school culture may become staff members whose strong connections to the community help responsive educators avoid missteps. For example, David, from Haiti, clearly recalled a moment in school that mattered for him as a student in science class. Instead of plowing through the periodic table when students were dealing with political and economic issues and natural disasters in their home countries, his chemistry teacher hit the pause button. During the pause, students were invited to share experiences and feelings. David recalled that "by the end of the class period, we saw a number of strong individuals sharing tears, hugs, and love. The class became very close and from that moment, I made a promise to myself to always be present and aware of creating space when space is needed in a school environment." This experience set the stage for his later work as a community associate.

David was hired specifically to make connections with some young men at BIHS. The school was in the midst of planning its 25th anniversary celebration and had invited him to serve on the planning committee. As a young Black immigrant man, David felt the weight of George Floyd's murder. He struggled through planning meetings but held his tongue, not wanting, as he said, "to stir the pot." When he could no longer remain silent, he expressed his discomfort with the idea of a celebration at that historical moment. Based upon his knowledge of the community, he suggested that instead the school community "hold space" for reflection. Both former and current students showed up to this event to express the fear and anxiety caused by the murder. Like that day in chemistry class when he was in 11th grade, David again witnessed a number of students share tears, love, and support for one another. He reflected, "Holding that space reminded everyone of the importance of community building, representation, and empowering young voices in times of tragedy. As an alum, I know the importance of not being excluded when things are not going right; when the world is facing a difficult time, the worst thing to do to young people is shut them out." By "growing their own" multilingual, culturally informed and responsive, community-grounded staff, BIHS was better able to connect with students and families, build community, and process grief.

Alums underscore how critical it is for all school staff, in the words Lilia Bartolomé (2010), not only to master the technical skills and content associated with their roles but also to critically "deconstruct the so-called natural and commonsense perceptions they may have of low socioeconomic status (SES) immigrant, refugee, and other linguistic-minority students" (p. 508). Furthermore, Bartolomé reminds us of the need for school staff to identify and address unconscious and acritical "beliefs and attitudes about the existing social order that reflect dominant ideologies that are harmful to many students" (p. 509) in order to create structures that would both enhance immigrant and refugee youth's ability to "learn English academic discourse" and "create spaces in which their own respective cultural voices can emerge" (p. 512). The scenarios described above clearly reflect a structure rooted in such notions.

David and Orubba are only two of 20 alums working throughout BIHS in some capacity. The school makes a concerted effort to cultivate this pool of talent. Kathleen, as school leader, intentionally sets aside funds and seeks out grants and other partnerships to fund these positions. Within the official school structure, she has regularly hired alums as substitute teachers, substitute paraprofessionals, school secretaries, school aides, and computer technicians. These positions often serve as a springboard for other opportunities. The school also has a group of alums attending graduate school whom BIHS supports through employment and mentorship to become social workers, teachers, and school leaders. Beyond the formal school structures, alum work as instructors through partnerships with community organizations, running a variety of after-school activities, including the Makers Club, Bollywood Dancing, African Club, SAT Club, Conversational English, and a Dreamers Club (see also Strategies 18 and 20).

SUMMARY

- BIHS, Wellstone, Rudsdale, and other schools serving immigrant and refugee youth hire multilingual educators and intentionally develop multilingual staffing by recruiting alum. Alums reach, understand, and communicate with students and families in ways that sometimes other school staff cannot.
- To develop staffing that reflects students' communities, school leaders should initiate an alum organization to identify those with interest in working in public schools who have the linguistic and cultural resources to serve youth and their families.
- Leaders should identify existing roles within the school and district that could be filled by alum and/or community members, consider what a career ladder within the school district might look like, and do what they can to support alums as they pursue higher education and credentials to return to work in the school.

ADDITIONAL RESOURCES

All resources are linked at the book's companion website: www.bit.ly/Immig RefugeeEd

- Re-imagining Migration has great resources for educators of immigrant and refugee students. See https://reimaginingmigration.org/
- The Refugee Educator Academy, focused on both the United States and international contexts, provides useful information and professional development opportunities. See https://ceinternational1892.org/cpl/ refugee-educator-academy/

Strategy 10

Integrate Coaching for Culturally Responsive Teaching

Joanna Yip With Daniel Walsh

School-based coaching offers educators the opportunity to collaborate and innovate in a supportive environment committed to growth and continual improvement. Coaching is a critical but often missing ingredient in the quest to improve the culture of learning for immigrant and refugee students and in the meaningful uptake of responsive practices. Schools such as New World High School in the Bronx, New York, and Rudsdale Newcomer High School in Oakland, California, integrate coaching into their ongoing professional development plans for teachers. Coaching involves building confidence among teachers, a penchant for experimentation and failure without judgment, and intentional systems and structures for individual and collective efficacy to take hold and meet the needs of underserved students. Without coaching, few teachers will implement new pedagogical practices introduced to them and even fewer will sustain them over time (Joyce & Showers, 2002).

Current paradigms for teacher development involve superficial training without coaching, or coaching that is compliance-driven, delivered in the form of supervisory feedback. This cursory approach does little to support teachers (Kraft et al., 2018). Substantial shifts in values, beliefs, and practices require time and space for learning and commensurate investment in teacher development. Hence, coaching activities need to simultaneously address a system of interrelated gaps between current ability and desired ability that include skill, knowledge, capacity, will, commitment, cultural competence, and emotional intelligence (Aguilar, 2020). Coaching too often involves a lot of telling but little modeling, rehearsing, experimenting, or collaboration. It is no surprise within these old paradigms that teachers feel frustrated and become skeptical of many professional learning opportunities. However, with the right elements, coaching can change not just teacher practice but organizational culture. Great coaching shifts an organization's belief in how it collaborates and what it is capable of achieving for students (van Nieuwerburgh, 2012). We use a case study to show how coaching in schools can meet the needs of immigrant and refugee students.

COMPONENTS OF EFFECTIVE COACHING FOR CULTURALLY AND LINGUISTICALLY RESPONSIVE TEACHING

Coach Allen (pseudonym), an instructional coach within the district, first met Ms. Franco (pseudonym) in her English Language Development class of 18 English learners. Ms. Franco requested coaching with Allen because she wanted to do better by her students and saw that many of them were stagnating. She had incredibly strong ties with her students, with many of them stopping by her classroom to give her an update or to ask for encouragement. She had a sense of where students were struggling and believed that a slow-paced curriculum, a focus on vocabulary, and ample read-alouds for complex texts was what they needed. But she was not sure where to go next. What support did Ms. Franco need and what strategies would Coach Allen use to effectively support changes in her instructional practice for the students?

Embedded as a Systemic Organizational Strategy

Coaching that is implemented as isolated classroom support is insufficient and will not lead to widespread changes in teacher practice to address the unique linguistic and cultural needs of immigrant and refugee students. Coaching should be embedded throughout a school's professional development and utilized as a key strategy for schoolwide goals and the instructional vision. The instructional focus for immigrant students needs to attach to a strong pedagogical framework that guides the larger instructional vision. Coaching should then be used to coordinate across various points of collaboration in order to systematically develop shared practices to meet the goals. Over time, these structures socialize a common pedagogical understanding of language and literacy instruction among practitioners. Coaching should be available consistently in a variety of formats:

- team coaching
- peer coaching, with external and internal coaches
- coaching from supervisors (Kraft et al., 2018; van Nieuwerburgh, 2012)

Coaching should not be implemented with language specialists in integrated English language development (ELD) classrooms alone, or only in designated ELD or tier 2 instruction (in a Response-to-Intervention model, tier 2 is targeted small group instruction); it should take place in collaboration with content teachers in the instructional core, where the real acceleration of learning happens to meet academic standards. Without an integrated system, coaching is just a siloed initiative that sidelines immigrant students to the margins of a school's priorities and rarely leads to success for teachers or for their immigrant students.

Implemented Within a Dynamic Culture of Learning

Effective coaching is possible when adult development is at the heart of organizational culture. Even the most skilled teachers are usually ill equipped to serve immigrant and refugee students. Few teachers have sufficient exposure to language instruction or culturally responsive teaching. Closing this gap requires an evolving culture of learning that encourages the deprivatization of practice, or opening classroom doors, and maintains psychological safety to normalize risk taking and vocalizing concerns (Edmondson, 2018). Schools mature as learning organizations when teachers contribute to the professional growth of their colleagues and when leaders support learning instead of compliance (see also Strategy 8). In a coaching culture, leaders create environments for open dialogue and courageous conversations about the challenges teachers face and how they might contribute to or support inequitable practices (New Teacher Center, 2018). As leaders set expectations to raise the achievement of immigrant students, they should also hold themselves accountable for providing sufficient support for teachers to reach those expectations.

Guided by How Adults Learn

Adults cannot change in themselves what they are not able to notice or recognize (Kegan & Lahey, 2009). This is likely to be especially true if they do not come from the same place as their students, hold implicit biases, or are not taught how to support language and literacy as they teach content (Benson & Fiarman, 2020; Gomez & Diarrassouba, 2014). To support these substantive shifts in practice, identity, and beliefs, coaches need a teacher-driven and inquiry-based framework for coaching that helps teachers see the current reality of their practice (Knight, 2017). Coaching structures need to be *experiential*, helping teachers to make sense of concrete experience and taking action and experimentation, as well as *reflective*, facilitating the active observation, integration, and interpretation of the person's experience (McDonald et al., 2013). Effective coaching frameworks use immediate and observable data, and support teachers to analyze the data and then make decisions and implement a small number of high-impact strategies that can lead to great results, even in complex teaching environments (Knight, 2017; Lampert et al., 2013; Panero & Talbert, 2013). Coaching that connects teachers to what they already know how to do and to their inner purpose, and maintains a solutions-focused approach, can also inspire teachers to grow (van Nieuwerburgh & Love, 2019).

In the case study mentioned earlier, Coach Allen used a number of methods to identify student needs in Ms. Franco's classroom. After an initial needs assessment that included lesson observation, student work analysis, and review of the literacy assessment data, Coach Allen could see that Ms. Franco lacked a plan of action for how to accelerate language and literacy growth. Ms. Franco and Coach Allen agreed to collect recordings of students' oral reading fluency, use a data protocol to make sense of what they learned about her students in the recorded reading observations, and track their findings on component reading skills in a spreadsheet. The recordings identified specific gaps in language skills that Ms. Franco wanted to address but also provided evidence that her students could do more than she realized. She and Coach Allen discussed how she might target specific skills in an upcoming lesson and what success would look like. This set of activities exemplifies how a coach can successfully collaborate with a teacher to learn about students and set learning goals for instruction with a focus on language and literacy.

Coaches cannot simply give feedback, addressing only behavior or skill through the communication of evaluative information. Such coaching conversations rarely result in changes in mind-sets, and may not even result in changes in technical skills. To get transformational results for immigrant and refugee students, teacher practice is not the only thing that needs to change; the manner of coaching itself and how coaches support teachers also needs to shift.

Focused on Equitable Outcomes for Immigrant Students

Coaching that supports teachers to become culturally responsive practitioners involves helping teachers learn to be curious about the identities and communities of immigrant students and build human connection with them (Aguilar, 2020). Teachers need to collect evidence from their students to examine their own assumptions about what practices are working, and to confront whether their planning and teaching is supporting or impeding student learning (Knight, 2017). Coaching conversations that center the needs of immigrant students tackle the instructional system from curriculum planning to instructional methods to assessment. The conversations do not focus solely on basic language skills or differentiation, which are necessary but insufficient to alter the status quo. Instead, coaching conversations focus on embedding language and literacy support into all aspects of instructional planning, implementation, and especially formative assessment, so that immigrant students learn rigorous content and language in tandem. Equity-focused coaching should also surface the assets of immigrant students and affirm their linguistic and cultural practices, not just focus on whether students are meeting instructional objectives.

THE IMPORTANCE OF COACHES WHO ARE WILLING
TO LEARN AND CHANGE

Coaches can be teachers, districtwide professionals who support multiple schools, and/or school leaders; regardless of who the coach is, school leaders play an important role in fostering a culture of coaching and growth in a school environment. And school administrators can also become effective coaches in their school settings, even if they lack the content expertise to support immigrant students. When these leaders acknowledge gaps in their own knowledge and skills, they embody the disposition and the stance needed to bring their teachers along for the challenging journey of changing practice. When leaders are continually growing in their coaching and instructional practice, they model what it takes to become culturally responsive practitioners. These leaders refine their coaching skills and strategies, and their way of being and leading, in order for linguistically and culturally responsive teaching to take hold in their buildings. Here are some questions leaders can ask themselves to become better coaches for teachers of immigrant students (see New Teacher Center, 2018, for additional tools):

- How do I analyze data from observations, and do these practices surface the assets and needs of immigrant and refugee students?
- Do my observation skills and coaching strategies identify inequities in the lesson to pursue equitable outcomes for immigrant students?
- Which of my coaching practices are particularly effective in helping teachers be successful in addressing the needs of immigrant students?
- What can I learn from the educators of color in my school about how we can better serve linguistically and culturally minoritized students in our community?
- How actively am I committed to improving my coaching to serve linguistically and culturally minoritized students?
- How often do I facilitate courageous conversations with teachers so that we are collectively working toward equitable outcomes for all students?

In the coaching case study, Coach Allen realized adjustments were needed in the coaching cycle to support Ms. Franco. During the next observation, Coach Allen saw Ms. Franco frequently explain the central text instead of supporting students to unpack the meaning for themselves. She did not implement any activities to address the target skills surfaced through their data analysis. What happened? Where was the breakdown? What did Coach Allen need to better understand Ms. Franco's lesson decisions? This scenario indicates the need for ongoing reflection and monitoring within the coaching cycle on the part of the coach. Figure 10.1 lists strategies that can be used with teams or in one-on-one coaching in order to elevate the assets and needs of immigrant and refugee students (Aguilar, 2020; Knight, 2017).

In summary, coaching for culturally and linguistically responsive teaching asks coaches to rethink what teacher development looks like when schools live up to their potential as learning organizations. Coach Allen had an opportunity to help transform Ms. Franco's understanding not only of her students but of her own self-efficacy and values. With additional coaching conversations focused on Ms. Franco's perceptions and acknowledgment of her strengths, as well as modeling and codesigning practices, Coach Allen greatly improved the coaching cycle to make a real difference.

SUMMARY

- Coaching can be a transformational school design strategy, not only for individual teachers but school organizations as a whole, when the focus is centered on the needs of teachers and on supporting students who are not being served well by the status quo.
- When coaching is positioned as an organizational strategy as opposed to a short-term intervention, it supports a culture of learning for teachers and ultimately facilitates school improvement in other problem areas related to access, equity, inclusion, and belonging within a school community.

Figure 10.1. Strategies for Culturally and Linguistically Responsive Coaching

Purpose	Examples
Surface current reality and gaps	Collect varied language samples that show how students speak and write in English and in their primary language (Auslander, 2022; Auslander & Yip, 2022): • Data from classroom discussion or student work related to grade-level content • Video of collaborative discussions or student participation in tasks and activities • Recordings of oral reading fluency and comprehension
Reflect on impact of teaching practices	• Conduct empathy interviews with immigrant students to hear about their experience as participants in the classroom (Anaissie et al., 2021) • Use observation or student shadowing tools that focus on classroom culture and participation in grade-level content and tasks (Soto, 2012) • Discuss successes and distribute examples of small victories (National School Reform Faculty, 2017)
Explore competing commitments and assumptions	• Discuss the internal saboteur that shows up during lessons to undermine teachers' ability to reach equity goals (Kimsey-House et al., 2018) • Use coaching tools to help teachers see where they are getting stuck (Kegan & Lahey, 2009)
Codesign and experiment with new practices	• Deconstruct the language demands and opportunities in texts and tasks when planning lessons, and align instructional supports (e.g., intellectual prep protocols) (Lucas et al., 2008) • Identify instructional goals specifically for immigrant and refugee students • Model, plan/modify, and rehearse high-impact methods with teachers to support immigrant students (Lampert et al., 2013) • Design new practices to test a hypothesis or try something new (Knight, 2017) • Create an instructional playbook with a few high-impact strategies for language and content integrated instruction (Knight, 2019)

ADDITIONAL RESOURCES

All resources are linked at the book's companion website: www.bit.ly/Immig RefugeeEd

- The Internationals Network for Public Schools provides resources on their website and professional development for schools and educators within and outside of their network. See https://www .internationalsnetwork.org
- Quintero, D. (2019). *Instructional coaching holds promise as a method to improve teachers' impact.* Brown Center Chalkboard, Brookings Institution.

Strategy 11
Address School Language Policies

Esther Bettney and Lesley Bartlett

The term *language policies* refers to guidelines that inform how individuals use language within various contexts. Language policies are a critical consideration when determining how to equitably support refugee and immigrant youth in schools. While English is the language of instruction in the vast majority of schools across the United States, many immigrant youth studied in languages other than English prior to their arrival in the United States and/or speak a language (or languages) other than English at home. Fifty-six percent of the children of immigrants are bilingual; of these bilingual children, 71% speak Spanish, and the remaining students speak a wide range of languages, including Hindi (4%), Mandarin/Cantonese (3%), Arabic (2%), French (2%), and Vietnamese (2%), among others (T. Woods & Hanson, 2016, p. 5). Equitable language policies provide multilingual students with the opportunity to leverage their linguistic repertoire as a learning *resource*, rather than a problem to be eliminated.

OVERVIEW OF SCHOOL LANGUAGE POLICIES

In 2001, the United States enacted the No Child Left Behind Act (NCLB), which required states to identify students with what federal legislation then called "limited English proficiency" and increase their English proficiency as measured (imperfectly) by yearly statewide standardized tests (Menken, 2008). NCLB encouraged English-only instruction (Menken, 2008; Wright & Ricento, 2016). Title III of the Every Student Succeeds Act, the 2015 reauthorization of the Elementary and Secondary Education Act (ESEA), vests the responsibility for maintaining accountability systems at the state (rather than district) level; it aims to ensure that English learners, including immigrant children and youth, attain English proficiency, develop high levels of academic attainment in English, and achieve at high levels in academic subjects to meet the same challenging state academic standards that all children are expected to meet (Sections 3101 and 3102). In the U.S. federal system of governance, states determine specific educational language policy (Wiley & García, 2016). They must ensure that English learners are meeting federal accountability metrics: currently, 41 states assess ELL student achievement through the annual administration of ACCESS for ELLs assessment (WIDA, 2020). Each state is required to include progress toward meeting the goals of Title III as part of their education department's ESEA state plan.

While federal and state-level policies mandate approaches to ensure that multilingual students are progressing toward English proficiency, educators and administrators at the district, school, and classroom levels adapt policies in accordance with their views of students' needs and the constraints of their institutional contexts. What school- and classroom-level language policies best serve the needs of immigrant youth? Within schools and classrooms, language policies typically fall into two categories: (1) language allocation policies that dictate the program model, such as a bilingual instructional model, and (2) language use policies that inform how teachers and students use language inside the classroom.

Language Allocation Policies

Guidelines generated by a local educational agency for language use in classes are termed language allocation policies. They recommend when, how, and why English and other languages are taught. There are three widespread models in use. First, transitional bilingual education (TBE) programs provide academic instruction in both languages, supporting and gradually increasing the dominance of English as students "transition" into English instruction over a period of several years. Second, schools may establish an English as a second language (ESL) program, in which students receive specialized and intense ESL instruction. Some large schools have self-contained ESL classes, where all academic instruction is provided in English with specialized teaching methodologies to support English language acquisition. In other situations, an ESL teacher may "push in," or co-teach, with the content teacher, or schools may employ a "pull out" model, where students spend most of their day in a mainstream classroom but are pulled out for a period of intensive ESL instruction. Notably, neither TBE nor ESL maintain students' home languages. Third, some schools use a "dual language" bilingual model, which mandates the structure, curriculum, and allocation of time in teaching two languages (e.g., Sánchez et al., 2018). Most dual language programs are located in elementary schools, where they have been immensely popular with middle-class families who want their children to learn two languages, meaning such programs do not always serve immigrant youth, even when they are available; they are gradually spreading to middle and high school levels (Watzinger-Tharp et al., 2021). There are a few bilingual high schools for immigrant youth. For example, Gregorio Luperón High School in New York City accepts newcomer immigrant and refugee students from Latin America. They provide intensive ESL classes for all students and use a translanguaging pedagogy in content classes, integrating Spanish and English (Bartlett & García, 2011). Their work is made possible in part because, in New York state, students can elect to take their content-area state exams in languages including English, Arabic, Bengali, Korean, Spanish, Haitian Creole, Russian, or Mandarin. The decision to make exams available in multiple languages means that they are less of a barrier to graduation for (some) immigrant students and to bilingual education (see also Strategy 6).

Language Use Policies

In comparison, language use policies typically outline appropriate purposes and times for teachers and students to use specific languages within, and at times outside of, their classrooms. Language policies may be explicit, formally recorded in a handbook or posted on signs at the school, or they may be implicit, known by students and teachers, but not formally written or stated. Within a classroom space, an explicit language use policy might require teachers to speak only in English with their students or might penalize students for speaking in their home language, while an implicit language policy might be evident when teachers encourage students to use online translators to clarify a task.

Teachers exert influence over language use policies. Teachers who value the language resources of multilingual learners seek to make space in their classrooms for students to use and sustain their languages (Blackledge & Creese, 2014; Prasad, 2014). More flexible language policies allow learners to "utilize the totality of their linguistic repertoires as learning resources" (Beeman & Urow, 2013, p. ix), as opposed to attempting to suppress one or more of their languages to match a language policy.

School administrators and teachers play an important role in both the creation and the appropriation of language policies. While they are accountable to state and district policies, there is space for policy negotiation. Classroom teachers are often the final arbiters of language policy implementation. Teachers can advocate for equitable language allocation policies that support the needs of multilingual students. Even when working within a system of language allocation policies that may not be beneficial for most multilingual students, administrators and classroom teachers can establish language use policies that encourage multilingual students to draw on their entire linguistic repertoire to engage in content and language learning (see also Strategy 1).

SCHOOL AND CLASSROOM STRATEGIES

In this section, we provide school administrators and teachers with a number of strategies to support the creation of equitable language policies that serve the needs of their multilingual students.

Utilize a Home and Community Language Questionnaire

As part of the initial school registration process, the school may ask students and their families to complete a home language questionnaire about the languages spoken by various family members, and levels of proficiency and/or schooling in each of the languages. The questionnaire should be as open-ended as possible, recognizing that language use varies widely. Whenever possible, written translations should be provided or families should have the option of completing the questionnaire with a translator to ensure accuracy (this questionnaire could also be completed at the same time as the initial intake interview suggested in Strategy 2). The purpose of the questionnaire is to better understand the linguistic background of the student, to identify possible resources in the school community, and to inform the creation of multilingual policies and programs at the school. The questionnaire should not penalize students in any way if they speak languages other than English at home. New York state recommends that schools use a home language questionnaire, and provides the questionnaire in 44 languages (New York State Education Department, 2019).[1]

Teachers may wish to conduct a home and community language questionnaire with their entire class. For example, teachers could ask students to take photos of instances when they see language used at home or in their community to share with the class. Asking all students to reflect on the use of written and spoken languages in their homes and communities serves various purposes:

- to increase students' awareness of the prevalence of multilingualism
- to provide the teacher with more information about all of the students' language backgrounds to encourage connections between students
- to create a classroom community in which interacting with multiple languages is seen as beneficial and the norm, as opposed to just the reality of newcomer students

Assess Student Language Proficiency

While home and community language questionnaires provide a snapshot of the languages students interact with, more in-depth student language assessments provide further insight into the needs of multilingual students. In many states, newcomer students will take a state-mandated English language assessment, such as the WIDA Screener. While providing essential information to guide English language support, multilingual students should be provided with an opportunity to demonstrate proficiency across all of their languages, not just English. For example, the Bridges to Academic Success (2019) program in New York state has developed assessment recommendations, including how to assess languages that are less commonly used in the United States, and those in which students may have oral, not written, proficiency (see also Strategy 5, which discusses the Bridges Curriculum and SLIFE students). By assessing students' linguistic proficiencies holistically, teachers are able to leverage students' oral and written literacy skills as a foundation for English language development.

Cocreate Classroom Language Norms

As a step toward creating a schoolwide language policy, teachers can cocreate classroom language norms with their students. These norms provide the opportunity for teachers to explicitly welcome all of students' languages and languaging practices as useful learning resources. For example, teachers might discuss with students a norm for the use of online translation tools or for how to ensure all students feel included in classroom discussions. Classroom language norms should take a strong stand against linguistic discrimination, committed by both staff and students, in all of its forms.

Offer Flexible Language Instruction Models

As noted above, language allocation policies are powerful tools that guide when, how, and why languages are taught. While districts and states may typically prefer certain models, schools often have some flexibility to create models that suit the needs of their students. For example, La Follette High School in Madison, Wisconsin, offers a dual language immersion (DLI) model, primarily as a continuation for students enrolled in the elementary DLI programs throughout the district. Spanish-speaking newcomers can also enroll in DLI courses, in which they are able to take social studies or Spanish literature and engage in academic content in Spanish.

Engage Multilingual Staff and Community Members

While the majority of teachers and school staff in the United States are monolingual (Deroo & Ponzio, 2021), multilingual staff and community members play an important role in supporting newcomer students. For example, Wellstone International High School (see School Profile 3), Brooklyn International High School, and Rudsdale Newcomer High School (see School Profile 4) make judicious use of multilingual assistant educators and community associates (see also Strategies 9 and 20).

As well, employing multilingual staff provides further possibilities for some home language instruction, even within an English instructional model. In this approach, as noted by Goldenberg (2013, p. 8), while content is taught in English, "the home language is used to help facilitate learning content and skills in English." Multilingual staff play an essential role in providing this helpful support to newcomers.

Position Every Teacher as a Language Teacher

While employing multilingual staff helps create a school environment that celebrates linguistic diversity and allows for home language support, schools can engage all teachers in supporting newcomers' language, regardless of the teachers' own linguistic proficiency. While newcomer students are at times seen as the responsibility of the English as a second (or additional) language teacher, in reality, newcomer students benefit from language development across all of their classes, at all stages of linguistic proficiency. As noted by Nordmeyer and Honigsfeld (2020), "all teachers need to share responsibility for both engaging all learners in the core curriculum and developing essential language skills" (p. 1). To do so, it is imperative that teachers learn about topics related to multilingual development, including: "the basic units of language," how oral language competency is developed, building background knowledge, developing vocabulary, developing sociolinguistic knowledge, "why English spelling is so complicated," "what makes a sentence or text easy or difficult to understand," and the latest in research on structuring instruction for English learners, among others (Adger et al., 2018, pp. 2–3).

Create a Schoolwide Language Policy

While it may seem that creating a schoolwide language policy should be the first recommendation, it is often both complex and, potentially, controversial. We therefore recommend beginning to engage in some of the supportive strategies outlined above that support multilingual learners and move toward creating an environment conducive to equitable language policies, while at the same time beginning schoolwide, and possibly districtwide, conversations about explicit, formal language policies.

According to Hamayan and Freeman Field (2012), very few schools or school districts have a clear, coherent language policy. The authors outline a process for creating a language policy, including reviewing current policies and procedures, identifying important gaps or contradictions, and making recommendations based on current research about best practices for multilingual students. Menken's (2008) work further strengthens the need for explicit and coherent language policies, stating they are essential to protect programming that serves the needs of multilingual students, even in the midst of changing, and possibly problematic, top-down reforms. Menken provides a number of useful recommendations for teachers and administrators in creating school language policies, including the following:

- starting from a mindset of multilingualism as an asset
- allowing for instruction and learning in students' home languages whenever possible
- acknowledging the importance of languages that are less common in the United States
- providing the necessary supports for students to be successful in high-stakes testing

In sum, even within the context of English-only instruction, multilingual language policies position students' entire linguistic repertoires as a tool for learning content and for developing language proficiency (see also Strategy 1). Intentional language policies, at both the classroom and the school level, make space for students' languages as resources and as rights.

SUMMARY

- Educators should envision their students' languages as resources and make space for students to draw upon their entire linguistic repertoires.

- Teachers are critical language policy actors, with much influence over language use policies.
- Educators should learn about students' language backgrounds, assess their language needs, cocreate classroom language norms, and utilize flexible language instruction models.
- Schools best serve newcomer youth when they employ multilingual staff, distribute responsibility for language instruction across all teachers, and create a schoolwide language policy.

ADDITIONAL RESOURCES

All resources are linked at the book's companion website: www.bit.ly/Immig RefugeeEd

- New York State Home Language Questionnaire (available in 44 languages). http://www.nysed.gov/bilingual-ed/ell-identification -placementhome-language-questionnaire
- Adger, C., Snow, S., & Christian, D. (2018). *What teachers need to know about language.* Multilingual Matters.
- Goldenberg, C. (2013). Unlocking the research on English learners: What we know—and don't yet know—about effective instruction. *American Educator, 37*(2), 4–11.

Strategy 12

Promote a Positive School Climate and Culture

Lesley Bartlett and Ariel Borns

Interviewer: ¿Qué es lo que más te gusta de los profesores del Liceo Luperón? [What do you like most about the teachers at Luperón High School?]

Eduardo: Confianza, siempre ha habido confianza. [The trust, there has always been trust.]

—Interview with a student at Gregorio Luperón High School, May 21, 2008

Students, and especially immigrant and refugee students, do best when they experience a sense of belonging and community at school. According to the National School Climate Center (2021), a positive school climate features shared beliefs and values that are directly communicated by educators and reinforced through social interactions; school connectedness, including positive teacher–student relationships and high staff morale; discipline practices perceived by students as fair; and safety. While these features matter in every school, they are particularly important for immigrant and refugee students. In this strategy, we discuss the need for educators to develop a deep understanding of their newcomer students and discuss the actions that can be taken to ensure a positive and productive school climate for immigrant and refugee youth.

DEEP UNDERSTANDING OF IMMIGRANT AND REFUGEE STUDENTS

Recognize Diversity Within National Groups

Good educators recognize that immigrant and refugee populations are incredibly heterogeneous. Educators must "refrain from essentializing" refugees or ignoring differences among conationals; students' "personal histories and current needs must take precedence" (Sarr & Mosselson, 2010, p. 553). Students' experiences vary significantly by the specific context of reception, including how peers perceive the immigrant or refugee student's nation of origin; levels of discrimination and racism; the prevailing ethos toward immigrants; economic opportunities; and

111

city and state social policies. Immigrant and refugee students may face more or fewer difficulties depending on income, status, family composition, social capital and social networks, religious background, race/ethnicity, languages and language abilities, legal status, gender identity, and sexual orientation.

In order to help students integrate into their new environments, educators should avoid binary, static, or homogeneous notions of culture (Bartlett et al., 2017). Schools too often hinder affiliation and belonging among transnational immigrant youth by perpetuating dichotomous notions of citizenship as defined by nation-state boundaries (Abu El-Haj, 2015). While groups may claim homogeneity for strategic reasons, group members do not necessarily share the same customs and beliefs. Culture does not make individuals act in certain ways; it is an ever-changing, active, productive process of sense-making in concert with others. Furthermore, power relations are recast and perpetuated through cultural practices. This more flexible notion of culture can avoid problematic dichotomies about "home culture" or "American culture."[1] Students feel more included when schools promote a processual notion of cultural production and reinvention as the norm, portray "home" and "American" cultural practices as heterogeneous, and emphasize how personal cultural repertoires vary situationally and relationally.

Acknowledge Different Histories and Cultures of Schooling

Before arriving in the United States, immigrant and refugee students have attended schools with different policies, procedures, and expectations (see, for example, the profiles of former students placed throughout this book). They may have attended a school premised on cooperation and collectivism; they may have studied in a situation where asking a question of the teacher was seen as disrespectful, discouraged, and/or even punished (see also the Profile of Ko). School cultures offer a specific and somewhat arbitrary set of expectations and rules, such as sitting still for long periods, the wearing (or not) of a uniform, raising a hand to speak, rotating classrooms or teachers, or determining when it is or is not permitted to cooperate on a task. Recognizing that students have likely experienced a different set of norms in their previous educational settings, the International Newcomer Academy in Fort Worth, Texas, provides an orientation to U.S. culture and the school environment. Similarly, the Newcomer Youth Summer Academy run by the International Rescue Committee explicitly teaches the norms and expectations of New York schools, including information such as a clear description of the roles of different adults in schools, an explanation of school rules and routines, and a description of different types of classroom activities (e.g., the difference between collaborative and independent work) (interview, Caitlyn Griffith, December 6, 2021).

Get to Know Students' Prior Schooling, Needs, Interests

To prepare a welcoming environment for immigrant and refugee students, educators should continuously seek new information about the countries and cultures from which their newcomer students hail. While respecting privacy, they should work to get to know each student—their life story, their family situation, and their interests. This effort helps to develop trust while allowing teachers to differentiate instruction and build on students' motivations. In Strategy 2, Figure 2.1 provides a sample intake interview form that educators can use to get to know students and their families better; ideally the interview would take place in the student's home language.

At the same time, to ensure students receive adequate academic support, it is critical to "assess students' educational needs, including the need for appropriate language assistance services and whether the student requires an evaluation to determine if he or she has a disability and as a result requires special education and/or related aids and services under the Individuals With Disabilities in Education Act (IDEA) or Section 504 of the Rehabilitation Act of 1973 (Section 504)" (U.S. Department of Education, 2016, ch. 2, p. 4). This information will help staff develop a comprehensive set of academic, social, and emotional supports for each child.

Become Aware of the Impact of Anti-Immigrant Rhetoric and Policies

School culture is not only about food and folkways; it is also, and quite centrally, about recognizing the serious political and economic constraints facing immigrant and refugee students. Students from mixed-status families fear the potential impact of forcible removals and the casual violence of others, particularly in political moments when federal or state officials are fomenting xenophobic rhetoric (see also Strategies 2 and 17). One survey of school administrators found that immigrant student attendance, and therefore learning (as well as funding), were negatively affected by increases in immigration enforcement activity (Gándara & Ee, 2018). Police cooperation with immigration enforcement officials negatively affects the persistence of Latinx students (Kirksey & Sattin-Bajaj, 2021; Kirksey et al., 2020; Mitchell, 2018). During the 2016 presidential campaign season, an online survey of a voluntary sample of educators conducted by Teaching Tolerance (now Learning for Justice) found that, across the country, teachers reported a marked increase in fear and anxiety among immigrant students, particularly Mexican, Muslim, and/or undocumented students (Costello, 2016). Schools need to plan carefully for how to support students when parents or caregivers are threatened with deportation (Breiseth, 2019; see also Strategy 17).

Educators may believe that students learn about democratic processes and/or current immigration issues primarily in social studies classes. However, in truth, students learn about democratic engagement and belonging through everyday curriculum and pedagogy throughout the school day. As Jaffe-Walter et al. (2019) explain, "when teachers remain silent on immigration policy, students interpret their silence as an implicit sanctioning of those policies. This can lead to the continued marginalization and exclusion of immigrant and undocumented students. . . . [W]hen xenophobic and false ideas about immigrants echo through public discourses and schools, teachers must actively challenge these dehumanizing discourses" (pp. 252–254). Communicating such stances may take different forms. Some schools run "Know Your Rights" workshops; some set up safe zones or sanctuary districts, as did public schools in Milwaukee, Wisconsin, in 2017 (Waxman, 2017b); some alert mixed-status families about the presence of ICE officers in areas surrounding the school (see also Strategy 17 for more information on these efforts).

ACTIONS TO ENSURE A POSITIVE SCHOOL CLIMATE

Provide Newcomer Families With Key Information

By law, schools are obligated to share information with families in a language that they understand (Colorín Colorado, 2019). Families with lower levels of literacy may need information shared orally. Schools should develop plans for how to communicate with families, using different channels and appropriate languages. In the earliest days of school, parents need to receive information, written and, when possible, orally in the home language(s), about topics such as the following:

- course schedules (e.g., child will have more than one teacher and more than one classroom)
- physical layout of the school
- homework policy and purpose
- attendance policy (e.g., mandatory phone call and note when child is sick)
- discipline policy
- immunization policy
- dress code, winter clothing, physical education uniforms
- cafeteria options
- subsidized lunch applications
- transportation options to and from school
- Back to School Night information
- progress report and report card descriptions
- parent–teacher conference dates and purpose
- after-school clubs and sports options
- special education services
- summer school availability
- the role of guidance counselors and other nonteaching staff (Short & Boyson, 2012, p. 52)

Later communication should remain cognizant of family needs. For example, relying solely on email to communicate may exclude some caregivers.

Cultivate a Sense of Belonging and Safety

Schools should actively and persistently cultivate a sense of belonging. Students need to experience strong, respectful connections with teachers. For example,

Castellón et al. (2015) described New World High School in the Bronx, New York, as a school "characterized by a strong culture of high expectations for all students" (p. 199). As they explained:

> Teachers frequently communicate their belief that every individual student is capable of success, and are constantly pushing and encouraging students to believe in their potential. The school is also built on a culture of mutual respect. Students, teachers, and staff reported feeling valued and appreciated by each other. . . . Overall, the school staff has built a safe, caring, and nurturing environment for students. The attendance clerk likened the school to a "second family" for students and faculty. . . . The goal is to establish trust, rapport, and a sense of consistency. As the technology consultant stated, "One of the things that really works well here is that the staff, at any level, tries to connect with the kids. Not just with individuals but also with the families. You can ask any staff member about any kid, and they know what is going on." (p. 199)

This sense of connection is a strong feature among schools that successfully prepare newcomer students. As one student from Gregorio Luperón High School in New York City said, "From the time a student arrives, the teachers here give a hand. They want to help you, as if they aren't here just for the salary but because students really matter to them—helping students advance matters. Many of them came at the same age, young. They had to learn English and there was no bilingual education. So they understand our situation" (interview, May 21, 2008).

Students also need to experience a strong sense of connection with other students. Schools may use different strategies to facilitate that culture. The International Newcomer Academy in Fort Worth uses a "house system," dividing students into smaller groups with designated teachers for social support and helping students develop social connections; this is akin to the advisory or homeroom structures discussed in Strategy 7. At Wellstone International High School in Minneapolis (School Profile 2), educators have developed a "buddy" program, connecting newcomers to more experienced students who share their home language.

Further, to promote a sense of belonging, schools must ensure that students feel safe. To prevent bullying, educators must set (and post) clear expectations of all students; provide clear examples of what constitutes bullying; encourage students to report bullying of themselves or someone else, with clear reporting mechanisms; establish consequences for bullying behavior; look for and document signs of bullying; and ask families not to normalize or excuse bullying.

A sense of safety and belonging is crucial for the success of restorative justice, an approach to resolving conflict that focuses on "strengthening individual and community relationships to create a sense of belonging and provide a system of communal accountability that sets the stage for repairing harm that may arise from student or educator behavior" (Collins, 2021). One crucial part of restorative justice is a strong school culture, "so that when conflict and challenges arise, there is something to restore and there are relationships to work through those challenges" (Castellón et al., 2015, pp. 48–49). For example, Gregorio Luperón

High School in New York City had a student-run mediation service to arbitrate disagreements. Many students were trained to work in the system as peer counselors. This system encouraged a sense of safety; students reported feeling very safe at their school, which they contrasted to what they had heard about the schools that their siblings, cousins, and neighbors attended (Bartlett & García, 2011). Rudsdale Newcomer High School in Oakland (see School Profile 4) also used restorative justice circles to manage conflicts that arose among students or with teachers (see Figure 12.1). One teacher in a Brooklyn high school reported, "We started a circle keepers program to train students. We train staff in circle keeping and restorative justice practices and integrate them, especially in our advisory curriculum. We have used reentry circles and harm circles as well. We had two restorative justice co-coordinators for a short time but funding and the pandemic ended this" (interview, July 9, 2021).

Develop an Asset-Based Stance: Build on Students' Languages, Talents, and Knowledge

A productive school culture adopts an asset-based stance that builds on the knowledges, talents, and languages of students and their families (see also Strategy 2). Schools can pursue this stance in a number of ways. Schools should develop a multilingual ecology and increase "multilingualism in schoolscapes" (Menken et al.,

Figure 12.1. Restorative Justice (RJ) Guidelines Posted in a Classroom at Rudsdale Newcomer High School, Oakland, California

RJ Circle Guidelines

 Respect the person talking
Respetar a la persona que habla

 Speak form the heart
Habla desde el corazón

 Listen with respect
Escucha con respeto

 Stay in the circle
Quédate en el círculo

Note: Recreated with permission.

2018) with welcome messages, in multiple languages, posted at entrances, and languages visibly and audibly present (see also Strategy 1).

Many schools establish extracurricular arts or interest clubs. For example, Lincoln High School in Nebraska (School Profile 1) has a section of Las Razas Unidas (a Latinx student organization), a Middle Eastern club, a Karen/Zomi/Karenni club, as well as a Native American caucus and a student chapter of the NAACP (Welner & Kelley, 2018). The library and classrooms should include books by diverse authors from the countries and languages represented in the school. A school might incorporate important visual symbols, such as flags from different countries, artwork, or photographs. At Wellstone International High School in Minneapolis, visitors are greeted by colorful murals representing the student populations and their languages (see Figure 12.2).

Other schools pursue an asset-based stance through celebratory cultural events, such as international festivals or talent shows. For example, South Division High School in Milwaukee, Wisconsin, where 55% of students are classified as English language learners, holds a World and Wellness Fair, which has featured Laotian music, African dance, a Hmong fashion show, and many of the 26 languages spoken on campus. Oakland International High School has an annual International Festival where students perform songs, dances, and poetry, and present other aspects of their home cultures for the school community coupled with a feast of foods from the more than 35 nations represented at the school.

Figure 12.2. Murals Representing the Diverse Populations and Their Languages at Wellstone

Note: Wellstone International High School photo from Minnesota Public Radio News. © 2019 Minnesota Public Radio®. [Used with permission. All rights reserved.]

Schools can also feature stories from students' lives. Green Card Voices, a Minneapolis-based nonprofit, publishes books with videos that showcase the narratives of recent immigrant and refugee youth. They have worked with youth from St. Paul and Minneapolis, Minnesota; Atlanta, Georgia; upstate New York; Fargo, North Dakota; and Milwaukee and Madison, Wisconsin, producing books that can be read in the school, community, and beyond (www.greencardvoices.org).

SUMMARY

- To create a positive school climate and culture, educators must take steps to ensure immigrant and refugee students feel a sense of belonging, community, and safety.
- Educators should avoid dichotomous notions of culture; acknowledge different histories of schooling; learn more about students' previous schooling experiences; share pertinent information, in accessible languages, with students and families; adopt an asset-based stance to build on and honor students' backgrounds in myriad ways; and communicate stances that acknowledge and challenge anti-immigrant rhetoric and policies.

ADDITIONAL RESOURCES

All resources are linked at the book's companion website: www.bit.ly/Immig RefugeeEd

- Bridging Refugee Youth and Children's Services. (n.d. c). *Welcoming and orienting newcomer students to U.S. Schools.* https://brycs.org/schools/welcoming-and-orienting-newcomer-students-to-u-s-schools/
- Office of English Language Acquisition. (2016). *Newcomer tool kit.* U.S. Department of Education. https://www2.ed.gov/about/offices/list/oela/newcomers-toolkit/index.html
- Language Lizard. (2011). *8 Tips to protect ELLs from bullying in your classroom and school.* Colorín Colorado. https://www.colorincolorado.org/article/8-tips-protect-ells-bullying-your-classroom-and-school

Strategy 13

Emphasize Students' Health and Wellness

Monisha Bajaj and Sailaja Suresh

The idea of a full-service community school is that schools should be a hub for services which are colocated on campus. Traditionally, academics happen in schools, health happens at a doctor's office or at a community clinic, food access happens at the food bank or the food stamps office. If you need health care access, that is something that you usually have to go to social services to get. Newcomers come with so many needs, and having health, mental health, legal, and other social services available on campus—or off campus but with organizations or agencies with which the school has very intentional partnerships—makes so much sense. Many students have never been to a doctor except for the time that they went to a community clinic to get their immunizations for school. So we have partnerships with community health centers and provide a warm handoff so students don't have to navigate those systems without a contact there. If you're suffering from an undiagnosed health issue, you can't learn. If you're in the throes of posttraumatic stress, you're not gonna be able to focus on math, at least not very well.

A lot of newcomer students have traumatic backgrounds, especially unaccompanied minors who are generally fleeing some kind of violence. We have students who have been sexually assaulted, or physically assaulted by gangs, so mental health interventions are incredibly important. Usually, school mental health is connected to insurance and a lot of our students are not insured; through our Wellness Center we have been able to establish partnerships with multilingual providers to support our students at school.

—Staff interview, Oakland International High School, 2016

Access to health (including mental health) services in a school setting has been shown to effectively increase well-being, especially for students living in poverty (Bundy et al., 2006), and, in the United States, particularly for those who are new to the country and may be uninsured. Existing school infrastructure and established relationships with families can allow for students to receive trusted information and services that the school has arranged with community organizations and other service providers without fear of being defrauded, overcharged, or reported if they are unauthorized immigrants. Additionally, mental health services can often be stigmatized in immigrant and refugee communities despite the need for interventions to address the trauma youth and families may have experienced or continue to be experiencing.

PROVIDING HEALTH SERVICES AT SCHOOL

Health services at school can consist of health centers or mobile clinics colocated on school campuses that offer services such as primary medical care, mental/behavioral health care, dental/oral health care, health and/or nutrition education, substance abuse counseling, case management, or other services (Health Resources and Service Administration, 2017). School-located vaccine clinics can also increase access to immunizations and have been advocated by the Centers for Disease Control and Prevention (CDC), particularly at the time of this writing during the COVID-19 pandemic. Other ways to provide such services can be through referrals to organizations that partner with schools to serve their student population, whether funded through state programs (such as Medi-Cal in California) or charitable organizations that provide no- or low-cost services to communities.

Another component of health is access to nutritious and fresh food, particularly in urban communities with limited access to healthy foods. As at Rudsdale Newcomer High School (School Profile 4), schools can provide bridges to food pantries or other social services, but the school campus can also be a place to grow and distribute nutritious foods. At South High School in Denver, Colorado, parent and student volunteers have set up a food bank run out of a classroom so that families can access healthy food (Thorpe, 2017). At a newcomer-focused school in North Carolina, a teacher shared with us the following: "We have a school garden where we grow vegetables for students to bring home to their families. We can grow whatever the garden can support, so we can have students' input in what we grow" (survey, July 29, 2021). Schools across the country have also partnered with the International Rescue Committee (2021a) and their New Roots Garden Project, which advances food security for refugee communities. As of 2021, this project boasts a network of 62 gardens where more than 5,000 people (mostly refugees) "grow, prepare, share, buy, and sell local, healthy foods in their community" (para. 2).

ADDRESSING MENTAL HEALTH

Destigmatizing mental health services and facilitating easy access to them on school campuses can offer newcomer students important support to address trauma that can impede learning, as noted in the opening quote by a staff member at Oakland International High School. Shown in Figure 13.1 are several core stressors and their causes that have been identified for newcomer students.

Being able to identify the stressors facing students requires educators and other school staff to assume a trauma-informed approach and have adequate

Figure 13.1. Definitions and Causes of Core Stressors for Newcomers

Stressor	Definition	Possible causes
Trauma	Child experiences an intense event that threatens or causes harm and trauma to their emotional and physical well-being	• War, persecution • Displacement from home • Flight and migration • Poverty • Family and/or community violence
Acculturation	Children and families experience acculturation as they try to navigate between their new culture/society and their culture/society of origin	• Conflicts between children and parents over new and old cultural/societal values • Conflict with peers related to cultural misunderstandings • Problems trying to fit in at school • Struggle to form an integrated identity including elements of their new culture/society and their culture/society of origin
Resettlement	Children and families who have relocated try to make a new life for themselves	• Financial stressors • Difficulties finding adequate housing, employment, access to services • Loss of community support
Isolation	Children and/or families experience isolation as new immigrants in a new country	• Discrimination/racism or anti-immigrant attitudes • Experiences of harassment from peers, adults, or law enforcement • Feelings of not "fitting in" • Separation from extended family, or immediate family in the case of unaccompanied minors • Loss of social status

Note: Adapted with permission from the *Refugee Services Toolkit* by the National Child Traumatic Stress Network. Copyright 2011.

resources and services available for students. Some ways that schools have done this are through the following:

- advisory periods where one teacher is closely monitoring advisees over one or more years (see also Strategy 7)
- joint meetings of teachers to discuss students in common and their needs
- school social workers who are in contact with students and able to refer them to partnering organizations (or those who come to campus) to address the needs of students
- services that are accessible in the home languages of families and that understand their cultural backgrounds and migration histories

TAKING A WELLNESS APPROACH

A whole-school approach to wellness for newcomer students can coordinate and align efforts toward student well-being. A unique approach we identified was the establishment of a "Wellness Center" at Oakland International High School. Despite it taking a few years to find physical space to locate this center on campus, OIHS launched the Wellness Center in 2016 and also offers peer support through Wellness Ambassadors. Other programs that operate at the school, such as its after-school soccer program, also assume a trauma-informed approach with the students (see also Strategy 15).

With newcomer student populations, many of whom may be unaccompanied minors, refugees, asylees, and/or students with interrupted formal education (see also Strategy 5), integrating a trauma-informed approach is essential to building successful relationships with students. At OIHS, the school's professional development is tailored to foster staff understanding of students' cultures and communities, but administrators have also made a concerted effort to ground their collective work in an understanding of how trauma affects the brain and learning. Within the school, adults strive to make students feel safe, welcome, and trusted in big and small ways. Advisors check in with their students daily about their grades and weekly about their lives through community circles. The Wellness Center at OIHS is open throughout the day for drop-in visits by students who may need help with social service applications or health appointments, or who just need a snack or a socioemotional breather (see Figure 13.2). The intentional focus on building safe spaces and trusting relationships with adults is evident in the strong community at the school. According to the 2016 California Healthy Kids Survey, 80.8% of students surveyed at OIHS responded to the question "How safe do you feel when you are at school?" with a response of Safe or Very Safe, as opposed to only 54.8% of students at all schools throughout the district. More recent data on inclusion, even after the COVID-19 school closures, indicates differences as well: 73% of students at Oakland International High School in 2020–2021 indicated they felt a part of their school, compared with 56.4% of students across the district (California Department of Education, 2021a).

Each year, OIHS has strengthened the socioemotional services available to students by expanding partnerships and by intentionally finding staff with linguistic and cultural competency to address students' many and varying needs (see also Strategy 9). OIHS has worked with a local agency called Partnerships for Trauma Recovery to provide an Arabic-speaking mental health counselor—one of the only ones in the entire district at the time of this writing. She had a regular caseload of more than a dozen students, meeting on a weekly basis. In fact, more than half of the student population at the school regularly receives counseling services during the school year through culturally specific individual and group counseling in English, Arabic, Spanish, Farsi, Karen, Burmese, Mandarin, and Cantonese. Receiving counseling services is remarkably unstigmatized at the school, as so many students do so each year.

Figure 13.2. Flyer from Oakland International High School

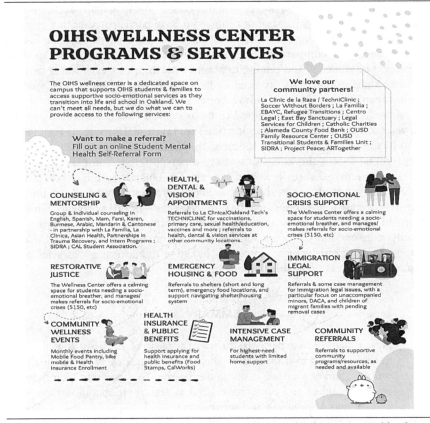

Note: Flyer provided by Madenh Ali Hassan, Community School Manager, Oakland International High School, 2022.

Each week, teachers meet to case manage and design academic and social interventions for struggling students. During this time, they make referrals to the Coordination of Student Services Team (COST), which includes all the mental health counselors working at the school through partner agencies. The COST team then meets together each week to manage the different interventions that are being coordinated for each individual student, matching them to counselors based on language need, to home-based tutors for extra academic support, or to other partner agencies, as needed (Bajaj & Suresh, 2018).

Soccer Without Borders (SWB) is one partner agency that has been working at the school since its opening in 2007 (and is discussed more fully in Strategy 15). Founder Ben Gucciardi and his staff have an office at the school where they meet weekly with the COST team, and where they plan their daily soccer practices with all six OIHS teams. The SWB mission is to use soccer as a vehicle for positive change, providing underserved youth with a tool kit to overcome obstacles to growth, inclusion, and personal success. "We've actually seen, over the last 5 years, [that] 95 percent of our kids who have participated in this program have graduated from high school," said Gucciardi (as cited in Bajaj & Suresh, 2018, p. 94). "You compare that to Oakland-wide, [where] that's closer to about 60 percent of students, and among newcomer youth, it's an even lower percentage than that" (Cate, 2017 as cited in Bajaj & Suresh, 2018, p. 94). José, an unaccompanied minor from Central America in 12th grade at the time he was interviewed, stated, "The first time I came to school, Coach Ben asked me, 'Do you want to play soccer? We have practice Tuesdays and Thursdays.' That helped me to stay in school. It was hard for me in the beginning to stay in school because of everything I went through, but to have a person telling you that you belong in this community, that really helped" (as cited in Bajaj & Suresh, 2018, p. 94).

An explicit focus on health and wellness in school contexts can improve students' overall well-being as well as address acute health problems. Trauma-informed approaches with newcomer populations offer schools a chance to identify stressors and provide resources for students to address them. Academic attainment and persistence are integrally linked with addressing obstacles posed by physical and mental health challenges.

SUMMARY

- Newcomer youth experience the usual adolescent stressors as well as those related to trauma from their home countries, the migration journey, and/or violence in communities they live in within their new country; conflict and problems related to acculturation and settlement; and feelings of isolation and separation.
- A whole-school wellness approach and colocated services can offer newcomer immigrant and refugee students resources and supports to address the various health and wellness challenges they may face.

ADDITIONAL RESOURCES

All resources are linked at the book's companion website: www.bit.ly/Immig RefugeeEd

- An article and short film from Colorín Colorado discuss supporting the social and emotional health of newcomer immigrants: Robertson, K., & Breiseth, L. (n.d.). *How to support refugee students in your school community*. Colorín Colorado. https://www.colorincolorado.org/article /how-support-refugee-students-ell-classroom
- The Centers for Disease Prevention and Control (CDC) offers guidance on providing vaccinations at school campuses. See https://www.cdc.gov /vaccines/covid-19/planning/school-located-clinics.html

Strategy 14

Establish Dual Enrollment and Early College Programs

Daniel Walsh, Yvonne Ndiaye, and Asmaa Amadou

[Throughout this dual enrollment program], I learned about primary and secondary data, which websites to use for accurate information, how to conduct interviews, how to write a paper. . . . Most of my [college] classes required so much writing and research. Still, it wasn't difficult because I knew what to do; so if it weren't for this experience, I would have suffered in college.

—Yvonne, former dual enrollment student, now 30 years old

I learned about ethics in research and how to apply them. . . . The research knowledge I acquired helped in my English composition and anthropology courses in college. Sometimes I wonder how difficult college would have been for me if I didn't have this learning experience.

—Asmaa, former dual enrollment student, now 27 years old

For refugee and immigrant students, college may seem a difficult if not impossible goal. They are likely to be the first in their family to consider college in the United States, and they may not know much about how to navigate the college selection, application, and financial aid processes. Students' perceptions of the viability of postsecondary goals may be limited by the xenophobia and racism they experience (Fenner, 2014; see also Fouad & Byars-Winston, 2005). Proficiency in English is a limiting factor for many newcomer students (G. M. Rodriguez & Cruz, 2009). Undocumented students face specific barriers, as they are denied access to federal financial aid and, in many states, government-subsidized tuition (Gonzales, 2010).

Schools may pursue a range of strategies to prepare students for college, including hosting alum panels; mentoring; organizing bilingual information sessions, meetings with college admissions counselors, and college visits; establishing a central location for college information; and having dedicated college counselors on staff to ensure that students are taking the necessary courses and to assist students with preparing for postsecondary transitions to higher education (Colorín Colorado, 2008; Fenner, 2014; Jaffe-Walter & Lee, 2011).

OVERVIEW OF DUAL ENROLLMENT

One useful strategy is dual enrollment. Dual enrollment programs exist in educational systems across the country as a way to prepare high schoolers for college and gain credits. Dual enrollment courses vary in their conceptualization and pedagogical approaches; however, most share an emphasis on preparing students for college by teaching them content, familiarizing them with the demands of college courses, and helping them earn credits and experiences that will assist them in the future both personally and professionally. Costs vary by state (and sometimes within states, depending on the programs); the school, district, college, or state may pay all or some of the costs (Mehl et al., 2020). Approximately 86% of dual enrollment students take classes at a high school, taught by a college instructor or high school instructor who is credentialed to offer the course; another 17% take courses on a college campus; and 8% take classes online (Mehl et al., 2020, p. 6).

Dual enrollment has expanded dramatically in the past decade, moving from approximately 200,000 to almost 750,000 students (Fink et al., 2017). The National Early College Initiative, supported by the Gates Foundation, was designed to increase postsecondary access for underrepresented groups; "280 Early Colleges were started in 31 states and the District of Columbia" under the initiative (Edmunds et al., 2017, p. 297). Forty percent of students in that Early College program are Latinx, and 60% come from low-income families. A study of 12 Early Colleges in North Carolina showed that, thanks to the program, "students attained significantly more college credits while in high school, and graduated from high school, enrolled in postsecondary education, and received postsecondary credentials at higher rates" (Webb & Gerwin, 2014). Minnesota's Post-Secondary Options program, which offers free college courses for high schools in grades 10 through 12, greatly benefits many immigrant, refugee, and first-generation students who can earn credits toward their undergraduate degree at no cost (Hodge, 2021). Texas has a large dual credit program: According to one evaluation, its benefits far exceed the cost, and participation increases college access and completion while decreasing time to degree (T. Miller et al., 2018). However, students of color and immigrant students are less likely to benefit from dual enrollment, in part because they may not be aware of such opportunities (Edmunds et al., 2017; see also Giani et al., 2014).

One study of nine dual enrollment programs in Florida, Ohio, and Washington with high participation rates for historically underrepresented students of color identified five core principles for equitable dual enrollment partnerships: (1) "Set a shared vision and goals that prioritize equity; (2) Expand equitable access; (3) Connect students to advising and supports that ensure equitable outcomes; (4) Provide high-quality instruction that builds students' competence and confidence; (5) Organize teams and develop relationships to maximize potential" (Mehl et al., 2020, p. 7).

Some schools have successfully prepared students for college and developed dual enrollment partnerships. For example, Oakland International High School offers newcomers community college English courses in partnership with Laney College where the college instructors come to the high school campus for instruction during the school day. As discussed in School Profile 3, Wellstone International High School in Minneapolis partners with a local college (MCTC); Wellstone employs a full-time coordinator who spends several days a week at MCTC coaching and tutoring students. Here we describe one dual enrollment experience, using it to draw broader lessons for educators and administrators who wish to consider this strategy.

DUAL ENROLLMENT THROUGH COLLEGE NOW

College Now (CN) is a long-term partnership between the City University of New York (CUNY) and the New York City Department of Education (NYCDOE). CN offers dual enrollment in CUNY courses to high schoolers in order to enhance college readiness. Usually, students must meet particular GPA and standardized testing thresholds. Unlike Advanced Placement and International Baccalaureate programs, no high-stakes summative assessment is associated with CN; rather, it functions more as a project-based college course. In this case, we describe a "foundations" course, which, once students have passed, allows them to automatically enroll in college-credit-bearing courses at CUNY without completing the required college application. The CN program allows NYCDOE teachers who possess a master's degree to teach both foundations and college-credit-bearing courses. Teachers are paid as adjuncts through CUNY to teach CN courses. Dual enrollment courses may meet on the college campus to provide students with the full experience or, to reduce transportation barriers, courses may also be taught on a high school campus or in a community center.

In fall 2009, Danny initiated his dissertation research by developing an early college, dual enrollment course entitled "Action Research." In spring 2010, he met with Brooklyn College's CN program director. Brooklyn College was the ideal sponsor given the campus's relative proximity to two high schools from which a cohort of students could be drawn. In addition, CN at Brooklyn College offered some flexibility in courses, given the program's desire to more equitably provide English learners access to the program. The proposal for the Action Research course was enthusiastically received because Danny is a certified English as a second language teacher; CN recognized a lack of accessibility to its courses for English learners, and the course was designed specifically for immigrant and refugee youth learning English. The students who enrolled in this particular course were not screened for academic ability, as is typically required—and the course was offered for both enrichment and credit recovery. Asmaa and Yvonne were students in that class; subsequently, later in the spring of 2010, through their high school's internship program and with Danny as their mentor, they conducted the research projects conceived during the class.

Course Design

The Action Research course taught by Danny through the CUNY College Now program was undergirded by Freirean notions of reading the word and the world (Freire, 1970), sociocultural learning theory (Lave & Wenger, 1991; Vygotsky, 1978) that sustains linguistic and cultural resources (Paris & Alim, 2017), and the tenets of youth participatory action research (YPAR) (Cammarota & Fine, 2008; S. Lee & Walsh, 2017; Walsh, 2018). Such a foundation eschews deficit approaches that frequently result in program and instructional models for immigrant and refugee youth that are devoid of meaningful content. Instead, YPAR seeks to foreground student voices to reveal "wisdom about the history, structure, consequences, and the facture points in unjust social arrangements" (Cammarota & Fine, 2008, p. 215).

The Action Research course met at Brooklyn International High School for 1.5 hours two times a week for 15 weeks. The course was designed for students at all academic and English proficiency levels; it incorporated differentiated support and extensive scaffolding for a variety of learners. The guidance counselor and assistant principal at BIHS recruited students for whom the course would provide an enrichment opportunity, as well as those who needed to recuperate credit for courses they did not pass. For all students, the course offered either the opportunity to recover high school credits or prepare them for enrollment in college-credit-bearing courses. In this course itself, students discussed the purpose of education, the nature of student–teacher relationships, and the nature of learning. Students were asked to become observers of their own environments as a way to begin to ask critical questions about what they saw. Some observed their school's hallways and classrooms, others their neighborhoods, and some even the dynamics in their own families.

In a particular lesson, after watching and discussing *The Problem We All Live With: Inequalities Between Boston's Urban and Suburban Schools* (Fedestin et al., 2004), the group discerned the research questions and methods to inform their own mini-research projects to conduct in their schools and communities. The students also developed their own mini-research projects to conduct in their schools and communities. To spur sociological analysis, the group completed Freirean problem trees (see Figure 14.1), with roots (systems, ideologies, and deeply held beliefs and values that underlie the issue), a trunk (the central issue, and the attitudes, goals, and policies that perpetuate or enlarge the issue), and leaves (the visible part of the problem) (see Walsh, 2018, for more information).

In the following semester, four students chose to complete their 11th-grade internship requirement by continuing to work with Danny on their research projects (see also Strategy 19); Asmaa and Yvonne were among them. During the internship, the students conducted the following:

- refined the research questions crafted during the course
- identified potential research sites
- negotiated entry into the field
- completed a certification to conduct research with human subjects as required by the Institutional Review Boards

Figure 14.1. Problem Tree Created by Action Research Class

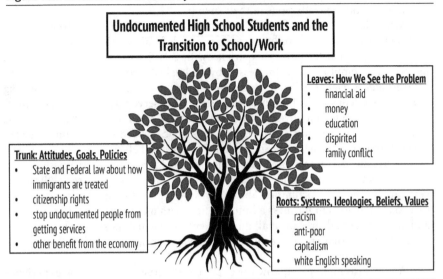

Undocumented High School Students and the Transition to School/Work

Leaves: How We See the Problem
- financial aid
- money
- education
- dispirited
- family conflict

Trunk: Attitudes, Goals, Policies
- State and Federal law about how immigrants are treated
- citizenship rights
- stop undocumented people from getting services
- other benefit from the economy

Roots: Systems, Ideologies, Beliefs, Values
- racism
- anti-poor
- capitalism
- white English speaking

Note: Recreated from an image provided by Danny Walsh.

- spent time at the research site introducing the project to the school community
- identified potential research participants
- designed interview and focus group protocols
- learned new techniques, like photovoice, a qualitative research method that asks research participants to document their lives with digital photography and then share their understandings of the images
- collected, analyzed, and interpreted qualitative data

Using the YPAR process, Asmaa, Yvonne, and the other students developed powerful and provocative analyses of immigrant school experiences and how undocumented high school students navigate transitions to college and/or work after graduation (Walsh, 2018). After completing their research projects, Danny and the students submitted an article to the *Harvard Educational Review*; though it was not ultimately published, the journal sent the young people a certificate to recognize their contribution. Additionally, the young people presented their research projects at immigration conferences at both CUNY's Medgar Evers College and City College.

Student Reflections

The early college course and subsequent research experience benefited participants in multiple ways. They helped the students develop advanced reading, writing, conversational, and analytical skills that were required in their postsecondary studies. They also helped students critically analyze education and its purpose, limitations, and contradictions in their own lives.

More than a decade after this experience, Asmaa and Yvonne drew connections between this dual enrollment course, its role in aiding them in college readiness, and more contemporary experiences. In 2019, for example, during a job interview, an employer was impressed by and asked Yvonne about the *Harvard Educational Review* certificate appearing on her resume. It is also worth noting that each student's contribution to the article also served as their college admissions essay. Yvonne initially studied human services as an undergraduate, and she recalled how the Action Research course experience helped her "tap into the sensitivity" required in the field. She added, "I honestly believe it would have been harder for me if I didn't have that training and knowledge to sympathize and handle sensitive information." Today, Yvonne is using those research skills to investigate business opportunities. She currently works at Bremer Bank and, having earned a bachelor's in business administration with a concentration in marketing and an associate's degree in small business entrepreneurship, she has launched an online business that specializes in Ankara style earrings and waist beads (www.afrikaanista.com).

Asmaa also highlighted how the experience "served as a solid job experience apart from customer service jobs on my resume. And it was always a highlight in my post-college interviews when I was applying to jobs or creative opportunities. In some ways it served as a bridge from college to professional life," despite occurring during high school. After earning a bachelor's degree in cultural anthropology, Asmaa started her own fashion brand, Caméléon, which she has slowly built while also working to sustain herself (see also the profile of Asmaa in this book). Asmaa applied to the Fashion Institute of Technology's MFA program so that she can sustainably create art-wear garments in collaboration with artisans in her home country of Togo (at the time of this writing, Asmaa was waiting to hear about the admissions decision).

Early college and dual enrollment, along with other strategies for college readiness, give immigrant and refugee newcomer students the chance to practice college-level reading, writing, and discussion; learn content; become familiar with the demands of college classes; and garner experiences, build networks, and earn credits. Although immigrant college students may enroll and begin taking college courses after high school completion, many never finish their degrees (Suárez-Orozco & Osei-Twumasi, 2019). Early college and dual enrollment courses can help remedy this challenge and bridge the gap by offering insights, relationships, strategies, and economic support for students to complete postsecondary credits.

SUMMARY

- Educators initiating or further developing a dual enrollment program for immigrant and refugee youth can leverage preexisting relationships that the district may have with higher education institutions to provide high school students with access to college courses, ideally free of charge. These institutions often see these courses as contributing to their diversity, equity, and inclusion or community engagement missions.

- Content in dual enrollment courses for immigrant and refugee youth should take into account their linguistic and cultural resources and their language development needs.
- Dual enrollment programs should identify teachers, either at the high school or college level, who (1) have relevant linguistic and pedagogical content knowledge, (2) possess the dispositions to work with young people in such courses, and (3) can actively engage young people with the content and recognize the importance of depth over breadth in curricula.

ADDITIONAL RESOURCES

All resources are linked at the book's companion website: www.bit.ly/Immig RefugeeEd

- Bridging Refugee Youth and Children's Services. (2020). *What now? Post-high school, college and career readiness for refugee youth.* https:// brycs.org/schools/what-now-post-high-school-college-career-readiness -for-refugee-youth/
- Colorín Colorado. (2008). *Creating a college-going culture for English language learners.* https://www.colorincolorado.org/article/28915/

Profile of Miguel
As Told to Gabriela Martínez

Miguel was 14 when he and his mother migrated to the United States from Mexico. In 9th grade, he started at Oakland International High School, a school exclusively for newcomers. Miguel shared how he began to learn English:

> During the summer vacations, I went to work in my cousin's car shop and he used to push me to learn English by saying, "We have a new customer, go and ask them what they need." I told him "I don't know any English yet," but he would say, "Just go and tell them, 'How can I help you?'" And, little by little, at the shop I started actually practicing what I was learning in school and getting the hang of the language. At school, too, all the classes were in English; some teachers spoke a little bit of Spanish, but by 12th grade, it was awesome because I could talk, I could write, and I could understand English.

Outside of school, Miguel's life was difficult: His stepdad was abusive to his mother and him, and the violence at home often was a lot to bear. Miguel mentioned that one day, when a teacher found him distraught from all the stress at home,

> There was one time that I was crying in the cafeteria. I felt really, really bad. Ms. Raquel sat next to me and asked, "How do you feel?" I said, "I feel numb. I don't feel anything [any] more." She said, "I've got the perfect song for you—'Comfortably Numb' by Pink Floyd. Listen to it and thank me later." That literally changed my life. It gave me my life back.

Teachers sought mental health support for Miguel, and he noted that "if it wasn't for the support of teachers and for finding a psychologist to talk to me, I don't think I would have made it. I owe them a big thank you" (see also Strategy 13).

Two months before graduation, Miguel's mother informed him they were moving back to Mexico. Teachers tried to intervene and convince his mom to let him finish high school, but she wouldn't relent. Miguel was heartbroken to leave the United States, where he had made so many friends and integrated many aspects of U.S. culture into his identity. Back in Mexico, living with his family also didn't suit him anymore given the conflicts at home. He began to look for work and found an opportunity at a call center in Guadalajara. He now fields calls from customers in the United States, the U.K., and Australia about the nutritional supplements the company he works for sells. Miguel noted that, at the call center, "I didn't feel like such an outcast [any] more because I could relate to people like me who had come back from the States either on their own or those who were deported back here, and we could share a lot of common experiences." He met his wife at the call center; she had been in the Bay Area from ages 4 through 12, so they shared many similar experiences growing up transnationally.

Now 28 years of age, and having been back in Mexico for 10 years, Miguel is still trying to find a way to complete his last credits and get his high school diploma (or some sort of equivalency) conferred so that he can pursue higher education.

When asked what advice he had for educators of newcomers, Miguel suggested they should "have a lot of patience because for us newcomers, we are starting a new life, in a new language. Try to put yourself in our shoes." Miguel also advised that "I think more therapy and psychologists will help students, because we really do not know what goes on in a student's life once they leave school. If schools can implement that for every student if possible, not just the students that they think need it, that will be amazing and that will make such a huge impact in the students' lives."

STRATEGIES FOR EXTRACURRICULAR PROGRAMS, AND COMMUNITY AND ALUM PARTNERSHIPS

School Profile 4

Rudsdale Newcomer High School in Oakland, California

Monisha Bajaj and Emma Batten-Bowman

December 17, 2021: It's Rudsdale Newcomer High School's Winter Exhibition and Graduate Celebration. Students, teachers, and community partners are gathered in the hallway, welcomed by school leader Emma Batten-Bowman. Martha, an alumna who is now working as an AmeriCorps volunteer at the school, follows with a trilingual (in English, Spanish, and Mam) introduction of a dance presentation that the Indigenous Guatemalan students have prepared to kick off the day. After the dance, everyone disperses into classrooms to view the videos, presentations, written products, and demonstrations that have been prepared to showcase learning from the fall term. There is a bicycle-powered smoothie station where students can select their ingredients and then ride the stationary bicycle to blend their drinks.

On one wall of the hallway, students have written "youth perspectives" modeled after a popular local public radio segment where listeners share their perspectives. In one student's perspective piece, he shared that when he initially came to the United States and worked as a day laborer, his employer refused to pay him and threatened to report him to immigration officials if he complained. Another student shared how her former school in Mexico was shot up by drug cartels and how that prompted her family to flee. And another wrote about the heartbreak of losing his father, who was back in El Salvador, to COVID-19 and not being able to go back to be with family to mourn the loss because of travel restrictions and his own tenuous immigration status.

On another wall of the hallway (and in multiple classrooms) hung a poster from the school district with the image of a butterfly in front of a globe, stating in big block letters that "Oakland Schools are Sanctuary Schools" and that all students "are welcome here." Students and teachers continued to move through the different classrooms during the Winter Exhibition to hear about what students in the different classes have learned over the semester such as a screening of video poems created by students and a presentation of interviews that students conducted in English. After, everyone reconvened in the hallway for the presentation of awards to the recent graduates; students were commended for their perseverance in completing high school as recent immigrants in the face of pandemic-related hardships, most of them working full time, and some of them parents of young children.

—Observation notes, December 2021

Rudsdale Newcomer High School was established in 2017 by Oakland Unified School District as the first "continuation" or "alternative" high school exclusively for newcomer immigrant and refugee students. Coauthor Emma Batten-Bowman helped design the school and has served as its lead administrator since 2017. In the state of California, continuation schools provide an alternative and more flexible pathway to a high school diploma for "students who are sixteen years of age or older, have not graduated from high school, are still required to attend school, and who are at risk of not graduating" (California Department of Education, 2021b, para. 1). Rudsdale Newcomer High School (a public, non-charter high school) became part of an already existing continuation school, but operates largely independently to serve the specific needs of the school's newcomers, almost all of whom are unaccompanied minors from Central America.

The legacy of Cold War interventionist U.S. foreign policy toward Central America in decades past has contributed to the destabilization of the region. Current violence and insecurity have fueled the widespread desire for out-migration from the Central American nations of El Salvador, Honduras, and Guatemala. In 2009, approximately 3,000 unaccompanied minors from Central America were apprehended at the U.S. border; by 2014, that number increased to approximately 55,000, and available data indicated more than 60,000 unaccompanied minors from Central America arrived in the United States in 2019. Unaccompanied minors are youth under the age of 18, usually boys, who migrate without their parents or legal guardians. After the apprehension of these minors, U.S. immigration laws (despite their widespread violation during the Trump administration) allow them to be placed with a relative while their asylum cases proceed through the courts (see also Strategy 17).

In Oakland, California—home to a large Central American immigrant community—the school district has seen a large influx of unaccompanied minors entering their schools over the past decade; according to a local news report, "Nearly one in five high school students in the district is new to the country" (Rancaño, 2020). While certain programs for newcomer students that previously existed were able to integrate some of these students, the school district realized that it was difficult to meet the needs of students most at risk of dropping out or being pushed out, namely, students who had to work to support themselves and their families (and to pay off debts related to coming to the United States).

SCHOOL DESIGN AND PRACTICES

Given the very low levels of school completion for unaccompanied minors in Oakland, an innovative continuation program, Rudsdale Newcomer High School, opened its doors in 2017 with the express purpose of providing a flexible and tailored approach to meeting the needs of newcomer youth. The school serves approximately 200 students, all of whom have arrived in the United States within the 3 years prior to enrolling at the school. The structures and practices of the school, designed deliberately in recognition of the needs of these students and their families, included the following:

- a later start time and shorter school day than most schools (9:30 a.m. to 2:30 p.m.), since almost all students work after school and late into the night as dishwashers in restaurants, as part of night-time office cleaning crews, or at other low-wage jobs
- six-week, credit-bearing courses that allow students to take leaves of absence if necessary and be able to integrate back into their academic program (see also Strategy 5)
- year-round admission that can accommodate students whenever they arrive throughout the school year, with an orientation for new students held every 6 weeks
- a focus on social–emotional learning, restorative justice, and trauma-informed approaches to address migrant students' distinct realities (see also Strategies 12 and 13)
- daily lunch provided at school, since all the students qualify for free lunch (which is one measure utilized in the United States to determine levels of student poverty)
- a social worker and other case managers at the school (funded through partnerships between nonprofit social service providers and the district) who support students and families. These staff organize workshops every month to assist students and the families they are living with to share information about government programs and also cultivate partnerships with food banks and legal aid organizations to help students with their immigration cases and court hearings (see also Strategies 17 and 18).

Rudsdale Newcomer High School pairs students with mental health services both on site and through community organizations. It also assigns staff (whether case managers or stipended volunteers hired through the AmeriCorps program) to accompany students to navigate accessing dental care, signing up for health benefits available through the state (Medi-Cal), getting a driver's license, showing up for court hearings, and working through other systems and processes that are particularly difficult for newcomer youth to understand.

COLLABORATIONS

In recent years, the school has worked with AmeriCorps to provide opportunities to recent alum of the school who want to gain paid experience working in education and also earn the educational benefit (up to $6,500 at the time of this writing) to pay for further higher education after completion of the 1-year AmeriCorps program. These alum staff members—which cost the school a fraction of what a full-time staff member usually would, through the AmeriCorps cost-sharing model—are particularly well suited to assist students who are in the same position that the alum once were a few years prior (see also Strategies 9 and 20). They often have linguistic competency in English, Spanish, and Mam (the Indigenous Guatemalan language many students at the school speak) and know how to reach out to students and families because they reside in the same communities. The school also organizes regular pickups of donations from the Alameda County Community Food Bank, and students can then take groceries home directly from school (see also Strategy 18). These efforts are managed by the AmeriCorps volunteers and family liaisons that the school has hired through its various partnerships.

With the nonprofit East Bay Agency for Children that partners with Oakland Unified School District to secure countywide grants as well as private donations to offset costs, Rudsdale Newcomer High School is able to hire part-time counselors, a family liaison, and a case manager for the school. Through a partnership with the organization Bay Area Community Resources, the school can hire a safety specialist who works with students to promote a healthy and safe school environment, particularly given the presence of gangs—both U.S.-based gangs and some extensions of gangs from Central America—that operate in the under-resourced neighborhoods students live in.

Community partnerships also help support after-school programs. Run by the organization Soccer Without Borders, Rudsdale Newcomer High School has an after-school soccer team with a trauma-informed and culturally competent approach to support students academically and holistically through their engagement with the sport (see also Strategy 15). One Rudsdale student from Honduras who had recently crossed the border with a *coyote* as an unaccompanied minor noted that "When I got here, I didn't know English. One thing that helped me to adapt was joining the soccer team. I met new friends and I tried to speak English there." Additionally, through a partnership between Oakland Unified School District and the International Rescue Committee, Rudsdale Newcomer High School also has an after-school garden program that combines the running of a vibrant and productive school garden and students cooking (usually Central American foods) with support of an after-school teacher who comes to campus each Wednesday (see also Strategy 15). The school has plans to construct a simple outdoor kitchen in the courtyard to support the gardening/cooking program.

The school has also partnered with a unique nonprofit check cashing agency (Community Check Cashing) in East Oakland that offers financial literacy training for students, helps them set up bank accounts, and has also provided a way to offer students direct aid, particularly during the COVID-19 pandemic. The school raised over $100,000 in contributions through crowd-funding, donations from private foundations, and a social media campaign for the school's well-wishers to donate some or all of their stimulus checks to the school's students, who were mostly ineligible for COVID-19 relief funds because of their immigration status (see also Strategy 18). Getting these funds to students to meet their most basic needs proved difficult until this partnership with Community Check Cashing was established. The agency offered a way to provide students short-term cash grants to pay rent, buy food, and keep their electricity on, especially since COVID-19 hit the industries most students and their families worked in extremely hard, and their unauthorized immigration status also made accessing any unemployment and other COVID-19 relief benefits difficult.

By centering the needs of the student population, Rudsdale Newcomer High School focuses on flexibility in their educational model and building close-knit relationships with students, so that when emergencies or crises arise, the school can respond meaningfully to help students and the communities they are part of. At Rudsdale, students—who have been enrolled at the school because they are at the highest risk of dropping out—are greeted by name daily by school staff, receive text messages if they don't show up to school, have culturally and linguistically competent staff who are sometimes also alum of the school, and are supported to meet their material, livelihood, and legal needs through the partnerships the school has established. The school is a hub of community resources and support that many continue to stay connected to even after graduating.

Strategy 15

Provide After-School and Summer Programming

Lesley Bartlett and Mary Mendenhall

After-school and summer extracurricular programs provide critical academic and language support that complements what happens in the classroom. Participation in these activities can lead to higher academic achievement, lower dropout rates, and continued studies after high school. Social, civic, cultural, and sports activities help to build students' personal development, self-confidence, and interpersonal and leadership skills (Deutsch et al., 2017; Mendenhall & Bartlett, 2018). Programs also help youth to think about the future and to explore academic and professional pathways after high school. Teachers and school leaders need to think creatively about how they might provide these opportunities by recruiting educators and volunteers, as well as developing partnerships with local organizations (see also Strategy 18).

LANGUAGE SUPPORT AND HOMEWORK HELP

Trained volunteers from a local organization or a university offering community-based or service learning courses may provide excellent tutoring support, language practice, and homework help. For example, the International Rescue Committee (IRC) in New York City partners with area universities to recruit volunteers for their tutoring programs. For many years, they met on Saturdays in the IRC offices. During the pandemic, the IRC shifted its Saturday tutoring program to Zoom meetings 5 days a week, supporting students at multiple schools across the city. They serve 100 students per year with one-on-one tutoring.

To maximize participation, tutoring should be held at the schools, as transportation often poses challenges. Colocation also makes it possible for tutors to check in with teachers, if necessary. It is important to consider how best to recruit and train tutors to help with specific subjects while offering language support. When possible, schools should seek tutors who speak the same languages as the students (see also the profile of Shaheen later in this book). Because it takes time for students to feel comfortable working with their tutors, when possible, tutoring program managers should consider how to build and sustain long-term relationships and opportunities for collaboration between tutors and students.

Peer tutoring offers another possibility. Schools that primarily or exclusively serve newcomers often pair them with more experienced same-language peers. The veteran students help to translate content and integrate new students into peer groups, and they often provide peer tutoring on specific subjects. Peer tutoring is efficacious (see, e.g., D. Miller et al., 2010), especially when peers receive training in how to tutor (see, e.g., Fuchs et al., 1994).

Weekend programming extends opportunities for newcomer students. Nebraska's Lincoln High School (see School Profile 1) runs Saturday School, staffed by teachers, to help students who need academic support; they also partner with a community organization, Lighthouse, to make tutors available to work with students on not only assignments but also job, college, and scholarship applications (Welner & Kelley, 2018).

AFTERSCHOOL PROGRAMS

Cultural, linguistic, sports, and leadership programs offer students valuable opportunities to participate, foster a sense of belonging, make new friends, learn to interact with people from different backgrounds, and manage stress. A study on newcomer and refugee students in Arizona and New York also found that students who participated in extracurricular activities and clubs, whether they were offered by their school or not, experienced a stronger sense of school belonging and inclusion (Russell et al., 2021). In one study we conducted (Mendenhall & Bartlett, 2018), students spoke about the importance of clubs that would help them preserve and celebrate their own cultural traditions and languages (e.g., African club, Arabic club). Students praised the chances provided by these clubs to interact with one another, speak in their home languages, and share and celebrate different aspects of their family and cultural traditions. The International High School at LaGuardia Community College in Queens, New York, offers various clubs and after-school programs that cultivate and celebrate students' home languages. The Chinese club, for example, meets weekly and publishes an annual magazine in Mandarin (Office of English Language Acquisition, 2016, p. 8).

Sports provide another vehicle for after-school programming that can directly serve immigrant and refugee youth. One sterling example is Soccer Without Borders (SWB), a nonprofit organization that since 2006 has used soccer to improve physical health and community-building among newcomer students. Founded on the core values of authenticity, development of the whole person, a culture of acceptance and inclusion, and equity, SWB uses soccer as a vehicle for positive change, providing underserved youth with strategies to overcome obstacles to growth and personal success. In an organization committed to gender equity, half of the coaches and 43% of program participants are women. SWB focuses on social inclusion, minimizing linguistic, cultural, logistical, and economic barriers to participation. Through strong relationships with coaches and other players, students build cross-cultural friendships, learn how to communicate in English, and engage with each other and with adults about difficult topics. SWB's programs in Baltimore, Boston, Colorado, Oakland, and Seattle incorporate graduates; many serve on the organization's Alumni Council, and almost one-third of staff are former program participants (Zaldivar, 2020). During COVID-19, the program adapted to online meetings with daily fitness challenges. As cofounder McVeigh Connor stated, "It was never about soccer. It was about belonging and a sense of belonging that people feel when they're part of a team that cares about you. And that was actually [what was] most needed in Covid and still is" (para. 28; for more information, see: www.soccerwithoutborders.org).

Supportive schools make space for student initiatives that respond to their needs and concerns. For example, in 2016, students at Oakland International High School were concerned by the homophobia they perceived among some peers. With a teacher advisor, they formed a Gay-Straight Alliance (GSA) club that, over time, created awareness and challenged heteronormativity and transphobia. Ko, a refugee student from Burma now studying in university, noted that the GSA allowed them to "discover who they were." Born the fifth child in a Karen-speaking Burmese Christian family, Ko joined and later became president of the GSA at OIHS. Ko noted that, at first, "I wasn't ready to come out to my parents or my teachers [yet]. I just wanted to explore" (Jacobson, 2020, para. 15). Through brief presentations, shared readings, and hearing the stories of other students, Ko came out during their senior year as transgender, facing some questions and resistance from their family. Ko noted that within the GSA, they "felt happy." Ko said the club "completely opened my mind to think about everyone's rights, because my family is very religious and for them, adopting new ideas is very challenging. I am the one that is bringing up sensitive topics and [sometimes] they will just not want to listen" (interview, November 2021). For Ko and for other newcomer students, after-school spaces can be important venues to explore identities and to find their own voices in their families and communities (see also the profile of Ko earlier in this book).

SUMMER PROGRAMMING

Summer instruction has a major impact on student achievement (e.g., Atteberry & McEachin, 2016; Gershenson, 2013). Summer opportunities are particularly valuable for immigrant and refugee students, who may have experienced interrupted formal education and are often working hard to develop English proficiency (see also Strategy 5). Summer programming can also positively influence students' sense of belonging (Symons & Ponzio, 2019). Some districts have developed newcomer academies to help students transition to the U.S. culture of schooling. For example, the City School District of Albany, New York, provides a Newcomer Summer School to help newcomers develop English language and acclimate to U.S. schools.[1] Some districts include instruction for bilingual development (Valentino & Reardon, 2015).

Summer programs not only help students develop their academic English but also give them a valuable chance to accumulate credits. Because English learners often spend extended time each day in English language classes, they may miss opportunities to complete courses that are recommended or required for high school graduation or college entrance (Kanno & Kangas, 2014; Umansky, 2016). Johnson's (2020) study of a summer credit recovery program in a large, urban California district found that such programs "resulted in significant increases in the number of ELA, math, science, and social science classes that newcomer English learners took" and led to improvements in English proficiency, but did not "significantly affect 4-year or 5-year graduation" rates, possibly because of the adoption of stringent state assessments (p. 1782). As a result of such successes, more districts are adopting summer programming. For example, San Juan Unified School District (2021) in Sacramento, California, runs a Newcomer Summer School program for high school students. It helps students develop their English, learn to navigate the technology platforms used by many schools, and complete credits required for graduation.

Newcomer Youth Summer Academy

One of the most comprehensive summer programs is run by the IRC in New York City—the Newcomer Youth Summer Academy (NYSA). Since 1999, IRC has worked to enhance the NYSA, a "linguistically supportive, culturally responsive and trauma informed" 6-week summer program that explicitly teaches U.S. school routines and expectations, supports and scaffolds English language development, and instructs in content area knowledge. Over the past 22 years, the Academy has served approximately 1,550 students speaking more than 30 languages and ranging in age from 4 to 20.

NYSA teaches school readiness skills, such as making friends; identifying grown-ups who can help; routines for participating in class and transitioning between classes; maintaining self-confidence, motivation, and a positive attitude toward school; and developing a positive support network. They measure growth in school readiness by surveying students and caregivers and asking teachers to complete an observation rubric at the beginning and conclusion of the program. The Academy also carefully measures academic growth, noting strong links between school readiness and academic gains. Further, NYSA works to develop among students strategies for emotional regulation and stress management. They explicitly teach 10 simple and easy-to-use strategies, including visualization, body scan, stretching, deep breaths, and pushing against a wall. IRC (2021b) hopes that students can learn these coping strategies and incorporate them in their future educational settings.

With a heavy emphasis on English language development, the Academy provides integrated and scaffolded content instruction. In addition, students enjoy weekly field trips to explore the city's cultural resources in places such as Central Park, the American Museum of Natural History, the financial district, the Statue of Liberty, Governor's Island, and the New York Hall of Science. The Academy features community-building events—such as an International Food and Fashion Show, a talent show, and an Arts Olympics—that showcase students' cultural backgrounds; the events are sequenced to gradually increase opportunities for students to take risks to stand out. Finally, thanks to their long-standing and carefully cultivated partnership with Artists Striving to End Poverty (ASTEP), the NYSA incorporates a strong arts component. According to Caitlyn Griffith, Education and Learning Manager at IRC, incorporating the arts offers two major benefits:

> First, it's a great nonverbal and linguistically accessible content area to instruct. Students who are reluctant to share in other spaces are more comfortable expressing themselves through arts. Second, arts classes are a way we can integrate cultural responsiveness and cultural representation. . . . We highlight traditions, art, and dance styles that are representative of students. This creates an entry point to discuss other styles. We can frame the conversation so everyone has something to contribute. (interview, December 6, 2021)

Recognizing that many immigrants and refugees have experienced trauma, NYSA strives to "create environments where all students feel safe—physically, emotionally, academically and socially" and to "foster positive connections to school" (Rowbottom et al., 2021, p. 4). The Summer Academy uses a multi-tiered system of support (MTSS) framework, which outlines three levels of support, depending on student behavioral needs. Facilitators engage all students in mindfulness and community building activities. Some students participate in restorative justice circles, while others with higher-risk behaviors are supported with individual behavior plans that are coordinated among caregivers, teachers, and social workers.

To achieve these complex goals, NYSA recruits experienced educators, particularly ESL instructors. The full staff in 2021 included almost 90 educators. According to Caitlyn Griffith, that included "volunteers, interns, and some paid alum of the program, who come and serve as role models in the classroom. They are usually rising high school seniors or college students. They participate as assistants but really as role models. They follow the instructions that the teacher provides . . . and help translate the key ideas in each lesson" (interview, December 6, 2021). NYSA offers extensive professional development for instructors, including five to 10 online training modules on topics such as trauma-informed care and language supports, and then three full days of training as a group. In addition to a Dean of Operations and a Dean of Student Support, the Academy has a Dean of Instruction who provides coaching and observes teachers, offering structured feedback on effective teaching.

Finally, NYSA actively engages caregivers with Know Your Rights and other relevant workshops, and parents are invited to events that showcase student work. NYSA staff find that family involvement matters significantly for teens. If staff can find ways to engage parents early on, then it is easier for them to stay engaged over the longer term, especially when parents are reticent about formal education amidst competing priorities and demands on their time.

IRC offices around the country have offered modified versions of the summer academy. In 2021, there were 12 IRC programs, including in Atlanta, Georgia;

Elizabeth, New Jersey; Seattle, Washington; San Diego, California; and Wichita, Kansas. For example, for over a decade the IRC Seattle has been delivering an NYSA as the newcomer program within the Tukwila, Washington, school district's summer school (Buhain, 2016), offering a comprehensive program including literacy, English, STEM, social–emotional learning, and the arts.

SUMMARY

- After-school and summer extracurricular programs support students to develop stronger academic, language, interpersonal, socioemotional, and leadership skills that help them overcome the daily challenges they face adjusting to new home and school environments. These programs also help young people think about and plan for future academic and professional opportunities.
- After-school and summer programs require careful planning by program developers to ensure that the opportunities are meaningful, inclusive, and sustainable.

ADDITIONAL RESOURCES

All resources are linked at the book's companion website: www.bit.ly/Immig RefugeeEd

- Bridging Refugee Youth and Children's Services. (n.d. b). *Refugee Youth Summer Academy.* https://brycs.org/promising/0123/
- A short video entitled *Sullivan* shows the power of soccer for newcomers at Sullivan High School in Chicago. See https://www.vimeo.com /247378786/4b5947d107

Strategy 16

Involve Families

Monisha Bajaj

There are many ways schools can facilitate the involvement of families at the school campus and in the community. At school, immigrant and refugee families' backgrounds and needs can be brought into school programming through cultural nights, parent–teacher meetings, workshops for families, and parenting classes. Additionally, some schools have designated spaces for parents/families on campus, whether a room that can serve as a family resource center or through providing families a small plot on campus to cultivate foods grown in their countries, as Oakland International High School does (the parents/guardians also regularly teach students how to cook these foods in partnership with the after-school cooking club). Most of these efforts bring families to the school campus to engage with school staff or to access resources; other initiatives take educators and other school staff out into communities (through home visits and community walks discussed later in this strategy). Oftentimes, these efforts are coordinated through a parent or family liaison who is employed by the school; however, even in the absence of such a staff member, educators and school leaders can develop robust and diverse strategies for family engagement.

Throughout the multiple forms and dimensions of family engagement, several processes and strategies have been identified that ensure meaningful participation of newcomer students and their families. Figure 16.1 shows five processes and some concrete strategies that align with each one that can facilitate schools' effective outreach and engagement with newcomer families.

Immigrant and refugee family structures are often highly diverse, especially since some children or parents migrate alone, with extended periods of family separation due to a variety of reasons. Many unaccompanied minors, for example, live with an aunt, uncle, or cousin as they await the results of their asylum petitions. Effective strategies for family engagement must take into account the needs and realities of diverse families from distinct regions, realities, and backgrounds. Family spaces at school, home visits, and community walks are three approaches to facilitate family engagement that can be utilized by educators, family liaisons, and schools serving newcomer populations.

Figure 16.1. Facilitating Effective Newcomer Family Engagement

Processes	Strategies
Collaboration	• Bring newcomer families and school staff together to coconstruct meaningful communications and resources for families and to collaborate in the delivery of learning and support activities for families. • In schools that don't exclusively serve newcomers, ensure newcomer families are represented on parent associations and school committees.
Capacity development	• Build staff capacity to challenge deficit mind-sets; shift toward an assets-based orientation or "community cultural wealth" model (Yosso, 2005). • Create family welcome kits (in students' home languages) with information about school (e.g., parent/guardian rights and responsibilities; school schedules/calendar, procedures). Consider alternative formats for parents/guardians with limited literacy levels.
Assets orientation	• Understand the cultural orientations and perspectives toward school in students' home cultures; draw from their backgrounds to establish culturally congruent family engagement approaches. • Incorporate the cultures, histories, and realities of families into the school curriculum and activities (see also Strategy 2).
Multimodal communications and language supports	• Use multiple methods (e.g., newsletters translated into languages spoken by families, telephone trees, text threads/WhatsApp groups, website, family liaisons, etc.) and structures to communicate. • Ensure adequate language supports are available for all families to be able to engage. • Create a buddy system for new families to pair with continuing families at school (or families of alum) from similar linguistic backgrounds to ask questions and integrate further into the school community.
Continuous improvement	• Create mechanisms in different languages for families to provide feedback (suggestion boxes, surveys, short interviews) on school issues and for continuous improvement of engagement strategies. • Consider how family involvement may be weighed against competing demands (work schedules, etc.) and strive to facilitate engagement that is supportive of and responsive to families.

Note: Adapted from *Newcomer Tool Kit* (pp. 136–137), by Office of English Language Acquisition, 2016, U.S. Department of Education (https://www2.ed.gov/about/offices/list/oela/newcomers-toolkit/index.html)

FAMILY SPACES AT SCHOOL

As mentioned earlier, family spaces at school can include a parent corner, re-source center, classroom, and/or family-run garden. Space is often very limited within schools, so the approach often depends on what space is available, and how active families and community partners can be in securing/maintaining/operating the space. Regardless of the size of the space, a designated family corner/center at school benefits all families, and especially immigrant and refu-gee families who may be new to the country and its educational norms and expectations.

Parent or family centers that are well designed carry out a number of func-tions. First, they welcome newcomer families by offering them a space where they know they can find information and—when regularly staffed by a volunteer or family liaison/family engagement coordinator—a sympathetic ear for problem solving. Second, family centers can be a central place of information that may be particularly relevant for newcomer families, such as how to locate food pantries, public assistance programs, free Internet/WiFi service, pro bono legal aid, and other social services. Even if a school doesn't have the space for a full-fledged center, a family corner or a bulletin board can offer some information for indi-viduals to follow up with if there are questions. Third, family centers can offer information about disability services for the students. Fourth, such centers or spaces can provide resources that may not be easily accessible in homes or com-munities, such as shared computers with Internet access or printers for families to use (Office of English Language Acquisition, 2016).

Additionally, family centers or classrooms can also be a space where com-munity partners come in to teach digital literacy or English classes to parents or guardians who may be interested and have time to attend. Oakland International High School has a designated family classroom where volunteers from the International Rescue Committee offer English and basic computer skills training multiple times during the week; family members as well as immigrant and refugee adults from the nearby community (even if their children don't attend the school) attend these free classes. Schools that serve newcomers are a hub for the com-munity to access resources and information; the more schools can embrace and facilitate this role, the more they can support their newcomer students and their families.

HOME VISITS

Teachers all do home visits at least twice a year. Mr. Chris, for example, gets on his bike and visits all his 25 advisees' homes in the fall and spring. He eats a lot of amazing food along the way! When you've made the effort to connect with families in their home, this person knows that the next time they come to school, there is at least one person that they've got a relationship with there. (interview with Oakland International High School staff member, 2016)

Home visits provide another way to bridge the gap between school and home for newcomer families. Mandy Manning, 2018 National Teacher of the Year, who teaches many immigrant and refugee students in Washington, has noted that home visits help families know "how much [educators] care about their children and that we are partners in helping their children achieve their potential. Students and parents learn that school is a second home for them, that they are supported, welcome, and that they matter" (2018, para. 8).

Home visits must be structured in a way that is respectful and supportive of families, because there is a history in the United States of home visits being a vehicle for the expansion of deficit views and sometimes the removal of children of color from families for placement into institutional care (McKnight et al., 2017). Given the sizable demographic, racial, and socioeconomic gap between educators and the students they serve, some educators may feel uncomfortable visiting the neighborhoods families live in. Educators can ascertain the best times of the day/week for visits, work in pairs, and also critically self-reflect on what fears may be warranted versus those that may be rooted in assumptions or stereotypes. Receiving a home visit is ultimately the choice of the families, and some may need more time to build trust with the school, especially in the case of unauthorized immigration status. That said, many immigrant and refugee families are very welcoming of educators who make the effort to visit their homes at a mutually convenient time that is not an imposition on work, faith practices, or other scheduled commitments.

Some tips for making home visits as effective as possible include the following:

- Learn about family norms and expectations for a visit to their home. Observe and follow the norms of the home (such as removing shoes, extended greetings, etc.). Learning some phrases in the home language, or having the student (or a community member who is multilingual) serve as interpreter may facilitate effective communication (Samway et al., 2020).
- If families do not want to meet in their home, suggest other places where a meeting can take place, such as a local library, park, cafe, and so forth.
- Home visits can have an agenda, such as orienting families to school routines or addressing an issue. However, an important goal of these visits is getting to know families, establishing rapport, and opening up two-way communication through as much listening as talking. Some initial questions to open the conversation, as suggested by Samway et al. (2020, p. 249), can include, "Tell me about your child." "What does your child like best about school?" "What are schools like in [family's country of origin]?" Another prompt could include, "What are your hopes and dreams for your child?" A question like this establishes the educator as a partner in the pursuit of these visions.
- Many families will offer food or drinks to guests (as mentioned in the quote above). Educators may also want to take a small token such as cookies or some fruit to offer to families to establish reciprocity (Samway et al., 2020).

It is also recommended that educators keep track of what they learn and observe about students and their families through home visits and other interactions (e.g., languages they speak, faith traditions, what the parents/guardians do, special interests, family stories, special skills or talents, etc.). Teachers should note these observations *after* the visit (taking notes *during* a home visit can unnecessarily alarm families, especially those who may be undocumented) so that they can track and refer back to this information over the course of the school year (Samway et al., 2020).

COMMUNITY WALKS

> Standing on a busy intersection in an industrial part of town, Juan, a senior at Oakland International High School and a leader of the community walk, discusses what it's like to work as a day laborer: how to get picked out from the crowd for jobs, how to avoid getting cheated, and how scary it is to operate heavy machinery. Juan worked as a day laborer for a year after arriving to the United States at the age of 16 before enrolling in high school, and still goes to look for work at the *parada* (a corner where day laborers assemble) on days he isn't in school or when making the rent is tight. One of the school staff asks if he's ever scared, and Juan says, "Yes, but we need the money so what can we do?" Ms. Janine, an English teacher who is a participant on the community walk, mentions that all the teachers are on different walks today as it is a mandatory professional development day. She says she loves these walks and that "it's good for us to know what our students are going through." (excerpt from fieldnotes, October 2015)

During a community walk, teachers and staff members visit students' communities, are introduced to important landmarks and cultural centers, meet with community leaders, and engage in discussion. "They also serve to immerse teachers in the home environments of their students, and give students and family members the opportunity to serve as leaders, inverting roles such that our teachers become the students, and our students and families become the teachers" (interview with staff member at OIHS, 2015). Community walks also help teachers better understand family and community language practices and see students' multilingualism as an asset (García & Menken, 2010).

At Oakland International High School in California, some seven simultaneous walks take place on the same day each fall during a professional development day focused on diverse communities such as Yemeni, Afghan, Burmese, and Central American immigrants who make up the school's population. Students who were unaccompanied minors from Central America, for example, showed a clip of *La Bestia* (the dangerous train many migrants take through Mexico on their journey north) from the movie *Sin Nombre*, and then shared stories about their own journeys across the border, riding the train, catching food from kind strangers alongside the railroad tracks, and watching helplessly as others fell off the train to their death during their migration journey (Bajaj & Suresh, 2018).

One of the student's moms who runs a small-scale catering business out of their home brought *pupusas* for the participants to have for lunch, and afterward, participants in this community walk visited *El Centro Legal*, a local nonprofit that has helped secure visas for unaccompanied minors from Central America.

Ricardo (pseudonym), an alumnus of Oakland International High School and a leader of the El Salvador walk when he was in high school, noted, "Because I was telling part of my life to teachers, I felt connected to them. Some of them actually cried when I shared my story. Community walks are a way to unify students and teachers, and share with them the beauty of where our people come from. Also, we got to share about how important it is for us to be here in this country seeking better opportunities" (personal communication, April 2019). Being able to share some of his story and the realities of his community, and see a visible empathic response from teachers, Ricardo found the experience of leading a community walk memorable even several years after graduating high school when asked to reflect back on the experience.

The community walks always include lunch at a community location or a family's home (the costs paid for by the school) and end with a circle back at the school, during which staff members can debrief their experiences and reflect with each other on their learnings (Bajaj & Suresh, 2018). Community walks center students' lived realities in their communities and offer educators insights on how to support them as they pursue their education. Further, community walks offer a lesson in cultural humility (Tervalon & Murray-García, 1998; Yosso, 2005) by replacing assumptions with first-hand interaction with students' communities and by inspiring the reflective practice needed by educators and social service providers when working with diverse populations.

Other scholars discuss the role of a *caminata* or community walk conducted in Spanish by teacher educators for preservice bilingual educators to learn about the neighborhood surrounding the schools where they student-teach (e.g., Heiman et al., 2021). Both the community walks and the *caminatas* offer teachers (or student teachers) an opportunity to better understand their students' realities and are ways to engage in critical place-based learning to bridge the distance between the school and the community.

The benefits of a community walk for educators, students, families, and the whole school community justify the significant preparation and planning required. Ahmed (pseudonym), an alumnus of Oakland International High School who also completed his bachelor's degree at the University of California–Berkeley, was greatly impacted by the willingness of the teachers to learn about his culture. During the community walk, school staff ate food prepared by some of the parents, visited the local mosque, and discussed the devastating war in his home country of Yemen, as well as the Islamophobia faced by some students in the United States. In reflecting on the experience of leading the community walk a few years later, Ahmed shared that this was an affirmation of his identity and increased his sense of belonging at the school (personal communication, May 2019). Further, for both Ahmed and Ricardo as well as others we spoke to during this research, the opportunity to be selected to lead a walk and work with a team of five other students to prepare the day served as a meaningful leadership experience.

Community walks can be a useful strategy in any type of school; fundamentally, they are about educators and school staff immersing themselves in the communities of the families they serve. Students, in leading a community walk, have the opportunity to offer their own stories and perspectives, demonstrating their expertise in being a member of their community. This reversal of customary roles can be extremely powerful for students. Schools that opt to do community walks can benefit from the greater engagement with parents, families, and community-based institutions in order to create more culturally and sociopolitically aligned practices and supports for students.

SUMMARY

- Educators should consider and address issues of accessibility with regard to language and forms of communication, times of events/meetings vis-à-vis family work schedules, and cultural expectations regarding school–family relationships.
- Effective ways to engage newcomer families include well-designed and operated family spaces at school, home visits, and community walks (ideally held in the fall so they can be used to guide instruction and provide services throughout the school year).

ADDITIONAL RESOURCES

All resources are linked at the book's companion website: www.bit.ly/Immig RefugeeEd

- Graff, C. S. (2017). *Home visits 101*. Edutopia. https://www.edutopia .org/article/home-visits-101-cristina-santamaria-graff
- Safir, S. (2017). *Community walks create bonds of understanding.* Edutopia. https://www.edutopia.org/blog/community-walks-create-bonds -understanding-shane-safir
- Bridging Refugee Youth and Children's Services. (n.d. a). *Family engagement with refugee populations* [Webinar]. https://www.brycs.org /webinar/family-engagement-with-refugee-populations

Strategy 17

Offer Legal Services

Monisha Bajaj

> The trauma some students are experiencing—from their home country, from the journey, from living here—is so complex and then, on top of that, the number of case management needs they have, especially unaccompanied minors, are so intense. It could be a kid that comes to school every day and is doing great in school, but still has 100 case management needs because that's just how complex all of our systems are.
>
> There is a lawyer from the Immigrant Family Defense Fund who does a lot of screening and case management for us; she will come to the school, and kids who don't have lawyers, she'll screen them and help match them with someone who offers pro bono or low-cost services. She does that throughout the whole district, which is really impossible but somehow, she's doing it. She and her team are making sure everyone's getting connected to services.
>
> —Interview with Emma Batten-Bowman, School Leader,
> Rudsdale Newcomer High School, January 2020

Centering the whole child in the context of their social, economic, and political realities requires an acknowledgment of the sometimes precarious immigration status that students and their families may have. Educators and schools that serve newcomers have begun to address the realities that face unauthorized migrant students in a variety of ways. Of the nearly 11 million undocumented immigrants in the United States, approximately 700,000 are children under the age of 18 (Kirksey et al., 2020); further, 5 million children—7% of the entire U.S. K–12 student population—have at least one undocumented parent (Passel & Cohn, 2018).

From 2009 onward, there has been a dramatic increase in deportations impacting immigrant and often mixed-status families. For example, in March 2017, 2,000 students stopped going to school after a raid by Immigration and Customs Enforcement (ICE) in Las Cruces, New Mexico. The school board then changed its policy to stop collecting information about students' documentation status and began rejecting ICE requests to access the school campus without a judicial warrant (Acevedo, 2018). As mentioned in the Introduction of this book, schooling is the only public good in the United States open to all—at least until now—regardless of immigration status; as such, it presents a unique opportunity for schools to reach and serve unauthorized immigrant families in ways that no other institution can (Wong et al., 2017).

In the charged political climate of the United States, local and state contexts may also influence schools' and school boards' responses. While there may be anti-immigrant sentiments in a school community, it is against the law to discriminate against undocumented students and their families at school:

> In 1982, the U.S. Supreme Court found in *Plyler vs. Doe* that because undocumented children are illegally in the United States through no fault of their own, they are entitled to the same K–12 educational opportunities that states provide to children who are citizens or legal residents. For this reason, U.S. public schools may not deny or discourage enrollment to any school-age children, regardless of their immigration status. In addition, such students are eligible for free and reduced-price meals, special education services, and school-sponsored events and activities. Federal law does not require school districts or their employees to report undocumented students to immigration authorities. Doing so would constitute a violation of the Family Educational Rights and Privacy Act (FERPA) if information in a student's education records is disclosed without consent. (National Association of Secondary School Principals, 2021)

The fear of deportation—their own or of family members—has negative impacts on school performance due to absenteeism and heightened risk of dropping out (Kirksey & Sattin-Bajaj, 2021), and also has detrimental effects on students' mental health. In a study by the Migration Policy Institute (2020) with data collected prior to the COVID-19 pandemic, researchers found that with regard to students' concerns about immigration, "two-thirds of the sample [of 308 Latinx high school students] met the clinical threshold for anxiety, 58% met the threshold for post-traumatic stress disorder (PTSD), and 55% met it for depression" (p. 3) (see also Strategy 13).

As a result, efforts taken by educators and schools to offer information and resources can improve students' academic engagement and overall well-being, and can offer them accurate information related to their or their family's legal status as well. Schools with immigrant populations have developed information sessions, school policies, and partnerships that seek to assist students and families with their legal status.

"KNOW YOUR RIGHTS" AND SAFE ZONE POLICIES

Many schools offer Know Your Rights workshops to students and their families at school, as well as posting information around schools. The U.S. legal system can be difficult to navigate, especially with policies and enforcement of laws shifting between presidential administrations and through state-level mandates. For example, in Texas, state law *requires* local law enforcement to cooperate with federal ICE agents, whereas states such as Rhode Island and California *prohibit* ICE officials from entering school premises (Ulloa, 2017). Further, hundreds of school districts around the country have declared themselves "safe zones" or "sanctuary districts" that refuse to cooperate with ICE officials either through data sharing or permitting entry to their school campuses. The National Educational Association (NEA) has resources such as sample resolutions for creating safe zones that can be modified for introduction in school districts, as well as a map of these districts nationwide (www.neaedjustice.org/safe-zones).

Other aspects of the declaration as a safe zone or sanctuary district, as in Oakland, California, can include the following:

- trainings for school workers (whether clerical, janitorial, or educators) about protocols for engaging with ICE
- a website with information for families in multiple languages on protocols (Oakland Unified School District has resources in English, Spanish, Arabic, Khmer, Mandarin/Cantonese, and Vietnamese)
- sessions on family preparedness in the case of detention or deportation about whose care the children will be placed under and families' rights if approached by ICE
- introductions to community legal partners that offer pro bono and low-cost legal services to families related to immigration (Oakland Unified School District, n.d.)

These partner organizations also run workshops and regularly come to school campuses to meet with students and/or family members they may be representing in their asylum cases, as noted in the opening quote of this strategy (Oakland Unified School District, n.d.). A good resource for educators and school personnel is also the book *What Educators Need to Know About Immigration Law: Supporting Immigrant, Undocumented, and Refugee Students* (Cunningham, 2021), which could form the basis of a reading group and/or professional development day for school staff.

The following checklist, excerpted from the organization Learning for Justice (Collins, 2020a), offers reflection and planning prompts for educators and school leaders as they consider the question, "How is your school supporting undocumented students and families?"

Enrollment

What information must be provided for students to enroll? How is your school or district ensuring you're not requiring students or families to disclose their citizenship status?

Student Services

What information must be provided for students to access extracurricular or support services? Check up on athletics policies, 504 and IDEA enrollment [for special services], free and reduced lunch enrollment, transportation policies, resources for students experiencing food insecurity or homelessness, and more.

Family Resources
How are translation services managed by your school or district? Who is responsible for ensuring all information is available in all home languages? What community resources are available to families—including connections to pro-bono legal supports, "Know Your Rights" clinics, and food and health care support for undocumented families? Where is this information available?

Discipline
Under what circumstances may law enforcement interact with students on your campus? Who serves as a point of contact for law enforcement? Who ensures FERPA guidelines are followed? (Collins, 2020a, para. 30–34)

LEGAL SERVICES PROVISION AT SCHOOL

Unauthorized immigrants may feel unsure about who to trust with regard to accurate legal information about their status or whether they can safely access state services such as health care or supplemental nutrition assistance programs (Colorín Colorado, 2018). The school as a "safe haven" and site for information as well as resources for families cannot be underestimated, and many have leveraged this role in innovative ways. Many schools bring community partners from local legal services centers to carry out workshops and individual assistance with cases on site at their schools (such as mentioned in School Profile 4). Additionally, the University of California–Los Angeles (UCLA) Law School runs an innovative legal clinic with a staff attorney and approximately a dozen law students each semester at an educational complex housing six public schools in Los Angeles that serves more than 4,000 students and their families.

UCLA's Immigrant Family Legal Clinic, "through integrated legal services in the school context, aims to help immigrant students and their family members flourish, and advocate for policies that promote the well-being of immigrant children and their families beyond the school campus" (UCLA Law, n.d.). Nina Rabin, who directs this legal clinic that was established in 2019, described the clinic's work in three areas. First, the clinic provides direct representation for a limited number of cases staffed by law students and clinic staff. Second, the clinic offers free and confidential consultations on legal matters for a larger number of students and families, on topics ranging from screening for immigration relief to workers' rights to housing and eviction issues. Third, the clinic offers community outreach and education on legal topics of importance to immigrant students and families, through classroom presentations as well as workshops that serve the entire school community (interview with Nina Rabin, July 2021).

According to Rabin, the clinic has expanded from an initial focus on immigration status to a broader range of legal challenges that face immigrant children and families:

> When our clinic first opened for consultations, the requests were almost entirely people who wanted immigration screenings. They wanted to know if they were eligible for status, or if they were in removal proceedings, what they should do to defend themselves. In our classroom presentations, we focused on legal orientations about the immigration system. There were a lot of students who were eligible for Special Immigrant Juvenile Status (SIJS) [a form of immigration status available to certain unaccompanied minors] who didn't know about it. So we spent some time explaining what it was—and it has been exciting to see that the outreach has really worked. A lot of our individual cases are actually students who, after hearing a presentation, have contacted our clinic to set up a consultation, and, with our help, filed for SIJS. Now they are on a path to a green card rather than looking at a future of legal uncertainty.
>
> Over time, we've expanded beyond just immigration screenings to try to empower the community more broadly, beyond immigration status. Our workshops for parents on a wider range of topics really picked up speed during the pandemic. We started to bring in community partners to help with virtual presentations on housing rights and public benefits. We also developed a curriculum for immigrant high school students on workers' rights, because so many of the students work, and we really wanted them to understand that they have rights, even if they're undocumented. (interview with Nina Rabin, July 2021)

Having a comprehensive legal clinic on a school campus like UCLA's Immigrant Family Legal Clinic is certainly effective, but it is a resource-intensive way to colocate legal services. Such an integrated approach may be beyond the scope of most schools, but there are replicable ideas to draw from this model, including having community partners visit the school campus regularly to provide information and legal services directly to immigrant students or family members (see also Strategy 18). For those who may have immigration-related or other legal questions, these visits can provide a bridge to other resources. The UCLA Immigrant Family Legal Clinic has found that regular trainings for school personnel at professional development days can help identify students who may need additional legal support and who may qualify for SIJS. Educators and school staff can then provide referrals or "warm handoffs" to organizations willing and able to offer legal assistance.

Schools serve an important role as a safe and trusted space within immigrant communities. Utilizing the school as a bridge to broader information, consultations, and direct legal assistance/representation can help counteract both misinformation and the many scammers who prey on the fear of unauthorized immigrants to make a profit. Educators, school leaders, and families can work together to make school sites "safe havens" from immigration enforcement; further, schools can also be repositories of accurate information and can provide connections to community agencies that offer support and resources.

SUMMARY

- Undocumented students are entitled to the same K–12 opportunities as citizens and legal residents (e.g., reduced-price lunch, special education services, etc.). Schools must protect their students' privacy if approached by immigration enforcement authorities.
- Know Your Rights workshops and legal services at school through community partners are important ways to ensure that students and their families have accurate information as well as access to legal representation.

ADDITIONAL RESOURCES

All resources are linked at the book's companion website: www.bit.ly/Immig RefugeeEd

- ACLU. (n.d.). *FAQ for educators on immigrant students in public schools.* American Civil Liberties Union. https://www.aclu.org/other/faq -educators-immigrant-students-public-schools
- Collins, C. (2020b). Toolkit for 'School as sanctuary.' *Learning for Justice Magazine 65.* https://www.learningforjustice.org/magazine/fall -2020/toolkit-for-school-as-sanctuary
- SPLC. (n.d.). *Resources for educators and school administrators: Protecting immigrant students' rights.* Southern Poverty Law Center. https://www.splcenter.org/resources-educators-school-administrators
- AFT. (2016). *Immigrant and refugee children: A guide for educators and school support staff.* American Federation of Teachers. https://www.aft .org/sites/default/files/im_uac-educators-guide_2016.pdf

Strategy 18

Develop Community Partnerships for Social Support and Civic Engagement

Lesley Bartlett and Claudia M. Triana

One strategy for serving refugee and immigrant youth is to develop community partnerships. Partnerships promise major benefits for students and their families, including learning support and after-school opportunities. Partnerships may complement, enrich, or extend the academic curriculum (Decker et al., 2007; Sanders, 2006).

Solid community partnerships share core characteristics. Based on their study of more than 30 successful partnerships aimed at supporting the needs of language minority students, Adger and Locke (2000) made the following recommendations for effective partnerships:

- Assure that potential partners are fully committed to the partnership.
- Maintain communication.
- Ensure strong leadership at the program level.
- Start small and build carefully.
- Look for opportunity. (pp. 23–24)

Schools can partner with a variety of community organizations, including those that focus on social services, health, arts, postsecondary and career exploration, and civic engagement, to name a few.

PARTNERSHIPS FOR THE PROVISION OF SOCIAL SERVICES AND HEALTH CARE

Partnerships with community-based organizations can provide access to important social services and health care. In Denver, Colorado, South High School partners with Jewish Family Services to provide school-based therapy for teens affected by trauma (Thorpe, 2017) (see also Strategy 13). In New York City, the International Rescue Committee (IRC), a humanitarian agency that works both internationally and domestically, has partnered with local universities to have social work and education students volunteer in extracurricular programs in public schools. The Immigrant and Refugee Community Organization (IRCO) in Portland, Oregon, offers vocational training, employment assistance, English lessons, youth academic support, and assistance for vulnerable elders, among other services. It partners with 14 Portland schools to distribute food through its Hunger Relief program (Giegerich, 2020). IRCO also organizes a school supplies drive each August, collecting donations such as backpacks, headphones, clothing, and shoes for 2,500 newcomer students. Fort Worth International Newcomer Academy provides a Food Pantry and Care Closet on site. They also track and announce on social media locations for mobile food pantries, mobile vaccine clinics, and free dental and vision clinics.

A school can partner with organizations and/or secure grants in order to become a central location of essential services. For example, Rudsdale Newcomer High School in Oakland works with a community organization to offer monthly workshops to assist students and their caregivers with information about government programs, such as Medi-Cal, which provides free health care to California residents living in poverty (see School Profile 4). They also partner with legal aid organizations, inviting lawyers to campus to help students with their immigration cases and court hearings (see also Strategy 17). The onset of COVID-19 made these resources even more essential, given the restrictions on many service-related jobs. Teachers and volunteers at Rudsdale Newcomer High School secured food from the school district and local agencies and delivered it to students and their families, given that many do not have cars or information about how to access such services. Through grants, crowd-funding efforts, and mutual aid, teachers and administrators secured Internet hot spots for families and Chromebooks for completing school work, since 80% of the students had no way to access remote schooling otherwise (Bajaj & Tow, 2021). Rudsdale Newcomer High School raised funds for direct financial assistance with rent, food, and other necessities, distributing an average of $10,000 per month in direct aid to students and their families from April 2020 through early 2021 (E. Batten-Bowman, personal communication, February 2021).

ARTS-BASED PARTNERSHIPS

Partnering with arts-focused nonprofits is another promising approach. The arts provide youth a chance to communicate their experiences, develop confidence, and potentially heal. The visual arts do not require communication in English, which can be a particular barrier for newcomer youth. Art education promises significant benefits for students (Caterall, 2009; Halverson, 2021; Hutzel et al., 2012).

Schools play an important role in connecting students to arts programs run through area organizations. For example, the Latin American Youth Center in Washington, D.C., offers youth classes in photography, radio, video, and fine arts (see www.layc-dc.org/arts-recreation). The Hmong American Partnership (HAP) in the Twin Cities of Minnesota works to "help Hmong grow deep roots in America while preserving the strength of our culture." They offer a range of programs for youth. For two decades, they produced *Hmoob Teen Magazine*, a quarterly e-zine founded in 1997 that shared news by and about area Hmong teens to more than 20,000 readers. Teens wrote the articles, short stories, and poems, and they produced the artwork, photos, and designs that were featured.

Other arts-based organizations that offer useful educational programs include Changing Worlds, which works with Chicago area schools. Their mission is to "foster inclusive communities through oral history, writing, and art programs that improve student learning, affirm identity, and enhance cross-cultural understanding" (www.changingworlds.org). The program uses music, dance, theater, and visual art "to help program participants explore their own backgrounds and learn about others while strengthening their academic skills" (Bridging Refugee Youth and Children's Services, 2018, para. 4). The Changing Worlds Arts, Cultural, and Literacy Connections (ACL) Program pairs teaching artists and writers with teachers to develop, in class, projects such as murals, art installations, or school performances that address cultural history, social issues, and personal identity. They also offer after-school programs that incorporate arts-based learning and field trips. One signature program, Adelitas: Women and Femmes of Courage, is described below and illustrated in Figure 18.1.

> During the Mexican Revolution in 1910, women, referred to as Adelitas, served dual roles as warriors and peacemakers; they fought for freedom and fought against the violence engulfing their families as leaders in their communities. Adelitas are symbols for hope, strength, and peace, and their legacy can be found in modern-day Mexican art and literature.
>
> Led by a Changing Worlds artist, this program explores the ideas of role models who may be local, national or historic Adelitas. Learning and using creative portraiture lessons and creative writing exercises, students create original art and writing in honor of their own personal Adelita. (Changing Worlds, 2022, p. 15)

Long-time teaching artist Diana Solís developed the "Adelitas: Women and Femmes of Courage" curriculum. This new branch of the Adelitas program reaches high school students and connects them with LGBTQ+ history (Schurz High School, 2022).

Changing Worlds also offers traveling art exhibits. One exhibit, "The Immigrant Experience Through the Eyes of Teens," features wall panels created by immigrant youth and can be used to prompt broader conversations about immigration, equity, and justice.

PARTNERSHIPS FOR POSTSECONDARY EDUCATIONAL AND WORK OPPORTUNITIES

Partnerships with organizations may provide valuable opportunities to plan for life after high school. Newcomer youth in particular need to be exposed to a range of ideas, opportunities, and resources as they consider their next steps and prepare to confront the challenges and opportunities that may await them after high school graduation.

Figure 18.1. Adelitas Poster from Schurz High School Gender & Sexuality Alliance (GSA) in Chicago

Note: Image by Diana Solís.

Schools may set up volunteer or internship opportunities with community-based organizations (see also Strategy 19). In New York City, the IRC provides a unique Leaders-in-Training initiative that draws students from schools across the city. The youth "identify their career goals and seek out opportunities for career day visits where [they] interact with New York professionals in different sectors while practicing their own interview and professional skills" (IRC, 2018). The International High School at LaGuardia Community College in Queens, New York, partners with a range of community-based organizations. Through their internship program, students may be placed at community organizations such as South Asian Youth Action, Make the Road New York (which advocates primarily in English and Spanish), Asian Americans for Equality, Desis Rising Up and

Moving, or Students for a Free Tibet. By maintaining active partnerships with these groups, the school connects students to communities and potential work sectors "where their home languages are an undeniable and indispensable resource" (Office of English Language Acquisition, 2016, ch. 4, p. 2).

School partnerships with local organizations can also provide opportunities for students to explore their options for the future, including college prep, job shadowing, or job training initiatives. For example, through an active job-shadowing program, students at Manhattan Bridges High School in New York City learn about work in companies like Verizon, AT&T, and American Express. Professionals from those companies also visit the school campus to offer workshops. These opportunities "expose students to new career fields and allow them to see the connection between what they are learning in school and their future goals" (Castellón et al., 2015, pp. 127–128).

School leaders in any region of the United States could cultivate partnerships with local, nonprofit, educational, or faith-based organizations in their communities to establish mutually beneficial partnerships. For example, teachers and counselors played an important role in connecting their students with the community-led initiatives and programs offered by Dreamers of Wisconsin (DoW), the first nonprofit organization in Wisconsin focused on higher education advocacy for undocumented students. The organization started as a college student-led group that evolved into a nonprofit committed to reducing educational access barriers across the state. Most college readiness programs assume that all students are U.S. citizens and impart advice on Free Application for Federal Student Aid (FAFSA) applications and other resources that are not usually available for undocumented students. Instead, DoW tailors information and support to students who are undocumented or hold Deferred Action for Childhood Arrivals (DACA) or Temporary Protective Status (TPS). DoW has invested significant time and effort to build networks with high school counselors, bilingual resource officers, and teachers who are knowledgeable about the challenges facing immigrant and refugee students. Recruitment of undocumented students poses a challenge since students have valid fears and concerns of divulging their status. These partnerships ensured that undocumented students received communication and information about college access programming from a trusted source.

PARTNERSHIPS FOR CIVIC ENGAGEMENT AND LEADERSHIP

Schools may find it useful to partner with community organizations to connect teaching and learning processes to civic engagement. In 2012 at Gregorio Luperón High School in New York City, one teacher piloted a bilingual curriculum developed through a partnership between The City College of New York and a widely circulating Spanish-language newspaper, *El Diario*. The curriculum, called "Social Justice and Latinos in NYC 1913–2013," used *El Diario* articles from the past century, along with other resources, to teach students about the history of Latinx communities in the city (Kleyn, 2013). Built on students' language resources, the curriculum encouraged students to develop a social justice perspective, deepen their historical and civic knowledge, and think critically about how political engagement and political representation for Puerto Ricans, Dominicans, Mexicans, and other groups had changed over time in New York (Bajaj & Bartlett, 2017).

Partners provide critical support for youth interested in engaging in immigration reform justice and mutual support among students in mixed-status families. For example, the New York State Youth Leadership Council has worked with high schools and colleges to support "Dream Teams," or student-led immigrant justice clubs that advocate for migration-related policies and programs.[1] Dream Teams develop public campaigns about immigration reform, sponsor informational events, organize conferences, and raise funds for scholarships. They can connect high school students to college groups, and they often help students with the abstruse college application process. In 2011, students at Flushing International High School in Queens, New York, formed a Dream Team and they have since spread to other area high schools.

Finally, community partners can provide opportunities to develop leadership skills. One powerful example comes from Youth Empowered in the Struggle, or YES!, the youth arm of Voces de la Frontera, a community organization in Milwaukee, Wisconsin, led by low-wage workers and immigrants that focuses on leadership development, community organizing, and empowerment. YES! is student-led, with school-based chapters in high schools across Milwaukee and Racine. YES! chapters aim to advance racial and social justice and support immigrant rights in their schools and communities. Additionally, chapters come together for retreats throughout the academic year and organize larger events with Voces de la Frontera, including the annual May Day march that takes place on International Workers' Day (May 1).

YES! leads a summer Freedom School, following the tradition of the civil rights movement, in which members learn about the principles of organizing and ways to share their narratives through storytelling. In planning for specific campaigns, students discuss systems of oppression and laws, policies, and practices impacting immigrant and refugee populations at the national, state, and local levels. For example, following the sanctuary school movements taking place nationwide, in 2017 Milwaukee Public Schools unanimously passed a resolution for the district to become a sanctuary district or "safe haven," by committing to put stronger protections in place to create a safe environment for undocumented students and their families (e.g., by refusing to share students' immigration status with authorities) (see also Strategy 17). YES! members were involved in organizing the campaign through lobbying and mobilizing efforts, and immigrant, refugee, and undocumented YES! members were among those who spoke in front of the Milwaukee school board (Waxman, 2017a; 2017b). Through campaigns and weekly organizing meetings, YES! fosters the civic engagement of immigrant, refugee, and undocumented students while supporting panimmigrant efforts for solidarity.

Community partnerships can extend the resources available to immigrant and refugee students and their families; such partnerships can also further integrate youth into their communities and provide networking and preparation for future professional opportunities.

SUMMARY

- Schools should partner with community-based organizations to expand programming and opportunities focused on academic support, social services, health, arts, postsecondary and career exploration, and civic engagement.

ADDITIONAL RESOURCES

All resources are linked at the book's companion website: www.bit.ly/Immig RefugeeEd

- Adger, C., & Locke, J. (2000). *Broadening the base: School/community partnerships serving language minority students at risk.* Center for Research on Equity, Diversity, and Excellence.
- Scholar Tatyana Kleyn has produced several resources and curriculum guides tailored for educators of immigrant and refugee students: https://www.tatyanakleyn.com/guides

Strategy 19

Implement Internships and Career Preparation Programs

Dariana Castro With Daniel Walsh

In 2010, after just completing 11th grade, Lesly participated in an 8-week service-learning project on a sustainable coffee farm in Nicaragua through Global Potential, a nonprofit organization that partnered with his school, the International High School at Prospect Heights in Brooklyn, New York [see School Profile 2]. Armed with the confidence of a transformative summer experience in Nicaragua, Lesly returned to school determined to graduate and seek new experiences. When the school's internship program began while Lesley was in the 12th grade, he asked for a placement where he could leverage his artistic skills. He was placed at the Brooklyn Artists Gym, an artists' co-op and gallery space in Park Slope. Lesly recalled being pushed outside of his comfort zone. For the first time in his life, Lesly saw two men holding hands and recognized there was another world outside of his rural town where he grew up in Honduras and his new world in a Brooklyn apartment where he and his brother had recently reunited with his parents. He remembered leaning into the discomfort of this new community and allowing himself to be challenged by the new environment. Lesly left Brooklyn Artists Gym with a new understanding of the world around him and a broadened social network. These artists taught him about the possibilities that arise when one follows their passion with commitment.

—Interview with Lesly, October and December 2021

Educators often think of career development programs as an isolated component of a school, or an after-school program. However, such programs can be a thread that ties together key elements of a school's design and helps students expand their social networks within and outside of the classroom; doing so can help forge strong ties that can be activated to create new opportunities to advance career goals or learn new information (ACTE, 2021).

Career development can be closely aligned with college readiness (see also Strategy 14) and can involve opportunities for students to learn about different careers through alum and/or career panels, summer programs, shadow days with

167

individuals in the workforce, and/or internships. Some schools and districts require internships, while others make connections for students who wish to pursue them. In either case, intentional and well-planned strategies for career development can be especially important for immigrant and refugee students with often limited professional networks in their families who are new to the United States.

In the following sections we describe how the International High School at Prospect Heights (IHSPH) in Brooklyn, New York, created its dynamic career development experience for newcomer multilingual learners by focusing on four areas of the school's design:

1. *Center student assets.* Embedded structures within the school reveal the many assets of all multilingual learners and provide valuable information that teachers use to match students with the right career and youth development opportunities.
2. *Systematically surface and respond to the socioemotional needs of multilingual learners.* Many resources are allocated to socioemotional supports, including staffing and time to ensure students receive the supports they need to bring their full selves to their school experience.
3. *Use experiential learning to create strong social networks and valuable skill development around collaboration.* A classroom designed around assets, collaboration, and student choice results in greater autonomy and numerous transferable workplace skills.
4. *Employ a staff person dedicated to building and maintaining relationships with nonprofits and local businesses.* This role leverages multiple school structures to establish an internship program and connect students to opportunities outside of the school.

CENTER STUDENT ASSETS

Career development plans should use the intake process to gauge student interests and strengths soon after enrollment. At IHSPH, the process for documenting student assets and surfacing their needs starts as early as the intake process, which involves interviews regarding prior schooling, years in the United States, living arrangements, and a number of open-ended questions around the student's interests and passions (see also Strategy 2, Figure 2.1, for a sample intake survey). This information is logged into a database, and an index card is created from initial intake details for teachers to use when creating heterogeneous cohorts for their teams. Including questions about students' interests and passions in the intake process provides teachers a window into students' aspirations, and later informs decisions around enrichment and career development activities. An intake card for Lesly, who was introduced in the opening vignette, included the following notes:

Lesly is a talented artist who wants to be a lawyer. He didn't enjoy school and so he missed many days of school as he preferred to be on the farm where he grew up. Lesly arrived last year at 15 years old and was reunited with his parents, whom he hasn't seen since he was a toddler. Lesly misses home, especially his strong connections to his community—he said when he missed a few pesos at the grocery store, the grocer would trust him to return it, but here he is not trusted. He is excited to know there are many Honduran students at our school, and wants to take an art class.

The instructional approach at IHSPH relies heavily on collaboration. Multilingualism hinges on students' development of skills in their home and new languages (see also Strategy 1). This emphasis on collaboration, student discourse, and the use of the home language at IHSPH gave students like Lesly an opportunity to bring linguistic and cultural capital to the classroom, allowing him to display his strengths from the start of the 9th grade. Lesly's teachers noted his artistic abilities, public speaking skills, an interest in supporting his peers, and a willingness to seek out support when needed. This information became key to identifying opportunities for Lesly to use his strengths in new contexts outside of school. Failure to capture Lesly's interests and abilities would have made an already challenging transition to school in the United States that much more difficult.

PROVIDE SOCIOEMOTIONAL SUPPORT

Establish a Guidance Team Dedicated to Socioemotional Support

Multilingual learners face a myriad of challenges in their transition to their new homes. They may also experience deep trauma before or during their travels to the United States (or in their new homes and communities) that require immediate attention. At IHSPH, a guidance team of two licensed clinical social workers meets with students like Lesly either one-on-one or in small groups to support the challenges of their transition (see also Strategy 13). Additionally, a parent coordinator remains in close contact with families and organizes parent events, and a college counselor manages the college application process, while a coordinator of special programs leads the career development program and connects students to resources through partnerships with nonprofits and businesses across the city.

Many of the students' challenges surface quickly through the intake process, while other issues make their way to the guidance team via an advisor or teacher. In Lesly's case, living with his parents after so many years of independence was highly challenging, as was the exhausting transition from life in a small community in rural Honduras to walking 15 city blocks in all types of weather and finding metal detectors waiting at the school's entrance in New York City.

Share the Responsibility of Responding to Socioemotional Needs

While having a team dedicated to the socioemotional needs of multilingual learners is key to ensuring their full engagement in school, the caseload is immense. Responsibility must be shared across the staff. One structure for doing this is an advisory program (see also Strategy 7). At IHSPH all adults, including assistant principals, engage with a small group of approximately 15 students in restorative practices and a thematic curriculum to create a nonacademic space for students to develop close relationships. These close relationships developed in advisories or homeroom periods can facilitate educators guiding students toward their post-high school goals, whether in higher education and/or in other roles they may already occupy or aspire to in the labor market. Like many of his classmates, Lesly worked nearly a full day before the school day even began. He woke at 3 a.m. each day to help his father, a superintendent ("super") for a number of Brooklyn buildings, sweeping, mopping, and taking out the garbage. The advisor was aware of this. When Lesly appeared disengaged in class, his advisor would remind the teacher team of Lesly's other responsibilities. The advisor supported both Lesly and his teachers in managing his workload in and outside of school.

The advisory structure is also the main vehicle for implementing the school's mentoring program, the internship program, and support for the college application process (see also Strategy 14). One advisory session per week is dedicated toward these efforts.

ENGAGE AN EXPERIENTIAL INSTRUCTIONAL APPROACH

Create Learning Environments That Foster Collaboration

When Lesly reflected on his time at the school, the greatest highlights were his time working in groups and the collaboration skills that proved important during his internships. The 9th- and 10th-grade classrooms devote a great deal of time to explicitly teaching collaborative routines and roles. This translates into highly effective collaboration on the 11th- and 12th-grade teams. When these students enter their internships, they have had strong experiences working in groups, taking on leadership roles, and navigating conflict. Additionally, they appreciate the power of working in groups toward a shared goal.

Validate All Learning, Whether Inside or Beyond the Classroom

Lesly recalled the many experiences outside of the classroom that helped him develop the courage and validation he needed to persevere in an academic setting that demanded more than he was always ready to offer. Internships, youth development or volunteer opportunities, or even work experiences are often seen as "extracurricular" activities and are not given the same value as instructional time. These spaces, however, offer students deep opportunities for learning that can be brought back to instructional spaces and even create the motivation students need to persist in the classroom.

At IHSPH, internships are considered an integral component of the 12th-grade experience, one that all students are expected to complete. Students receive academic credit and complete a capstone project highlighting what they learned from their internships and reflecting on their performance as interns. This final project also gives students an opportunity to engage in a work performance review that, for many, is their first experience with such a review.

Implement Instructional Practices With Multiple Ways to Show Learning

As the school load increased, Lesly's academic skills, particularly reading and writing, lagged behind. Still, he was a talented artist and public speaker who thrived in such a close community, where relationships were valued. The experiential learning and group work structure allowed him to shine in ways he might not in a more traditional setting. He defended his ideas in Spanish and worked diligently to reach the same level of oral skills in English. Universal design for learning principles guided a lot of curriculum writing at IHSPH, giving students like Lesly an opportunity to select multiple avenues for tackling and showcasing their learning (see also Strategy 4). This level of autonomy placed Lesly in the driver's seat of his own learning, a skill he continues to utilize as an adult.

CULTIVATE COMMUNITY CONNECTIONS

Allocate the Appropriate Resources

The allocation of school resources indicates what a school leader prioritizes. IHSPH has a full-time position dedicated to establishing partnerships. Lesly remembered making many visits to this office to seek opportunities or to share new experiences from his internships.

Partner With a Wide Range of Nonprofits and Businesses

Students at IHSPH have access to video production programs after school, volunteer opportunities at local nursing homes and hospitals, part-time jobs in local businesses, and even international service-learning programs. They have more than 50 internship sites in numerous fields available each spring. This wide array of opportunities allows students to find a strong match for their interests and to expand their social networks in a variety of settings.

Each new partnership requires relationship building (see also Strategy 18). The school leadership ultimately chose to partner with Global Potential as one of their first pilot sites, investing the time and commitment to bring this unique opportunity to IHSPH students. Through Global Potential's program in Matagalpa, Nicaragua, Lesly expanded his network to include coffee farmers and exporters. Lesly was later hired by that nonprofit and mentored on how to start his own coffee business by the same farmers he supported during his service-learning project through Global Potential.

Highlight Multiple Definitions of Student Success

Lesly started at the Borough of Manhattan Community College in 2013 and, in 2015, decided to walk away from college and dedicate himself completely to his coffee business by working and saving the funds necessary. He has worked multiple jobs and built countless relationships by doing so. He attributes his success to the many people he has learned from along the way, ranging from a financier he met while bartending and then served as an interpreter for in Guatemala and who taught him about the stock market, to the farmers in Nicaragua who taught him all that he knows about coffee.

Emphasizing college as the sole pathway to a fulfilling career in the United States has often come at the expense of exploring other pathways—often entrepreneurial and/or transnational as in Lesly's case—for students (see also the profiles of former students in this book). For many multilingual learners, college can be an expensive option that rarely values their multilingual skills. Encouraging and supporting students on the path to college while also allowing students to find new pathways toward success is a difficult balancing act for schools.

From his initial intake interview, it was clear that Lesly wanted to return to the mountains of Honduras where he grew up. Today, Lesly owns his own coffee farm and has exported 6,000 pounds of specialty coffee from the northwestern mountains of Honduras. His coffee *El Emperador* is brewed and distributed by specialty coffee vendors, including a shop in Soho where Lesly spent time working as a barista; he built a strong relationship with the owner, who was thrilled to distribute Lesly's first import batch. (For more information, see the Instagram account of @elemperadorcoffeefarm.)

Lesly's example demonstrates the value of supporting students to explore career pathways through internships and through collaborative peer groups at school. Lesly has bridged his social networks in Central America and the United States to turn his dream into a reality. Every harvest, Lesly employs 30 members of the Cortes community where he grew up in Honduras, including family members, who help with the milling process. He owns 120 acres of land and will expand to nearly 200 acres by the end of 2022. Lesly can quickly calculate the return on investment of the fluctuating coffee market values on Wall Street, which he keeps a very close eye on. Career development and internships that expose students to a range of possible pathways, aligned with their talents and interests, offer immigrant and refugee students the chance to chart their future in expansive and often unexpected ways that can be deeply fulfilling for them.

SUMMARY

- Strategies for career development should explore the many directions students may want to pursue after graduation, whether in the United States or transnationally.

- Internships can help immigrant and refugee students expand their networks and knowledge about different career pathways, especially those unfamiliar to them as newcomers to the United States.

ADDITIONAL RESOURCES

All resources are linked at the book's companion website: www.bit.ly/Immig RefugeeEd

- Minero, E. (2016). *Real-world learning with internships.* Edutopia. https://www.edutopia.org/practice/learning-through-internships -connecting-students-passions-real-world
- Immigrants Rising provides career pathway resources for undocumented students. See https://immigrantsrising.org/
- Santos, M., Castellón Palacios, M., Cheuk, T., Greene, R., Mercado-Garcia, D., Zerkel, L., Hakuta, K., & Skarin, R. (2018). *Preparing English learners for college and career: Lessons from successful high schools.* Teachers College Press.

Strategy 20

Engage Alum in Schools and Community Building

Monisha Bajaj and Gabriela Martínez

> Most of our students stay local whether they go to either community college or to a 4-year college, or find work. We have school social media accounts that students stay connected through. Every spring, we have an alumni panel where we invite former students to come back and talk to 11th- and 12th-graders about "this is what I went through in high school and is what I'm going through now after high school," and to answer questions. . . . There are certain times when we need a translator for a family meeting or event, and we use our growing network of alumni and offer them a stipend to translate. In the future, I'd love to have alumni here running the school.
>
> —Interview with Sailaja Suresh, former coprincipal of
> Oakland International High School, October 2016

Newcomer schools and programs have sought to maintain contact with alum and include them as resources and mentors for current students. Having alum—who have been in the same position previously as the current students are—offer advice, insights, and perspectives can be a powerful way for students to envision themselves in higher education or professional settings in the future. Schools have used social media to stay in touch with alum (as mentioned in the opening quote), WhatsApp or text messaging, and where available, designated staff members liaise with alum and include them through alum panels, mentoring programs, or as staff in the school itself (see also Strategy 9).

Despite the positive impacts of alum engagement noted by staff, students, and alum we have talked to, little research exists on alum engagement in high schools, especially in public schools and especially among immigrant and refugee student populations. One of the few studies on public high school alum engagement conducted by researchers at the University of California–San Diego found that alum expressed a "desire to give back and reconnect. Some also conveyed a sense of identity that linked them to both the school and the neighborhood and the desire to help, advise and/or inspire students. Several alum said that they knew from their own experience how high school graduates are often unaware of opportunities available to them, and ill-prepared for college. By volunteering, they hoped to help reverse these outcomes" (UC San Diego Center for Research on Educational Equity, Assessment & Teaching Excellence, 2019, p. 8). Some alum may feel comfortable just "stopping by" the campus from time to time to greet teachers, whereas others may feel less comfortable making such visits, not knowing how to engage at the school when no longer a student. However, formal volunteering, mentorship, and/or part-time work opportunities can engage alum in productive ways in the life of their former school (or alma mater) and offer current students role models who have been in their shoes just a few years prior (UC San Diego Center for Research on Educational Equity, Assessment & Teaching Excellence, 2019).

ALUM AS MENTORS AND STAFF

Alum can provide useful advice to students and valued administrative or academic support to school programs. Coauthor Gabriela Martínez describes her engagement as an alum of Oakland International High School:

> After I finished high school and was at college nearby, a teacher reached out to a few of us to be part of a video that would offer tips to current students. I remember I shared in the interview for the video about how I used to write in the corner of my notebook all the English words I didn't understand during a lesson so I could look them up later and how that can help students build their English vocabulary and some other tips for preparing for college. I also spoke on a couple of alumni panels where about 10 of us advised all the 12th-graders about the college application process.
>
> At that time, I had all my college courses packed onto Tuesdays and Thursdays from first thing in the morning until late at night, because I worked cleaning houses on Mondays, Wednesdays, Fridays, and sometimes on the weekends to be able to pay for school and to help with family expenses. In my third year of college, my former high school principal texted me and asked if I wanted to help them out with some administrative work funded through a grant they had received; they remembered that I had helped them organize some information about the lockers when I was a high school senior and they had thought I did a good job.
>
> I switched my class schedule and I started working after-school at Oakland International High School (OIHS) for about 20 hours a week, tracking after-school attendance, supporting the after-school teachers, and delivering snacks to the classes. It was better money than cleaning houses. I worked there after school until I graduated from college. One day, the school's administrative assistant told me that she was planning to retire and asked if I would be interested in the job. I was able to work there after graduating for a few years and, in that time, I also saw other alum hired as instructional assistants for newcomers (a position the district created

to support students), as tutors, as soccer coaches through Soccer Without Borders, and in other roles that came open.

At other schools as well, alum have also found their way into roles at the school as mentors, part-time staff, AmeriCorps volunteers (as discussed in School Profile 4), or even full-time staff (as discussed in both School Profile 2 and School Profile 3). Alum who are working in community organizations or studying in allied fields, like social work or education, provide valuable networks and analytical perspectives. Joe Luft, the former director of the Internationals Network for Public Schools, noted that the 2012 Deferred Action for Childhood Arrivals (DACA) and subsequent state policies (such as the 2016 rule passed by the New York Board of Regents) opened the door for many undocumented alum to pursue teaching careers, including in schools with newcomer populations. He further noted that dozens of alum from Internationals Network for Public Schools (INPS) schools work as school staff, teachers, and even one alumna serves as the principal of an INPS high school in New York. Luft noted the following about these educators who were once newcomer students and are alum of newcomer schools: "It's such an amazing connection. They walk in the door with a lot more credibility than [others do] and they're so connected to the work in ways that you could not possibly create otherwise" (interview, July 2016).

ARISE High School in Oakland, California, utilized COVID-19 relief funds to hire 20 alum as academic mentors to support teachers with checking in on students during remote learning and ensuring they were making progress. Back at campus in the fall of 2021, the school has continued this academic mentoring program with alum of the school. Mentors, who work part-time, are required to be enrolled in college and must be able to support students in either math, science, or literacy (Gardner, 2022).

ALUM AS COMMUNITY BUILDERS

Alum can stay connected to newcomer programs and schools through events, such as reunions, celebrations, fairs, information sessions, and other occasions that include them and leverage their experience and expertise. Alum can also be involved in larger efforts that include students and benefit the entire community. One example we highlight comes from Henry Sales, who originally came to the United States from Guatemala at age 17 and attended Oakland International High School. While there, he was struck by the appreciation and respect accorded his Indigenous Mam language. Henry said,

> I felt comfortable speaking Mam at OIHS. In Guatemala, they stopped us from speaking Mam; they told us in school that if you didn't speak Spanish, you were stupid. At OIHS, everyone was speaking their language so I felt comfortable speaking Mam. They would say Mam is welcome here and I felt accepted as an Indigenous person. Everyone was accepted no matter where they were from. (interview, July 2021)

After graduation, Henry attended a community college and later transferred to a 4-year college. But he always wondered why no high school or college courses existed to teach the Mam language or to teach about Mayan Indigenous issues.

Thousands of Mam speakers have migrated to the United States from Central America due to high poverty, violence, and enduring legacies from the Guatemalan civil war (1960–1996), which targeted the nation's Indigenous populations. Encouraged by a professor, Henry began to offer Mam language classes at the community college. Henry noted,

> I began to offer classes on Mam and the history of Indigenous Mam people at Laney College. The first day, only 1 or 2 students came. That's how we began. Then 3 people came. I got discouraged by the numbers, but even linguists from UC Berkeley were contacting me, and I thought if even linguists are interested in this, let's do it. So we created a flyer to post around campus, and the next thing we knew, we had 10 students in the class. We were around a table, not even in our own classroom. Then 40 people came, then 50. Then when they saw people were coming, the college gave us a classroom. Doctors, lawyers, educators, people from San Francisco and Berkeley came. Then we had to start offering both beginner and intermediate level classes.
>
> Once they got news about what was happening over at Laney, the school district said, "We are going to contract Henry to offer Mam classes at Oakland schools with Indigenous Mam students," and they hired me to work across several schools. Everything started from wanting to create something that didn't exist. That's how it happened. We are now trying to get the community college classes accredited to have Mam become an official language recognized by the state of California.
>
> When we went online during COVID, the numbers in the Mam class went way up and we now have students from 10 different states, people from Utah, even students from Stanford and Harvard, attending. I want to create more opportunities for more people to teach Mam in different places. (interview, July 2021)

Henry, who is also the administrative assistant at Rudsdale Newcomer High School (School Profile 4), shared further about both the opportunities and the challenges posed for the Indigenous immigrant community during the COVID-19 pandemic. Many students and their family members who worked in restaurants were being laid off, not being paid, not eligible for unemployment because of employers' unwillingness to file paperwork, and generally lacked access to information that, even if targeted to Latinx communities, was offered in Spanish and not in Indigenous languages.

With a partner organization, Henry developed an idea to start a Mam language radio station (*Radio B'alam*) as a way to both celebrate the Mam culture and share information in the Mam language about access to benefits, resources, and other information. When the station went live in late 2020, it started by sharing segments on COVID-19 vaccines and testing, information about virtual schooling, troubleshooting common questions about how to get online for families with limited computer know-how, about unemployment benefits, and about where to access free groceries and/or food pantries (Hossaini, 2021). The radio station operates through an app and on Facebook, given that many Mam speakers across generations are on the social media platform. Many current newcomer students in California (and also across the country), alum parents, families, recent immigrants, and even people back in Central America have accessed *Radio B'alam* through the Internet. Henry is in the process of applying for a license and an antenna for the station to make the content more accessible across the United States (interview, July 2021). The radio station serves as a diasporic space for connection, pride, and resistance in the face of discrimination, as well as a central location for resources and information.

Whether as resources for the school community at periodic events to offer mentoring and support or as school staff or community leaders, alum who were once newcomers can inform and inspire younger students in meaningful ways. Through the humanizing, caring, and justice-oriented school communities that newcomer students are welcomed into, many alum develop a desire to give back and to pursue work in education or related fields. These individuals can further the vision of schools as community hubs where information, support, services, and resources can be accessed and strong bonds that unite diverse communities can be built.

SUMMARY

- Engaging alum who were once newcomers themselves as mentors in structured ways and as staff in schools, particularly those that serve newcomer students, can provide students role models and help students navigate systems that may be foreign to them.
- Maintaining strong connections with alum through messaging and social media platforms can allow for greater continuity and integration of alum into the ongoing life of the school.

ADDITIONAL RESOURCES

All resources are linked at the book's companion website: www.bit.ly/Immig RefugeeEd

- Gardner, T. (2022). *The benefits of an alumni mentorship program for students*. Edutopia. https://www.edutopia.org/article/benefits-alumni-mentorship-program-students
- Hossaini, S. (2021, March 27). *Indigenous-language radio show in Oakland promotes vaccine effort*. National Public Radio (NPR). https://www.wnyc.org/story/indigenous-language-radio-show-in-oakland-promotes-vaccine-effort

Profile of Shaheen

As Told to Gabriela Martínez

Shaheen was 16 when he arrived in the United States. His family fled Afghanistan because his father, who worked for the U.S. Embassy, had received multiple death threats from the Taliban and other extremist groups. They applied for and received a "special immigrant visa" and migrated to the United States in 2014. Shaheen enrolled in 11th grade at Oakland International High School, knowing hardly any English except the word *hi*. He was so frustrated not understanding anything at school in those first weeks, he almost dropped out. But his father told him, "You have to go to school, or you will end up at a job that you don't want." Shaheen took his father's advice to heart: "So I started paying more attention at school and staying up until like 3 a.m. translating sentences from my language to English and then practicing with my classmates. That was a big challenge—language; but when I got the language, it helped me a lot."

While still in high school, Shaheen took classes through dual enrollment on Tuesday and Thursday evenings at a nearby community college to accrue credits (see also Strategy 14). He also worked many evenings until 2 a.m. delivering pizzas to earn money. By taking advantage of dual enrollment, Shaheen was able to complete high school with several college credits that helped him finish his associate's degree and transfer to a 4-year university, earning a double major in construction management and civil engineering. Shaheen is now enrolled in an MBA program and works full-time at a large international construction firm as a project director. He makes time to tutor students through the community organization Refugee and Immigrant Transitions, which supports newcomers across several high schools in the Bay Area (see also Strategy 20).

Shaheen reflected on family members still living in Afghanistan after the Taliban's return to power in 2021: "I'm worried about my grandparents and one of my uncles who are still there. I actually have a bunch of family that are still there. Some used to work for the U.S. government and they have all their paperwork and everything, but there is no way to get out. They're moving from one village to another village to protect themselves."

Despite the threatening conditions that led his family to leave Afghanistan and the pressure to learn English and graduate high school within 2 years, Shaheen felt prepared for the transition to community college. He advises educators and students to take time to build strong connections while in high school, as he noted the transition to a 4-year university was a bit more challenging:

I wish I would have spent more time with teachers and classmates in high school because I saw some of these students later in my community college and university classes. There was one guy I saw and he looked familiar but we had never met in high school. Building a good connection with classmates helps a lot. One classmate, I knew her from high school, we used to help each other after class and get the homework done together. Our classmates from high school can end up with us for a long time until we're done with our education, and they can be good resources. We can help each other or team up for class projects. At university, the instructions for assignments are given so quickly, and teachers don't always repeat everything. So it helps us stay on track to have each other.

Shaheen aspires to complete a PhD after his MBA, and the firm he works for has an educational benefit that will pay for his doctoral studies. He advises newcomer students not to be shy or worry about someone making fun of them when learning English. He encourages students to work hard, take advantage of the resources available, and build strong relationships with teachers and classmates.

Conclusion

The 20 strategies presented in this book—interspersed with school profiles and advice from former newcomer students—offer educators and school staff various ideas and approaches for creating humanizing and CARING school communities. As discussed in the Introduction, CARING schools center students in the learning process, take an assets-based and trauma-informed approach to the educational process, and are *Compassionate, Achievement-oriented, Relationships-focused, Inclusive, Nurturing,* and *Genuine.*

We invite you to adapt and build upon the ideas presented here, tailoring them to your own contexts and the needs of students in your schools. The companion website (www.bit.ly/ImmigRefugeeEd) lists all the additional resources presented in the book and a video playlist for educators. We look forward to you sharing your own strategies and innovative approaches that have worked for immigrant and refugee students in your contexts. You can follow/tag us on Twitter at @ImmigRefugeeEd. Additionally, a vibrant online professional learning community (PLC) for conversation, presentations by experts, and additional information sharing can be found at the hashtag #PLC4newcomers (primarily on Twitter). This PLC was created by ESL teacher Emily Francis as a space for educators of newcomers to come together virtually.

According to Brazilian scholar Paulo Freire (1970), humanizing education is a process of "mutual humanization" (p. 56) that unfolds among educators and students rooted in dialogic and culturally relevant approaches that affirm the histories, heritages, and humanity of students and their communities. Ultimately, the process of humanizing education through the creation of deeply caring and committed school communities equips students to develop the skills, confidence, and knowledge to be agents of change; indeed, as Freire (1985) wrote, "to transform the world is to humanize it" (p. 70).

Immigrant and refugee youth continue to enter schools across the United States. Whether they are from Yemen, Afghanistan, Guatemala, Haiti, Senegal, Ukraine, or elsewhere, it is our job as educators to meet students where they are and to help them envision and navigate their next steps in their new countries of residence. Traditional educational approaches have sought to assimilate students, often in a process that regards their home cultures as inferior. Acknowledging students' transnational lives and communities necessitates approaches that honor students' languages and backgrounds and seek appropriate ways to make space for them as equal and active participants in building a more democratic and representative society.

This book has offered a compendium of ways for school leaders, teachers, school staff, and after-school providers to imagine new models of integration and welcome for newly arrived immigrant and refugee students. Schools, at their best, are beacons of hope, promise, and opportunity. We can and should offer newcomer students the skills, knowledge, and pathways to a bright and fulfilling future, one that affirms their backgrounds and cultures as integral to the diverse tapestry of this nation.

Additional Resources and Video Playlist

Within each strategy, we have listed additional resources that can help readers explore the topic further. We have also curated a video playlist of excellent resources that can help educators and school leaders further explore strategies, resources, and opportunities for working with newcomer youth. All of the links to additional resources and the video playlist can be found on this book's companion website at www.bit.ly/ImmigRefugeeEd; the site can also be accessed by scanning the QR code in Figure A.1 with any mobile device.

Figure A.1. QR Code to Access Book's Companion Website

Glossary of Key Terms

In this glossary we provide concise definitions of terms central to the themes in this book. Some terms are also pertinent to issues that are highly politicized in dominant discourse. In addition, we have included references to other sources where more extensive definitions can be found.

Asylees/Asylum: Asylees are individuals who travel on their own (without refugee status) to another country to apply for or receive a grant of asylum or protection from persecution. These individuals may enter the country they seek asylum from on student, tourist, or business visas, or without a visa (as undocumented or unauthorized immigrants); they then apply under the respective nation's laws for asylum. The United Nations Universal Declaration of Human Rights, adopted in 1948 and the cornerstone of international humanitarian law, enshrines the right for all people across the globe "to seek and enjoy in other countries asylum from persecution" (United Nations, 1948). In the United States, any individual can apply for asylum either within the United States or at a port of entry (air, land, or sea) (Office of English Language Acquisition, 2016; United Nations, 1948).

DACA: DACA is an acronym for Deferred Action for Childhood Arrivals, a U.S. program instituted under former U.S. President Barack Obama. DACA does not grant legal status, but it does offer protection from deportation for around 800,000 unauthorized immigrants who entered the United States originally as children. Applicants must have entered the United States under the age of 16 prior to 2012 and show proof of high school enrollment/ completion or military service (among other requirements). Once granted, DACA allows recipients to apply for a driver's license, a work permit, and a Social Security number. Another estimated 1 million people are eligible for DACA but have not yet received this temporary status. Many legal challenges were mounted to the DACA program under former U.S. President Donald Trump, and recent efforts at the time of this writing have been undertaken by U.S. President Joe Biden to strengthen DACA (Samuels, 2021).

Dreamers: Individuals who were born in another country but came to the United States as unauthorized immigrants when they were children are also sometimes referred to as *dreamers*, a term derived from a bill that was originally before the U.S. Congress in 2001 that was called the DREAM Act, an acronym for the Development, Relief and Education for Alien Minors Act.

Versions of this bill have come before the U.S. Congress several times and have never passed, and the term's second meaning refers to the dreams that many undocumented youth have for their future that are hampered by their inability to regularize their status (American Immigration Council, 2021). The term *dreamers* is not without contestation, as scholars have rejected the notions of selective deserving-ness that are associated with its categorization of some immigrants as "worthy" of protection while others remain outside of such policy discourses (Abrego & Negrón-Gonzales, 2020).

English Learner (EL)/English Language Learner (ELL): EL or ELL refers to an individual whose home language is not English and/or who comes from a place where English is not the dominant language, and is in the process of learning English. In the U.S. educational setting, students who are classified as English learners may be immigrants or refugees, or they may have been born in the United States within families that speak languages other than English. Additional programs and accommodations may exist to support students designated English learners in the classroom, though sometimes this designation has been used to track students of color and limit their educational opportunities (Callahan, 2005; Colorín Colorado, n.d.). The ELL term often appears in policy documents. However, by definition, it disregards students' home languages. For that reason, many prefer terms such as emergent bilingual (EB) or multilingual learner (ML), as we do in this text (unless referring to an EL or ELL policy or program).

English as a Second Language (ESL) or English as a New Language (ENL): ESL or ENL refers to a program designed for students labeled as ELLs to teach English language, sometimes in connection to content (and, increasingly, with the inclusion of their full linguistic repertoire, though this varies by site). Transitional bilingual education is a program where the home language is utilized to teach English, but diminished over time; other forms of bilingual education seek to have students achieve comparable literacy and fluency in two languages (Colorín Colorado, n.d.). Translanguaging, as discussed in Strategy 1, refers to the use of all of a student's linguistic and cognitive resources in any language to aid in the understanding of academic content in the new language (García & Kleyn, 2016; García & Wei, 2014).

Immigrant-Origin Students: In the United States, the term *immigrant-origin students* usually refers to those who were born abroad or born in the United States to immigrant parents. Immigrant-origin students constitute approximately 25% of the K–12 student population in the United States, and a 2018 report found that nearly 30% of students enrolled in U.S. colleges and university were of immigrant origin (Batalova & Feldblum, 2020); many of them were the first generation in their family to attend higher education.

First-generation immigrants refers to those that immigrate themselves while *second-generation* refers to the children of immigrants who are born in the country to which the parents migrate. The term *1.5 generation* refers to individuals who migrated as children or adolescents and, according to sociologist Rubén G. Rumbaut (2012), who coined this term, their "processes of acculturation and educational experiences can vary significantly depending on whether their migration occurred during early childhood, middle childhood, or adolescence . . . [and] historical circumstances (such as the case of war-torn refugees), the cultural distance traveled by migrant populations, their socioeconomic resources, legal status and contexts of reception in host countries" (p. 982).

Newcomers: The term *newcomer* in its broadest definition refers to anyone who is new to a place; for students, this usually refers to any student who was born abroad and is attending school in another country. Some government definitions categorize newcomers as anyone who has arrived in the United States within the previous 10 years, whereas many newcomer programs or schools in the United States utilize arrival within the past 4 years as a criterion for inclusion. Research has shown that newcomer students, on average, live in greater poverty and have higher dropout rates than their U.S.-born peers in the same neighborhoods (Suárez-Orozco et al., 2015; Sugarman, 2019).

Refugee: The United Nations Convention on the Status of Refugees was adopted in 1951 and added to through a 1967 Protocol that applies its tenets universally; 146 nations (including the United States) are party to the Convention and/or the Protocol. This landmark legal document defines refugees as "someone who is unable or unwilling to return to their country of origin owing to a well-founded fear of being persecuted for reasons of race, religion, nationality, membership of a particular social group, or political opinion" (UNHCR, 2021). In the United States, an individual who meets the definition of a refugee can be granted refugee status and resettled in the United States through a lengthy process undertaken by the United States Citizenship and Immigration Services (USCIS).

SIFE/SLIFE: The term *SIFE* stands for Student With Interrupted Formal Education and is a designation that can help offer additional services and resources to students usually arriving from other countries where violence, conflict, the migration journey, or other factors have resulted in extended out-of-school periods (sometimes also written as *SLIFE* for Student With Limited and Interrupted Formal Education). The New York State Education Department (NYSED, 2016) assigns the SIFE designation to "English Language Learners (ELLs) who have attended schools in the United States (the 50 States and the District of Columbia) for less than twelve months and who, upon initial enrollment in such schools, are two or more years below grade level in literacy in their home language and/or two or more years below grade level in Math due to inconsistent or interrupted schooling prior to arrival in the United States" (p. 1). This definition is "inclusive of 'Low Literacy SIFE,' students who have literacy at or below third grade in their home language. This means that they are not yet fluent readers in any language and do not independently use text as a resource to build new knowledge" (NYSED, 2016, p. 1). (Strategy 5 in this book discusses educational strategies specifically for SLIFE students, though many of the approaches in this book are also tailored to this subset of the newcomer student population.)

Unaccompanied Minor: The term *unaccompanied minor* refers to a child under age 18 who travels to the United States without a parent or legal guardian with them. Since 2011, the number of unaccompanied youth—a majority of them boys—arriving at the U.S. border has increased significantly from previous years (a majority of these youth are from the Central American nations of El Salvador, Honduras, and Guatemala, where violence and instability have resulted in the decision to flee). The 1997 Flores Settlement Agreement outlined the standards to which the U.S. government must abide (previously through the Immigration and Naturalization Service, now through the Department of Homeland Security, which oversees immigration) in the housing and care of immigrant minors who are apprehended and detained.

Unaccompanied minors can be released to "sponsors" (usually relatives who are in the United States), who agree to care for them while their cases are pending. These youth can attend schools while their cases are pending, since all children, documented or not, have a right (affirmed in *Plyler v. Doe*) to attend U.S. schools. Unaccompanied minors can often be eligible for Special Immigrant Juvenile Status (SIJS) as a path to regularizing their status in the United States (as discussed further in Strategy 17 on Legal Services) (Immigrant Legal Resource Center, 2021).

Undocumented/Unauthorized Immigrant: These terms refer to someone living in a particular country without the proper legal documents to be able to do so. In the United States, the terms refer to children or adults who are born outside the country and "who entered the U.S. without inspection and proper permission from the government, and those who entered with a legal visa that is no longer valid" (Immigrants Rising, 2020). Approximately 45 million out of the U.S. population of 330 million are foreign born; of this number, less than 25% are undocumented or unauthorized immigrants (approximately 10.5 million people) (Budiman, 2020). About half of the unauthorized immigrant population originally came from Mexico, with an additional 15% coming from the Central American nations of El Salvador, Honduras, and Guatemala; the remainder are from other countries, such as India, the Philippines, Canada, China, Colombia, Brazil, and elsewhere (Baker, 2021).

Notes

Preface

1. The Internationals Network for Public Schools (INPS) establishes schools and academies within larger schools tailored to the needs of newly arrived immigrant and refugee youth. Oakland International High School was founded in 2007 and was the first INPS school to be established outside of New York.

2. Some pieces are coauthored; in those instances, authors' names are connected by "and" to indicate equal contributions to the conceptualization and writing process. Other pieces were produced through thought partnerships and dialogues; in those cases, the "with" designation indicates that the piece was largely written by the first author(s), but the ideas were developed in consultation with the contributor listed after the "with."

Introduction

1. Latinx is a term that includes the full range of gender identity and diversity in referring to people of Latin American origin and descent.

School Profile 2

1. For more information, see https://strategicinquiry.com/workshops/

Strategy 3

1. For a brief description of several newcomer programs, see https://ncela.ed.gov /files/feature_topics/newcomers/ElevatingELs_ProgramsForNewcomerStudents.pdf

School Profile 3

1. On the bilingual seal program in Minnesota, see https://education.mn.gov /MDE/dse/stds/world/seals/; on the Seal of Biliteracy, see https://sealofbiliteracy.org

Strategy 11

1. For more information, see http://www.nysed.gov/bilingual-ed/ell-identification -placementhome-language-questionnaire

Strategy 12

1. The term "American" can, of course, apply equally to North and South America. Here, however, the term refers to problematic and often racialized assumptions about dominant forms of culture in the United States.

Strategy 15

1. For more information, see https://www.albanyschools.org/academics/summer-programs/enl

Strategy 18

1. A Dream Team is featured in a video about supporting immigrants in schools from the CUNY Initiative on Immigration and Education at https://vimeo.com/354056933, also linked at this book's companion website (www.bit.ly/ImmigRefugeeEd).

References

Abrego, L. J., & Negrón-Gonzales, G. (Eds.). (2020). *We are not dreamers: Undocumented scholars theorize undocumented life in the United States.* Duke University Press.

Abu El-Haj, T. (2015). *Unsettled belonging: Educating Palestinian American youth after 9/11.* University of Chicago Press.

Acevedo, N. (2018). *Immigration policies, deportation threats keep kids out of school, report states.* NBC News. https://www.nbcnews.com/news/latino/immigration-policies-deportation-threats-keep-kids-out-school-report-states-n938566

ACLU. (n.d.). *FAQ for educators on immigrant students in public schools.* American Civil Liberties Union. https://www.aclu.org/other/faq-educators-immigrant-students-public-schools

ACTE. (2021). *CTE works!* Association for Career & Technical Education. https://www.acteonline.org/wp-content/uploads/2021/02/CTE_Works_Research-Feb2021.pdf

Adger, C., & Locke, J. (2000). *Broadening the base: School/community partnerships serving language minority students at risk.* UC Berkeley, Center for Research on Education, Diversity and Excellence. https://escholarship.org/uc/item/8s47008n

Adger, C., Snow, C., & Christian, D. (2018). *What teachers need to know about language.* Multilingual Matters.

Advancement Project. (2010). *Test, punish and push out: How "zero tolerance" and high stakes testing funnel youth into the school-to-prison pipeline.* https://www.justice4all.org/wp-content/uploads/2016/04/Test-Punish-Push-Out.pdf

AFT. (2016). *Immigrant and refugee children: A guide for educators and school support staff.* American Federation of Teachers. https://www.aft.org/sites/default/files/im_uac-educators-guide_2016.pdf

Aguilar, E. (2020). *Coaching for equity: Conversations that change practice.* Jossey-Bass.

Alba, R., & Nee, V. (2003). *Remaking the American mainstream: Assimilation and contemporary immigration.* Harvard Education Press.

American Immigration Council. (2021). *The Dream Act: An overview.* https://www.americanimmigrationcouncil.org/research/dream-act-overview

Anaissie, T., Cary, V., Clifford, D., Malarkey, T., & Wise, S. (2021). *Liberatory design.* http://www.liberatorydesign.com

Ancess, J. (2003). *Beating the odds: High schools as communities of commitment.* Teachers College Press.

Ansari, S. (2017, August 10). *How the partition of India happened—and why its effects are still felt today.* The Conversation. https://theconversation.com/how-the-partition-of-india-happened-and-why-its-effects-are-still-felt-today-81766

Antrop-González, R., & De Jesús, A. (2006). Toward a theory of critical care in urban small school reform: Examining structures and pedagogies of caring in two Latino community-based schools. *International Journal of Qualitative Studies in Education, 19*(4), 409–433. https://doi.org/10.1080/09518390600773148

Anyon, J. (1980). Social class and the hidden curriculum of work. *Journal of Education, 162*(Winter), 67–92. https://doi.org/10.1177/002205748016200106

Apple, M. W., & Beane, J. A. (Eds.). (2007). *Democratic schools: Lessons in powerful education.* Heinemann.

Ascenzi-Moreno, L., Hesson, S., & Menken, K. (2016). School leadership along the trajectory from monolingual to multilingual. *Language and Education, 30*(3), 197–218. https://doi.org/10.1080/09500782.2015.1093499

Atteberry, A., & McEachin, A. (2016). School's out: Summer learning loss across grade levels and school contexts in the U.S. today. In K. Alexander, S. Pitcock, & M. Boulay (Eds.), *The summer slide: What we know and can do about summer learning loss* (pp. 35–54). Teachers College Press.

Au, W. (2011). Teaching under the new Taylorism: High-stakes testing and the standardization of the 21st century curriculum. *Journal of Curriculum Studies, 43*(1), 25–45. https://doi.org/10.1080/00220272.2010.521261

Auslander, L. (2022). Getting newcomer English learners off the sidelines: Strategies for increasing learner engagement while developing language and literacy. *TESOL Journal,* 00e1–6. https://doi.org/10.1002/tesj.647

Auslander, L., & Yip, J. (2022). *School-wide systems for multilingual learner success.* Routledge.

Ayers, W., Laura, C., & Ayers, R. (2018). *"You can't fire the bad ones!" And 18 other myths about teachers, teachers unions, and public education.* Beacon Press.

Bahruth, R. E. (2007, March 9). *Learning how to speak human* (Keynote). I-Shou University.

Bajaj, M. (2009). Why context matters: The material conditions of caring in Zambia. *International Journal of Qualitative Studies in Education, 22*(4), 379–398.

Bajaj, M., Argenal, A., & Canlas, M. (2017). Socio-politically relevant pedagogy for immigrant and refugee youth. *Equity & Excellence in Education, 50*(3), 258–274. https://doi.org/10.1080/10665684.2017.1336499

Bajaj, M., & Bartlett, L. (2017). Critical transnational curriculum for immigrant and refugee youth. *Curriculum Inquiry, 47*(1), 25–35. https://doi.org/10.1080/03626784.2016.1254499

Bajaj, M., Canlas, M., & Argenal, A. (2017). Between rights and realities: Human rights education for immigrant and refugee youth in an urban public high school. *Anthropology and Education Quarterly, 48*(2), 124–140. https://doi.org/10.1111/aeq.12189

Bajaj, M., & Suresh, S. (2018). The "warm embrace" of a newcomer school for immigrant & refugee youth. *Theory into Practice, 57*(2), 91–98. https://doi.org/10.1080/00405841.2018.1425815

Bajaj, M., & Tow, D. (2021). Towards a praxis of educational solidarity. *On Education, 4*(10), 1–7. https://www.oneducation.net/no-10_april-2021/towards-a-praxis-of-educational-solidarity

Baker, B. (2021). *Estimates of the unauthorized immigrant population residing in the United States: January 2015–January 2018* (Population Estimates). U.S. Department of Homeland Security, Office of Immigration Statistics. https://www

.dhs.gov/sites/default/files/publications/immigration-statistics/Pop_Estimate
/UnauthImmigrant/unauthorized_immigrant_population_estimates_2015_-
_2018.pdf

Bangura, R. (2014). In search of success: Where school and marriage meet in the educational lives of immigrant African girls with limited formal schooling. In J. Koyama & M. Subramanian (Eds.), *US education in a world of migration: Implications for policy and practice* (pp. 204–221). Routledge.

Barros, S., Domke, L., Symons, C., & Ponzio, C. (2021). Challenging monolingual ways of looking at multilingualism: Insights for curriculum development in teacher preparation. *Journal of Language, Identity, & Education, 20*(4), 239–254.

Bartlett, L. (2005). Dialogue, knowledge, and teacher–student relations: Freirean pedagogy in theory and practice. *Comparative Education Review, 49*(3), 344–364. https://doi.org/10.1086/430261

Bartlett, L., & García, O. (2011). *Additive schooling in subtractive times: Bilingual education and Dominican immigrant youth in the heights.* Vanderbilt University Press.

Bartlett, L., Mendenhall, M., & Ghaffar-Kucher, A. (2017). Culture in acculturation: Refugee youth's schooling experiences in international schools in New York City. *International Journal of Intercultural Relations, 60,* 109–119. https://doi.org/10.1016/j.ijintrel.2017.04.005

Bartlett, L., & Oliveira, G. (2018). Cruel optimism: Migration and schooling for Dominican newcomer immigrant youth. *Anthropology and Education Quarterly, 49*(4), 444–461. https://doi.org/10.1111/aeq.12265

Bartolomé, L. (1994). Beyond the methods fetish: Toward a humanizing pedagogy. *Harvard Educational Review, 64,* 173–195. https://doi.org/10.17763/haer.64.2.58q5m5744t325730

Bartolomé, L. (2010). Preparing to teach newcomer students: The significance of critical pedagogy and the study of ideology in teacher education. *Teachers College Record, 112*(14), 505–526. https://doi.org/10.1177/016146811011201410

Batalova, J., & Feldblum, M. (2020). *Immigrant-origin students in U.S. higher education: A data profile.* https://www.migrationpolicy.org/research/immigrant-origin -students-us-higher-education

Beeman, K., & Urow, C. (2013). *Teaching for biliteracy: Strengthening bridges between languages.* Caslon Publishing.

Benson, T., & Fiarman, S. (2020). *Unconscious bias in schools: A developmental approach to racism.* Harvard Education Press.

Bigelow, M., & Watson, J. (2013). The role of educational level, literacy and orality on L2 learning. In S. M. Gass & A. Mackay (Eds.), *The Routledge handbook of second language acquisition* (pp. 461–475). Routledge.

Blackledge, A., & Creese, A. (2014). Heteroglossia as practice and pedagogy. In A. Blackledge & A. Creese (Eds.), *Heteroglossia as practice and pedagogy* (pp. 1–20). Springer. https://link.springer.com/book/10.1007/978-94-007-7856-6

Blad, E. (2019). How schools can make advisories meaningful for students and teachers. *EducationWeek.* https://www.edweek.org/leadership/how-schools-can-make -advisories-meaningful-for-students-and-teachers/2019/03

Boaler, J., & Staples, M. (2008). Creating mathematical futures through an equitable teaching approach: The case of Railside School. *Teachers College Record, 110*(3), 608–645.

Bond, N. (Ed.). (2015). *The power of teacher leaders: Their roles, influence, and impact*. Routledge.

Bourdieu, P., & Passeron, J. (1977). *Reproduction in education, society and culture*. SAGE Publications.

Breiseth, L. (2019). *11 strategies schools can use to support students after an immigration raid*. Colorín Colorado. https://www.colorincolorado.org/article/11-strategies-schools-can-use-support-students-after-immigration-raid

Bridges to Academic Success. (2019). *Bridges sheltered program for SIFE with developing literacy*. CUNY. https://bridges-sifeproject.com/Prof_Dev/Publications/Bridges%20Sheltered%20Program%20Manual%202019.09.18.pdf

Bridging Refugee Youth and Children's Services. (n.d. a). *Family engagement with refugee populations* [Webinar]. https://www.brycs.org/webinar/family-engagement-with-refugee-populations

Bridging Refugee Youth and Children's Services. (n.d. b). *Refugee Youth Summer Academy*. https://brycs.org/promising/0123/

Bridging Refugee Youth and Children's Services. (n.d. c). *Welcoming and orienting newcomer students to U.S. schools*. https://brycs.org/schools/welcoming-and-orienting-newcomer-students-to-u-s-schools/

Bridging Refugee Youth and Children's Services. (2018). *Youth arts & voices: Expressive arts programs for refugee and immigrants*. https://brycs.org/youth-development/youth-arts-voices-expressive-arts-programs-for-refugee-and-immigrants

Bridging Refugee Youth and Children's Services. (2020). *What now? Post-high school, college and career readiness for refugee youth*. https://brycs.org/schools/what-now-post-high-school-college-career-readiness-for-refugee-youth/

Bristol, T., & Martin-Fernandez, J. (2019). The added value of Latinx and Black teachers for Latinx and Black students: Implications for policy. *Policy Insights from Behavioral and Brain Science, 6*(2), 147–153. https://doi.org/10.1177/2372732219862573

Budiman, A. (2020). *Key findings about U.S. immigrants*. Pew Research Center. https://www.pewresearch.org/fact-tank/2020/08/20/key-findings-about-u-s-immigrants/

Buhain, V. (2016, September 13). The fourth R: Refugee students get intensive course in resettlement. *The Seattle Globalist*. https://seattleglobalist.com/2016/09/13/the-fourth-r-refugee-students-get-intensive-course-in-resettlement/55614

Bui, T. (Ed.). (2012). *We are Oakland International*. Minute Man Press.

Bundy, D., Shaeffer, S., Jukes, M., Beegle, K., Gillespie, A., Drake, L., Lee, S.-h. F., Hoffman, A.-M., Jones, J., Mitchell, A., Barcelona, D., Camara, B., Golmar, C., Savioli, L., Sembene, M., Takeuchi, T., & Wright, C. (2006). School-based health and nutrition programs. In D. T. Jamison, J. G. Breman, A. R. Measham, G. Alleyne, M. Claeson, D. B. Evans, P. Jha, A. Mills, & P. Musgrove (Eds.), *Disease control priorities in developing countries* (2nd ed., pp. 1091–1108). World Bank; Oxford University Press. https://www.ncbi.nlm.nih.gov/books/NBK11783

Burris, C., Heubert, J., & Levin, H. (2006). Accelerating mathematics achievement using heterogeneous grouping. *American Educational Research Journal, 43*(1), 105–136. https://doi.org/10.3102/00028312043001105

Calderón, M. (2008, December). Expediting language, literacy and learning for adolescent ELLs. The STARlight—Research & resources for English learner achievement, 3(1). Santa Clara, CA: California STARlight Consortium.

California Department of Education. (2021a). *California Healthy Kids Survey*. http://calschls.org/

California Department of Education. (2021b). *Continuation education.* https://www.cde.ca.gov/sp/eo/ce/

Callahan, R. M. (2005). Tracking and high school English learners: Limiting opportunity to learn. *American Educational Research Journal, 42*(2), 305–328. https://doi.org/10.3102/00028312042002305

Callahan, R. M. (2013). *The English learner dropout dilemma: Multiple risks and multiple resources California dropout research.* Gevirtz Graduate School of Education. http://cdrpsb.org/researchreport19.pdf

Cammarota, J., & Fine, M. (2008). *Revolutionizing education: Youth participatory action research in motion.* Routledge.

CASEL. (2020). *CASEL's SEL framework: What are the core competence areas and where are they promoted?* https://casel.s3.us-east-2.amazonaws.com/CASEL-SEL-Framework-11.2020.pdf

CAST. (2013). *UDL intersections.* https://inclusive-live-storagestack-assetstorages3bucket-3uty0hejzw6u.s3.ap-southeast-2.amazonaws.com/public/inclusive-education/resources/files/UDL-intersections.pdf

CAST. (2018). *Universal design for learning guidelines version 2.2.* http://udlguidelines.cast.org

Castellón, M., Cheuk, T., Greene, R., Mercado-García, D., Santos, M., Skarin, R., & Zerkel, L. (2015). *Schools to learn from: How six high schools graduate English language learners college and career ready.* Stanford Graduate School of Education. https://www.lehman.edu/academics/education/middle-high-school-education/documents/SchoolstoLearnFrom-NewWorld-Gashi.pdf

Cate, R. (2017). *Soccer Without Borders: Bridging the culture gap for newcomers across US.* Fox News. https://www.foxnews.com/sports/soccer-without-borders-bridging-the-culture-gap-for-newcomers-across-u-s

Caterall, J. (2009). *Doing well and doing good by doing art: A 12-year longitudinal study of arts education—Effects on the achievements and values of young adults.* I-Group Books.

Celic, C. M. (2009). *English language learners day by day: A complete guide to literacy, content-area, and language instruction.* Heinemann.

Cenoz, J., & Gorter, D. (2011). A holistic approach to multilingual education: Introduction. *The Modern Language Journal, 95*(3), 339–343. https://doi.org/10.1111/j.1540-4781.2011.01204.x

Changing Worlds. (2022). *Arts programs and services 2021–2022.* https://static1.squarespace.com/static/58741895ff7c5095f82b32f5/t/61533c3bc719c45b562be7d3/1632844864108/CW+2022+Program+Book.pdf

Cherng, H.-Y. S., & Halpin, P. F. (2016). The importance of minority teachers: Student perceptions of minority versus White teachers. *Educational Researcher, 45*(7), 407–420. https://doi.org/10.3102/0013189X16671718

Cioè-Peña, M., & Snell, T. (2015). Translanguaging for social justice. *Theory, Research, and Action in Urban Education, 4*(1).

Coalition for Community Schools. (2020). *Community schools.* https://www.communityschools.org/

Collier, V., & Thomas, W. (2017). Validating the power of bilingual schooling: Thirty-two years of large-scale, longitudinal research. *Annual Review of Applied Linguistics, 37,* 203–217. https://doi.org/10.1017/S0267190517000034

Collins, C. (2020a). School as sanctuary. *Learning for Justice Magazine, 65*. https:// www.learningforjustice.org/magazine/fall-2020/school-as-sanctuary

Collins, C. (2020b). Toolkit for "School as sanctuary." *Learning for Justice Magazine, 65*. https://www.learningforjustice.org/magazine/fall-2020/toolkit-for-school-as -sanctuary

Collins, C. (2021). Toolkit: The foundations of restorative justice. *Learning for Justice Magazine, 66*. https://www.learningforjustice.org/magazine/spring-2021/toolkit -the-foundations-of-restorative-justice

Colorín Colorado. (n.d.). *ELL glossary*. https://www.colorincolorado.org/ell-basics /ell-glossary

Colorín Colorado. (2008). *Creating a college-going culture for English language learners*. http://www.colorincolorado.org/article/28915/

Colorín Colorado. (2018). *Immigrant students' legal rights: An overview*. https://www .colorincolorado.org/immigration/guide/rights

Colorín Colorado. (2019). *Fact sheet: Information for limited English proficient parents and for schools and school districts that communicate with them.* https://www.colorincolorado.org/guide/fact-sheet-information-limited-english -proficient-parents-and-schools-and-school-districts

Costello, M. (2016). *The Trump effect: The impact of the presidential campaign on our nation's schools*. Southern Poverty Law Center. https://www.splcenter.org /sites/default/files/splc_the_trump_effect.pdf

Cunningham, G. (2021). *What educators need to know about immigration law: Supporting immigrant, undocumented, and refugee students*. Teachers College Press.

Custodio, B., & O'Loughlin, J. (2017). *Students with interrupted formal education: Bridging where they are and what they need*. Corwin Press.

Darling-Hammond, L. (2000). Teacher quality and student achievement: A review of state policy evidence. *Education Policy Analysis Archives, 8*(1), 1–44. https://doi .org/10.14507/epaa.v8n1.2000

Decker, L. E., Decker, V. A., & Brown, P. M. (2007). *Diverse partnerships for student success: Strategies and tools to help school leaders*. Rowman & Littlefield Education.

De Jong, E., & Commins, N. (2006). How should English language learners be grouped for instruction? In E. Hamayan & R. Freeman (Eds.), *English language learners at school: A guide for administrators* (pp. 118–121). Caslon Publishing.

de Mejía, A. M., Peña Dix, B., de Vélez, M., & Montiel Chamorro, M. (2012). *Exploraciones sobre el aprendizaje de lenguas y contenidos en programas bilingües: Una indagación en la escuela primaria* [*Explorations about language and content learning in bilingual programs: An inquiry in elementary school*]. Universidad de los Andes.

Deroo, M. R., & Ponzio, C. M. (2021). Fostering pre-service teachers' critical multilingual language awareness: Use of multimodal compositions to confront hegemonic language ideologies. *Journal of Language, Identity & Education*, 1–17. https://doi .org/10.1080/15348458.2020.1863153

Deutsch, N. L., Blyth, D. A., Kelley, J., Tolan, P. H., & Lerner, R. M. (2017). Let's talk after-school: The promises and challenges of positive youth development for after-school research, policy, and practice. In N. L. Deutsch (Ed.), *After-school programs to promote positive youth development: Integrating research into practice and policy* (Vol. 1, pp. 45–68). Springer.

Duncan-Andrade, J. (2009). Note to educators: Hope required when growing roses in concrete. *Harvard Educational Review, 79*(2), 181–194. https://doi.org/10.17763/haer.79.2.nu3436017730384w

Dyrness, A. (2021). Rethinking global citizenship education with/for transnational youth. *Globalisation, Societies and Education, 19*(4), 443–455. https://doi.org/10.1080/14767724.2021.1897001

Dyrness, A., & Abu El-Haj, T. (2020). Reflections on the field: The democratic citizenship formation of transnational youth. *Anthropology & Education Quarterly, 51*(2), 165–177. https://doi.org/10.1111/aeq.12294

Echevarria, J., Vogt, M., & Short, D. J. (2008). *Making content comprehensible for English learners: The SIOP model* (3rd ed.). Allyn & Bacon.

Eckerson, J. M. (2015). *Teacher perspectives on professional development needs for better serving Nebraska's Spanish heritage language learners.* [Doctoral dissertation, University of Nebraska–Lincoln]. DigitalCommons@University of Nebraska–Lincoln. https://digitalcommons.unl.edu/teachlearnstudent/62/

EdBuild. (2019). *$23 Billion.* https://edbuild.org/content/23-billion#CA

Edmondson, A. (2018). *The fearless organization: Creating psychological safety in the workplace for learning, innovation, and growth.* John Wiley & Sons.

Edmunds, J., Unlu, F., Glennie, E., Bernstein, L., Fesler, L., & Furey, J. (2017). Smoothing the transition to postsecondary education: The impact of the early college model. *Journal of Research on Educational Effectiveness, 10*(2), 297–325.

Ellis, E. (2013). The ESL teacher as plurilingual: An Australian perspective. *TESOL Quarterly 47*(3), 446–471. https://doi.org/10.1002/tesq.120

Fass, P. (1989). *Outside in: Minorities and the transformation of American education.* Oxford University Press.

Fedestin, B., Jean, J., Phillips, M., Haferd, T., Fuoco, M., Posada, M., Madden-Fuoco, J., & What Kids Can Do (Organization). (2004). *The problem we all live with: Inequalities between Boston's urban and suburban schools* [DVD]. What Kids Can Do.

Fenner, D. S. (2014). *Advocating for English learners: A guide for educators.* Corwin.

Ferlazzo, L. & K. Hull Sypnieski. (2018). The ELL Teacher's Toolbox: Hundreds of Practical Ideas to Support Your Students. John Wiley and Sons.

Figlio, D., & Page, M. (2002). School choice and the distributional effects of ability tracking: Does separation increase inequality? *Journal of Urban Economics, 51*(3), 497–514. https://doi.org/10.1006/juec.2001.2255

Fink, J., Jenkins, D., & Yanagiura, T. (2017). *What happens to students who take community college "dual enrollment" courses in high school?* Teachers College. https://ccrc.tc.columbia.edu/publications/what-happens-community-college-dual-enrollment-students.html

Fishman, E. (2021). *Refugee High.* New Press.

Florian, L., & Linklater, H. (2010). Preparing teachers for inclusive education: Using inclusive pedagogy to enhance teaching and learning for all. *Cambridge Journal of Education, 40*(3), 369–386. https://doi.org/10.1080/0305764X.2010.526588

Ford, K. (2012). *Differentiated instruction for English language learners.* Colorín Colorado. https://www.colorincolorado.org/article/differentiated-instruction-english-language-learners

Forte, I., & Schurr, S. (1993). *Definitive middle school guide: A handbook for success.* Incentive.

Fouad, N. A., & Byars-Winston, A. M. (2005). Cultural context of career choice: Meta-analysis of race/ethnicity differences. *The Career Development Quarterly, 53,* 223–233. https://doi.org/10.1002/j.2161-0045.2005.tb00992.x

Fránquiz, M., & Salazar, M. (2004). The transformative potential of humanizing pedagogy: Addressing the diverse needs of Chicano/Mexicano students. *High School Journal, 87*(4), 36–53.

Freire, P. (1970). *Pedagogy of the oppressed.* Continuum.

Freire, P. (1985). *The politics of education: Culture, power and liberation.* Bergin & Garvey.

Fuchs, L. S., Fuchs, D., Bentz, J., Phillips, N. B., & Hamlett, C. L. (1994). The nature of student interactions during peer tutoring with and without prior training and experience. *American Educational Research Journal, 31,* 75–103. https://doi.org/10.3102/00028312031001075

Gándara, P., & Ee, J. (2018). *U.S. immigration enforcement policy and its impact on teaching and learning in the nation's schools.* The Civil Rights Project. https://www.civilrightsproject.ucla.edu/research/k-12-education/immigration-immigrant-students/u.s.-immigration-enforcement-policy-and-its-impact-on-teaching-and-learning-in-the-nations-schools

García, O. (2012). Theorizing translanguaging for educators. In C. Celic & K. Seltzer (Eds.), *Translanguaging: A CUNY-NYSIEB guide for educators* (pp. 1–6). CUNY-NYSIEB. https://www.cuny-nysieb.org/wp-content/uploads/2016/04/Translanguaging-Guide-March-2013.pdf

García, O., Johnson, S., & Seltzer, K. (2017). *The translanguaging classroom. Leveraging student bilingualism for learning.* Caslon.

García, O., & Kleyn, T. (2016). *Translanguaging with multilingual students: Learning from classroom moments.* Routledge.

García, O., & Menken, K. (2010). Moving forward: Ten guiding principles for teachers. In K. Menken & O. García (Eds.), *Negotiating language policies in schools: Educators as policymakers* (pp. 262–268). Taylor & Francis.

García, O., & Menken, K. (2015). Cultivating an ecology of multilingualism in schools. In B. Spolsky, O. Inbar-Lourie, & M. Tannenbaum (Eds.), *Challenges for language education and policy* (pp. 95–108). Routledge.

García, O., & Sylvan, C. (2011). Pedagogies and practices in multilingual classrooms: Singularities in pluralities. *Modern Language Journal, 95,* 385–400. https://doi.org/10.1111/j.1540-4781.2011.01208.x

García, O., & Wei, L. (2014). *Translanguaging: Language, bilingualism, and education.* Palgrave MacMillan.

García, O., Woodley, H. H., Flores, N., & Chu, H. (2013). Latino Emergent Bilingual Youth in High Schools: Transcaring Strategies for Academic Success. *Urban Education, 48*(6), 798–827. https://doi.org/10.1177/0042085912462708

Gardner, T. (2022). *The benefits of an alumni mentorship program for students.* Edutopia. https://www.edutopia.org/article/benefits-alumni-mentorship-program-students

Gay, G. (2000). *Culturally responsive teaching: Theory, research, and practice.* Teachers College Press.

Gershenson, S. (2013). Do summer time-use gaps vary by socioeconomic status? *American Educational Research Journal, 50*(6), 1219–1248. https://doi.org/10.3102/0002831213502516

Gershenson, S., Hansen, M., & Lindsay, C. (2021). *Teacher diversity and student success: Why racial representation matters in the classroom.* Harvard University Press.

Giani, M., Alexander, C., & Reyes, P. (2014). Exploring variation in the impact of dual-credit coursework on postsecondary outcomes: A quasi-experimental analysis of Texas students. *The High School Journal, 97*(4), 200–218. https://doi.org/10.1353/hsj.2014.0007

Gibbons, P. (2014). *Scaffolding language, scaffolding learning: Teaching English language learners in the mainstream classroom* (2nd ed.). Heinemann.

Giegerich, A. (2020, July 26). How a winning Portland nonprofit delivers vital goods to immigrants and refugees. *Portland Business Journal.* https://www.bizjournals.com/portland/news/2020/06/26/andy-column-6-26.html

Ginwright, S., & Cammarota, J. (2007). Youth activism in the urban community: Learning critical civic praxis within community organizations. *International Journal of Qualitative Studies in Education, 20*(6), 693–710. https://doi.org/10.1080/09518390701630833

Giroux, H., & Penna, A. (1979). Social education in the classroom: Dynamics of the hidden curriculum. *Theory and Research in Social Education, 7*(1), 21–42. https://doi.org/10.1080/00933104.1979.10506048

Gist, C. D., & Bristol, T. J. (Eds.). (2022). *Handbook of research on teachers of color and Indigenous teachers.* American Educational Research Association.

Gist, C. D., Bristol, T. J., Bianco, M., & Goings, R. (2021). Finding strategies to bring teachers of color and Indigenous teachers into the profession. *Phi Delta Kappan Special Report.* https://pdkmembers.org/members_online/publications/archive/pdf/PDK_2021_SpecialIssue/PDK_SpecialIssue_2021_RecruitementBrief.pdf

Glass, G. (n.d.). *Grouping students for instruction.* National Education Policy Center. https://nepc.colorado.edu/sites/default/files/Chapter05-Glass-Final.pdf

Glazer, N., & Moynihan, D. (1963). *Beyond the melting pot: The Negroes, Puerto Ricans, Jews, Italians, and Irish of New York City.* MIT Press.

Goldberg, C. A. (2007). *Citizens and paupers: Relief, rights, and race, from the freedmen's bureau to workfare.* University of Chicago Press.

Goldenberg, C. (2013). Unlocking the research on English learners: What we know—and don't yet know—about effective instruction. *American Educator, 37*(2), 4–11.

Gomez, M. N., & Diarrassouba, N. (2014). What do teachers need to support English learners? *English Language Teaching, 7*(5), 89–101. https://doi.org/10.5539/elt.v7n5p89

Gonzales, R. G. (2010). On the wrong side of the tracks: Understanding the effects of school structure and social capital in the educational pursuits of undocumented immigrant students. *Peabody Journal of Education, 85*(4), 469–485. https://doi.org/10.1080/0161956X.2010.518039

Graff, C. S. (2017). *Home visits 101.* Edutopia. https://www.edutopia.org/article/home-visits-101-cristina-santamaria-graff

Halverson, E. R. (2021). *How the arts can save education.* Teacher College Press.

Hamayan, E., & Freeman Field, R. (Eds.). (2012). *English language learners at school: A guide for administrators* (2nd ed.). Caslon Publishing.

Hantzopoulos, M. (2016). *Restoring dignity in public schools: Human rights education*. Teachers College Press.

Hantzopoulos, M., Rivera-McCutchen, R. L., & Tyner-Mullings, A. R. (2021). Reframing school culture through project-based assessment tasks: Cultivating transformative agency and humanizing practices in NYC public schools. *Teachers College Record, 123*(4), 1–38. https://doi.org/10.1177/016146812112300404

Hantzopoulos, M., & Tyner-Mullings, A. R. (2012). *Critical small schools: Beyond privatization in New York City urban educational reform*. Information Age Publishing.

Health Resources and Service Administration. (2017). *School-based health centers*. https://www.hrsa.gov/library/school-based-health-alliance

Heiman, D., Bybee, E. R., Rodriguez, H. M., & Urrieta, L. (2021). "Era como si esas casas no encajaban con la comunidad": Caminatas with futurxs maestrxs bilingües in a gentrifying Latinx community. *Journal of Language, Identity & Education, 20*(1), 30–44. https://doi.org/10.1080/15348458.2021.1864207

Herrera, S., Murray, K., & Cabral, R. (2013). *Assessment accommodations for classroom teachers of culturally and linguistically diverse students*. Pearson.

Hing, B. O. (2004). *Defining America through immigration policy*. Temple University Press.

Hodge, A. (2021, March 22). *A graduate's view: Minnesota's dual-enrollment college program was my ticket out of poverty. More HS students of color need access to it*. The 74. https://www.the74million.org/article/a-graduates-view-minnesotas-dual-enrollment-college-program-was-my-ticket-out-of-poverty-more-hs-students-of-color-need-access-to-it/

Holland, D., Nonini, D. M., Lutz, C., Bartlett, L., Frederick-McGlathery, M., Guldbrandsen, T. C., & Murillo, E. G. (2007). *Local Democracy Under Siege: Activism, Public Interests, and Private Politics*. New York University Press.

Hos, R. (2016). Caring is not enough: Teachers' enactment of ethical care for adolescent students with limited or interrupted formal education (SLIFE) in a newcomer classroom. *SAGE Journals, 48*(5), 423–443. https://doi.org/10.1177/0013124514536440

Hossaini, S. (2021, March 27). *Indigenous-language radio show in Oakland promotes vaccine effort*. National Public Radio (NPR). https://www.npr.org/2021/03/27/978592445/indigenous-language-radio-show-in-oakland-promotes-vaccine-effort

Huerta, T. M. (2011). Humanizing pedagogy: Beliefs and practices on the teaching of Latino children. *Bilingual Research Journal, 34*(1), 38–57.

Hutzel, K., Bastos, F., & Cosier, K. (2012). *Transforming city schools through art: Approaches to meaningful K–12 teaching*. Teachers College Press.

Immigrant Legal Resource Center. (2021). *Immigrant youth*. Immigrant Legal Resource Center. https://www.ilrc.org/immigrant-youth

Immigrants Rising. (2020). *Defining undocumented*. https://immigrantsrising.org/resource/defining-undocumented/

International Rescue Committee. (2018). *Leaders in Training explore new careers*. https://www.rescue.org/announcement/leaders-training-explore-new-careers

International Rescue Committee. (2021a). *IRC's New Roots program: Growing good from the ground up*. https://www.rescue.org/resource/ircs-new-roots-program-growing-good-ground

International Rescue Committee. (2021b). *Newcomer Youth Summer Academy.* https://www.rescue.org/sites/default/files/document/6549/2021nysafinalreport.pdf

Internationals Network for Public Schools. (2017). *The Internationals approach.* https://www.internationalsnetwork.org/about/#intls-approach

Internationals Network for Public Schools. (2021). *Re-engaging multilingual learners post-pandemic: Lessons from Internationals Network for Public Schools.* https://www.internationalsnetwork.org/wp-content/uploads/2021/07/Re-Engaging-Multilingual-Learners-Post-Pandemic.pdf

Internationals Network for Public Schools. (2022). *About us.* https://www.internationalsnetwork.org/about/#vision-mission

Irujo, S. (2004). *Differentiated instruction: We can no longer just aim down the middle.* Course Crafters. http://www.coursecrafters.com/differentiated-instruction-we-can-no-longer-just-aim-down-the-middle/

Jacobson, L. (2020). "I didn't want to change my name"—From spending six years in a refugee camp to coming out as a trans woman, how Ko Ser Lu Htoo came into her identity. *The California Aggie.* https://theaggie.org/2020/05/29/i-didnt-want-to-change-my-name-from-spending-six-years-in-a-refugee-camp-to-coming-out-as-a-trans-woman-how-ko-ser-lu-htoo-came-into-her-identity/

Jaffe-Walter, R., & Lee, S. J. (2011). "To trust in my root and to take that to go forward": Supporting college access for immigrant youth in the global city. *Anthropology & Education Quarterly, 42*(3), 281–296. https://doi.org/10.1111/j.1548-1492.2011.01132.x

Jaffe-Walter, R., Miranda, C., & Lee, S. J. (2019). From protest to protection: Navigating politics with immigrant students in uncertain times. *Harvard Educational Review, 89*(2). https://doi.org/10.17763/1943-5045-89.2.251

Jaffe-Walter, R., Walsh, D., & Lee, S. J. (2018). This issue. *Theory into Practice, 57*(2), 79–81. https://doi.org/10.1080/00405841.2018.1425818

Jiménez, R. T. (2020). Community cultural wealth pedagogies: Cultivating autoethnographic counternarratives and migration capital. *American Educational Research Journal, 57*(2), 775–807. https://doi.org/10.3102/0002831219866148

Jiménez, R. T., David, S., Fagan, K., Risko, V. J., Pacheco, M., Pray, L., & Gonzales, M. (2015). Using translation to drive conceptual development for students becoming literate in English as an additional language. *Research in the Teaching of English, 49*(3), 248–271. http://www.jstor.org/stable/24398702

Johnson, A. (2020). Summer credit recovery impact on newcomer English learners. *American Educational Research Journal, 57*(4), 1757–1790. https://doi.org/10.3102%2F0002831219883237

Jordan, A., Schwartz, E., & McGhie-Richmond, D. (2009). Preparing teachers for inclusive classrooms. *Teaching and Teacher Education, 25*(4), 535–542. https://doi.org/10.1016/j.tate.2009.02.010

Joyce, B. R., & Showers, B. (2002). *Student achievement through staff development* (3rd ed.). Association for Supervision & Curriculum Development (ASCD).

Kanno, Y., & Kangas, S. E. (2014). "I'm not going to be, like, for the AP": English language learners' limited access to advanced college-preparatory courses in high school. *American Educational Research Journal, 51*, 848–878. https://doi.org/10.3102/0002831214544716

Katzenmeyer, M. H., & Moller, G. V. (2009). *Awakening the sleeping giant: Helping teachers develop as leaders.* Corwin Press.

Kegan, R., & Lahey, L. (2009). *Immunity to change: How to overcome it and unlock potential in yourself and your organization.* Harvard Business School Press.

Kelley, R. D. (2002). *Freedom dreams: The Black radical imagination.* Beacon Press.

Kessler, J., Wentworth, L., & Darling-Hammond, L. (2018). *The Internationals Network for Public Schools: Educating our immigrant English language learners well.* Stanford Center for Opportunity Policy in Education. https://edpolicy.stanford.edu/sites/default/files/International%20Network%20v2.pdf

Kimsey-House, K., Kimsey-House, H., Sandhall, P., & Whitworth, L. (2018). *Co-active coaching: The proven framework for transformative conversations at work and in life.* Nicholas Brealey Publishing.

Kirksey, J. J., & Sattin-Bajaj, C. (2021). Immigration arrests and educational impacts: Linking ICE arrests to declines in achievement, attendance, and school climate and safety in California. *AERA Open.* https://doi.org/10.1177/23328584211039787

Kirksey, J. J., Sattin-Bajaj, C., Gottfried, M. A., Freeman, J., & Ozuna, C. S. (2020). Deportations near the schoolyard: Examining immigration enforcement and racial/ethnic gaps in educational outcomes. *AERA Open, 6*(1), 1–18. https://doi.org/10.1177/2332858419899074

Kleyn, T. (2013). *Social justice and Latinos in NYC 1913–2013: A social studies English/Spanish bilingual curriculum grades 6–12.* City College of New York. https://static1.squarespace.com/static/5ebc3e87f0b2e170fea06fa6/t/5f3d20fcf69bd73dc295a8c6/1597841705089/Social+Justice+%26+Latinos+FINAL.pdf

Kleyn, T. (2017). Centering transborder students: Perspectives on identity, languaging and schooling between the U.S. and Mexico. *Multicultural Perspectives, 19*(2), 76–84. https://doi.org/10.1080/15210960.2017.1302336

Kleyn, T. (2021). *Living, learning, and languaging across borders: Students between the US and Mexico.* Routledge.

Knight, J. (2017). *The impact cycle: What instructional coaches should do to foster powerful improvements in teaching.* Corwin.

Knight, J. (2019). *The instructional playbook: The missing link for translating research into practice.* One Fine Bird Press.

Korematsu v. U.S. (1944). https://supreme.justia.com/cases/federal/us/323/214/

Kraft, M. A., Blazar, D., & Hogan D. (2018). The effect of teacher coaching on instruction and achievement: A meta-analysis of the causal evidence. *Review of Educational Research, 88*(4), 547–588. https://doi.org/10.3102/0034654318759268

Ladson-Billings, G. (1995a). Toward a theory of culturally relevant pedagogy. *American Educational Research Journal, 32*(3), 465–491. https://doi.org/10.3102/00028312032003465

Ladson-Billings, G. (1995b). But that's just good teaching! The case for culturally relevant pedagogy. *Theory into Practice, 34*(3), 159–165. https://doi.org/10.1080/00405849509543675

Lampert, M., Franke, M. L., Kazemi, E., Ghousseini, H., Turrou, A. C., Beasley, H., Cunard, A., & Crowe, K. (2013). Keeping it complex using rehearsals to support novice teacher learning of ambitious teaching. *Journal of Teacher Education, 64*(3), 226–243. https://doi.org/10.1177/0022487112473837

Language Lizard. (2011). *8 tips to protect ELLs from bullying in your classroom and school*. Colorín Colorado. https://www.colorincolorado.org/article/8-tips-protect-ells-bullying-your-classroom-and-school

Lave, J., & Wenger, E. (1991). *Situated learning: Legitimate peripheral participation*. Cambridge University Press.

Lee, E. (2019). *America for Americans: A history of xenophobia in the United States*. Basic Books.

Lee, S., & Hawkins, M. (2008). "Family is here": Learning in community-based after-school programs. *Theory Into Practice, 47*, 51–58. https://doi.org/10.1080/00405840701764763

Lee, S. J. & Walsh, D. (2016). Welcoming immigrant students with a high-quality education. *Phi Delta Kappan, 97*(4), pp. 46–50.

Lee, S. J. & Walsh, D. (2015). Teaching (in)justice: One teacher's work with immigrant English learners. *The Urban Review, 47*(1), pp. 45–66.

Lee, S. J. & Walsh, D. (2013). Resistance and accommodation: Social justice education for immigrant youth in an era of high stakes testing. *Encyclopaideia: Journal of Phenomenology and Education, 43*, XVI.

Lee, S., & Walsh, D. (2017). Socially just, culturally sustaining pedagogy for diverse immigrant youth: Possibilities, challenges, and directions. In D. Paris & H. S. Alim (Eds.), *Culturally sustaining pedagogies: Teaching and learning for justice in a changing world* (pp. 191–206). Teachers College Press.

Loewus, L. (2017). The nation's teaching force is still mostly White and female. *Education Week*. https://www.edweek.org/ew/articles/2017/08/15/the-nations-teaching-force-is-still-mostly.html

Lomawaima, K. T. (1993). Domesticity in the federal Indian schools: The power of authority over mind and body. *American Ethnologist, 20*, 227–240. https://doi.org/10.1525/ae.1993.20.2.02a00010

Lomawaima, K. T., & McCarty, T. L. (2006). *"To remain an Indian": Lessons in democracy from a century of Native American education*. Teachers College Press.

Lucas, T., Villegas, A. M., & Freedson-Gonzalez, M. (2008). Linguistically responsive teacher education: Preparing classroom teachers to teach English language learners. *Journal of Teacher Education, 59*, 361–373. https://doi.org/10.1177/0022487108322110

Lukes, M. (2015). *Latino immigrant youth and interrupted schooling: Dropouts, dreamers and alternative pathways to college*. Multilingual Matters.

Macleod, C. (2021, September 17). *The changing concepts around immigrant integration*. Migration Policy Institute. https://www.migrationpolicy.org/article/changing-concepts-immigrant-integration

Manning, M. (2018, August 10). *How America's 2018 Teacher of the Year builds community for new immigrants and refugees*. Summit Learning. https://blog.summitlearning.org/2018/08/community/

Markham, L. (2017). *The Far Away Brothers*. Crown.

McDonald, M., Kazemi, E., & Kavanagh, S. S. (2013). Core practices and pedagogies of teacher education: A call for a common language and collective activity. *Journal of Teacher Education, 64*(5), 378–386. https://doi.org/10.1177/0022487113493807

McKnight, K., Venkateswaran, N., Laird, J., Robles, J., & Shalev, T. (2017). *Mindset shifts and parent teacher home visits*. Parent Teacher Home Visits. https://pthvp

.org/wp-content/uploads/2022/03/mindset-shifts-and-parent-teacher-home-visits.pdf

Mehl, G., Wyner, J., Barnett, E., Fink, J., & Jenkins, D. (2020). *The dual enrollment playbook: A guide to equitable acceleration for students.* The Aspen Institute; Community College Research Center. https://ccrc.tc.columbia.edu/media/k2/attachments/dual-enrollment-playbook-equitable-acceleration.pdf

Mendenhall, M., & Bartlett, L. (2018). Academic and extracurricular support for refugee students in the US: Lessons learned. *Theory Into Practice, 57*(2), 109–118. https://doi.org/10.1080/00405841.2018.1469910

Mendenhall, M., Bartlett, L., & Ghaffar-Kucher, A. (2017). "If you need help, they are always there for us": Education for refugees in an international high school in NYC. *The Urban Review, 49*(1), 1–25. https://doi.org/10.1007/s11256-016-0379-4

Menken, K. (2008). *English learners left behind.* Multilingual Matters.

Menken, K., Pérez Rosario, V., & Valerio, L.A.G. (2018). Increasing multilingualism in schoolscapes: New scenery and language education policies. *Linguistic Landscape, 4*(2), 101–127. https://doi.org/10.1075/ll.17024.men

Migration Policy Institute. (2020). *Frequently requested statistics on immigrants and immigration in the United States.* https://www.migrationpolicy.org/article/frequently-requested-statistics-immigrants-and-immigration-united-states

Miller, D., Topping, K., & Thurston, A. (2010). Peer tutoring in reading: The effects of role and organization on two dimensions of self-esteem. *British Journal of Educational Psychology, 80,* 417–433. https://doi.org/10.1348/000709909X481652

Miller, T., Kosiewica, H., Knight, D., Ratway, B., Delhommer, S., & Levin, J. (2018). *Dual credit programs in Texas: Phase II.* American Institutes of Research. https://reportcenter.highered.texas.gov/reports/data/dual-credit-education-programs-in-texas-phase-ii1/

Minero, E. (2016). *Real-world learning with internships.* Edutopia. https://www.edutopia.org/practice/learning-through-internships-connecting-students-passions-real-world

Mitchell, C. (2018, October 30). Latino enrollment shrank where police worked with federal immigration authorities. *Education Week.* https://www.edweek.org/leadership/latino-enrollment-shrank-where-police-worked-with-federal-immigration-authorities/2018/10

Mitchell, C. (2019, March 19). Bilingual teachers are in short supply. How can schools cultivate their own? *Education Week.* https://www.edweek.org/teaching-learning/bilingual-teachers-are-in-short-supply-how-can-schools-cultivate-their-own/2019/03

Moll, L., Amanti, C., Neff, D., & Gonzalez, N. (1992). Funds of knowledge for teaching: Using a qualitative approach to connect homes and classrooms. *Theory Into Practice, 31*(2), 132–141. https://doi.org/10.1080/00405849209543534

Moquino, T., & Blum Martínez, R. (2017). Keres Children's Learning Center: The search for a linguistically and culturally appropriate education. https://static1.squarespace.com/static/5dd21f53fc6b713e17aa9d19/t/5f06218ebd6cfa7c6b832d8a/1594237327014/Moquino_Martinez+article.+TPE.pdf

Morris, M. (2018). *Pushout: The criminalization of Black girls in schools.* The New Press.

Munter, J., Tinajero, J., & del Campo, A. (2007). Engaging parents as leaders in schools with English language learners. In D. B. Hiatt-Michael (Ed.), *Promising practices for teachers to engage families of English language learners* (pp. 119–134). Information Age Publishing.

Murillo, E. G., Jr. (2002). How does it feel to be a problem? "Disciplining" the transnational subject in the New South. In S. Wortham, E. G. Murillo, & E. T. Hamann (Eds.), *Education in the new Latino diaspora: Policy and the politics of identity* (pp. 215–240). Ablex.

Napolitano, J. (2021). *The school I deserve: Six young refugees and their fight for equality in America.* Beacon Press.

National Academies of Sciences, Engineering, & Medicine. (2015). *The integration of immigrants into American society.* https://doi.org/10.17226/21746

National Academies of Sciences, Engineering, & Medicine. (2017). *Promoting the educational success of children and youth learning English: Promising futures.* The National Academies Press. https://doi.org/10.17226/24677

National Association of Secondary School Principals. (2021). *Undocumented students.* https://www.nassp.org/top-issues-in-education/position-statements/undocumented-students

National Center for Education Statistics. (2017). Disability Rates and Educational Attainment. https://nces.ed.gov/programs/coe/pdf/coe_tad.pdf

National Center for Education Statistics. (2021). *Status and trends in the education of racial and ethnic groups: Indicator 6: Elementary and secondary enrollment.* https://nces.ed.gov/programs/raceindicators/indicator_rbb.asp

National Child Traumatic Stress Network. (2011). *Refugee services core stressor assessment tool: Refugee services toolkit* [Web-based tool]. https://www.nctsn.org/resources/refugee-services-core-stressor-assessment-tool

National School Climate Center. (2021). *National School Climate Center.* https://schoolclimate.org

National School Reform Faculty. (2017). *Success analysis protocol with reflective questions.* https://www.nsrfharmony.org/wp-content/uploads/2017/10/success_analysis_reflective_0.pdf

Nebraska Department of Education. (2021). *2020–2021: Lincoln High School, high school classification.* https://nep.education.ne.gov/Schools/Index/55-0001-001?DataYears=20202021&type=HIGH%20SCHOOL#program-participation

New Teacher Center. (2018). *Instructional coaching practice standards.* https://newteachercenter.org/resources/instructional-coaching-practice-standards

New York State Education Department. (2016). *Students with interrupted/inconsistent formal education (SIFE): Questions and answers.* http://www.nysed.gov/common/nysed/files/programs/bilingual-ed/sife_q_a_9_20_16.pdf

New York State Education Department. (2019). *ELL identification & placement/home language questionnaire.* http://www.nysed.gov/bilingual-ed/ell-identification-placementhome-language-questionnaire

Noddings, N. (1984). *Caring: A feminine approach to ethics and moral education.* University of California Press.

Noddings, N. (1988). An ethic of caring and its implications for instructional arrangements. *American Journal of Education, 96*(2), 215–231. https://doi.org/10.1086/443894

Noguera, P. (2003). *City schools and the American dream: Reclaiming the promise of public education.* Teachers College Press.

Nordmeyer, J., & Honigseld, A. (2020). *WIDA collaboration focus bulletin.* Board of Regents of the University of Wisconsin System.

Novak, K. (2018, March 9). Why UDL matters for English language learners. *Language Magazine.* https://www.languagemagazine.com/2018/03/09/why-udl-matters-for-english-language-learners/

Oakes, J. (1985). *Keeping track: How schools structure inequality.* Yale University Press.

Oakland Unified School District. (n.d.). *OUSD is a sanctuary district.* https://www.ousd.org/Page/15870

Office of English Language Acquisition. (2016). *Newcomer tool kit.* U.S. Department of Education. https://www2.ed.gov/about/offices/list/oela/newcomers-toolkit/index.html

Oliveira, G. (2018). *Motherhood across borders: Immigrants and their children in Mexico and New York.* New York University Press.

Osofsky, D., Sinner, G., & Wolk, D. (2003). *Changing systems to personalize learning: The power of advisories.* The Education Alliance at Brown University. https://repository.library.brown.edu/studio/item/bdr:7zd8y9q9/

Otero, L., & Cammarota, J. (2011). Notes from the ethnic studies home front: Student protests, texting, and subtexts of oppression. *International Journal of Qualitative Studies in Education, 24*(5), 639–648. https://doi.org/10.1080/09518398.2011.600267

Panero, N., & Talbert, J. (2013). *Strategic inquiry: Starting small for big results in education.* Harvard Education Press.

Paris, D. (2012). Culturally sustaining pedagogy: A needed change in stance, terminology, and practice. *Educational Researcher, 41*(3), 93–97. https://doi.org/10.3102/0013189X12441244

Paris, D., & Alim, S. (2017). *Culturally sustaining pedagogies: Teaching and learning for justice in a changing world.* Teachers College Press.

Passel, J. S., & Cohn, D. (2018, November 27). *U.S. unauthorized immigrant total dips to lowest level in a decade.* Pew Research Center. https://www.pewresearch.org/hispanic/2018/11/27/u-s-unauthorized-immigrant-total-dips-to-lowest-level-in-a-decade/

Patel, L. (2013). *In loco emporium*: Immigrant youth and educators in the social contracts of education. *Children & Society, 27*(4), 309–320. https://doi.org/10.1111/chso.12032

Payne, C. (1995). *I've got the light of freedom: The organizing tradition and the Mississippi freedom struggle.* University of California Press.

Portes, A., & Zhou, M. (1993). The new second generation: Segmented assimilation and its variants. *The ANNALS of the American Academy of Political and Social Science, 530*(1), 74–96. https://doi.org/10.1177/0002716293530001006

Prasad, G. L. (2014). Portraits of plurilingualism in a French international school in Toronto: Exploring the role of visual methods to access students' representations of their linguistically diverse identities. *Canadian Journal of Applied Linguistics, 17*(1), 51–77. https://journals.lib.unb.ca/index.php/CJAL/article/view/22126

Prasad, G. L., Hyun, J., & Bettney, E. (in press). Designing critical multilingual multiliteracies projects with teachers in two-way-bilingual education. *Canadian Journal of Applied Linguistics.*

Quinn, R., & Nguyen, C. (2017). Immigrant youth organizing as civic preparation. *American Educational Research Journal, 54*(5), 972–1005. https://doi.org/10.3102/0002831217712946

Rancaño, V. (2020). *Jobs, laptops, food: How Rudsdale High teachers are helping newcomer students during COVID-19.* KQED. https://www.kqed.org/news/11817366/jobs-laptops-food-how-rudsdale-high-teachers-are-helping-newcomer-students-during-covid-19

Robertson, K., & Breiseth, L. (n.d.). *How to support refugee students in your school community.* Colorín Colorado. https://www.colorincolorado.org/article/how-support-refugee-students-ell-classroom

Robertson, K., & Lafond, S. (n.d.). *How to support ELL students with interrupted formal education (SIFEs).* Colorín Colorado. https://www.colorincolorado.org/article/how-support-ell-students-interrupted-formal-education-sifes

Roc, M., Ross, P., & Hernández, L. E. (2019). *Internationals Network for public schools: A deeper learning approach to supporting English learners.* Learning Policy Institute. https://learningpolicyinstitute.org/product/deeper-learning-networks-cs-internationals-network-report

Rodriguez, A. (2008). Toward a transformative teaching practice: Criticity, pedagogy and praxis. *International Journal of Learning, 15,* 345–352.

Rodriguez, D., Carrasquillo, A., García, E., & Howitt, D. (2020). Factors that challenge English learners and increase their dropout rates: Recommendations from the field. *International Journal of Bilingual Education and Bilingualism.* https://doi.org/10.1080/13670050.2020.1722059

Rodriguez, G. M., & Cruz, L. (2009). The transition to college of English learner and undocumented immigrant students: Resource and policy implications. *Teachers College Record, 111*(10), 2385–2418. https://doi.org/10.1177/016146810911101004

Rodriguez, S. (2020). "I was born at the border, like the 'wrong' side of it": Undocumented Latinx youth experiences of racialization in the U.S. South. *Anthropology & Education Quarterly, 51,* 496–526. https://doi.org/10.1111/aeq.12357

Rodriguez, S., Monreal, T., & Howard, J. (2020). "It's about hearing and understanding their stories": Teacher empathy and socio-political awareness toward newcomer undocumented students in the new Latino South. *Journal of Latinos and Education, 19*(2), 181–198. https://doi.org/10.1080/15348431.2018.1489812

Rooks, N. (2020). *Cutting school: The segrenomics of American education.* The New Press.

Rosales, J., & Walker, T. (2021). The racist beginnings of standardized testing. *NEA Today.* https://www.nea.org/advocating-for-change/new-from-nea/racist-beginnings-standardized-testing

Rosario, V. P., & Cao, V. (2015). *The CUNY-NYSIEB guide to translanguaging in Latino/a literature.* City University of New York (CUNY)–New York State Initiative on Emergent Bilinguals (NYSIEB). https://www.cuny-nysieb.org/wp-content/uploads/2016/05/CUNY-NYSIEB-Latino-Literature-Guide-Final-January-2015.pdf

Rowbottom, S., Arndt, R., Curran, P., & Cauchois, B. (2021, May 19). *Newcomer youth summer academy multi-tiered systems of support, culture & climate contributors.* The IRC in New York Education & Learning Department.

Rubin, B. (2007). "Laboratories of democracy": A situated perspective on learning social studies in detracked classrooms. *Theory & Research in Social Education, 35*(1), 62–95. https://doi.org/10.1080/00933104.2007.10473326

Rumbaut, R. G. (2012). Generation 1.5, educational experiences of. In J. A. Banks (Ed.), *Encyclopedia of diversity in education*. SAGE Publications.

Russell, S. G., Persaud, A., Mantilla Blanco, P. L., Webster, K., & Elliott, M. (2021). *Fostering belonging and civic identity: Perspectives from newcomer and refugee students in Arizona and New York*. Teachers College, Columbia University. https://doi.org/10.7916/d8-zw9k-dv30

Sadowski, M. (2013). *Portraits of promise: Voices of successful immigrant students*. Harvard Education Press.

Saenz, R., Filoteo, J., & Murga, A. (2007). Are Mexicans in the United States a threat to the American way of life? A response to Huntington. *Du Bois Review: Social Science Research on Race, 4*(2), 375–393. https://doi.org/10.1017/S1742058X0707021X

Safir, S. (2017). *Community walks create bonds of understanding*. Edutopia. https://www.edutopia.org/blog/community-walks-create-bonds-understanding-shane-safir

Salazar, M. (2008). English or nothing: The impact of rigid language policies on the inclusion of humanizing practices in a high school ESL program. *Equity & Excellence in Education, 41*, 341–356.

Salazar, M. (2013). A humanizing pedagogy: Reinventing the principles and practice of education as a journey toward liberation. *Review of Research in Education, 37*(1), 121–148. https://doi.org/10.3102/0091732X12464032

Samuels, B. (2021, September 27). Biden administration moves to preserve DACA after court ruling. *The Hill*. https://thehill.com/homenews/administration/574057-biden-administration-moves-to-preserve-daca-after-court-ruling

Samway, K. D. (2006). *When English language learners write*. Heinemann.

Samway, K. D., Pease-Alvarez, L., & Alvarez, L. (2020). *Supporting newcomer students: Advocacy and instruction for English learners*. W. W. Norton & Company.

Sánchez, M. T., García, O., & Solorza, C. (2018). Reframing language allocation policy in dual language bilingual education. *Bilingual Research Journal, 41*(1), 37–51. https://doi.org/10.1080/15235882.2017.1405098

Sanders, M. (2006). *Building school–community partnerships*. Corwin Press.

San Juan Unified School District. (2021). *Newcomer Summer School Program 2021*. https://www.secctv.org/video/san-juan-usd-summer-program-highlight-newcomer-summer-school/

Santos, M., Castellón Palacios, M., Cheuk, T., Greene, R., Mercado-Garcia, D., Zerkel, L., Hakuta, K., & Skarin, R. (2018). *Preparing English learners for college and career: Lessons from successful high schools*. Teachers College Press.

Sarr, K. G., & Mosselson, J. (2010). Issues in teaching refugees in U.S. schools. *Yearbook of the National Society for the Study of Education, 109*(2), 548–570.

Schools of Opportunity. (n.d.). *Lincoln High School*. https://schoolsofopportunity.org/recipient-details/lincoln-high-school

Schurr, S. L. (1992). *How to evaluate your middle school*. National Middle School Association.

Schurz High School. (2022). *New program! Adelitas: Women & femmes of courage*. https://www.schurzhs.org/apps/bbmessages/show_bbm.jsp?REC_ID=79059

Schweisfurth, M. (2013). *Learner-centred education in international perspective: Whose pedagogy for whose development?* Routledge.

Seilstad, B. (2021). *Educating adolescent newcomers in the superdiverse Midwest: Multilingual students in English-centric contexts.* Multilingual Matters.

Shapiro, S. (2018). Familial capital, narratives of agency, and the college transition process for refugee-background youth. *Equity & Excellence in Education, 51*(3–4), 332–346. https://doi.org/10.1080/10665684.2018.1546151

Short, D. J., & Boyson, B. A. (2012). *Helping newcomer students succeed in secondary schools and beyond.* Center for Applied Linguistics. https://www.carnegie .org/publications/helping-newcomer-students-succeed-in-secondary-schools-and -beyond/

Sims Bishop, R. (1990). Mirrors, windows, and sliding glass doors. *Perspectives, 1*(3), ix–xi.

Sleeter, C. (2005). *Un-standardizing curriculum: Multicultural teaching in the standards-based classroom.* Teachers College Press.

Soto, I. (2012). *ELL shadowing as a catalyst for change.* SAGE Publications.

SPLC. (n.d.). *Resources for educators and school administrators: Protecting immigrant students' rights.* Southern Poverty Law Center. https://www.splcenter.org /resources-educators-school-administrators

Stewart, M. A., & Hansen-Thomas, H. (2020). Co-learning, translanguaging and English language acquisition. *Research OUTREACH, 116.* https://researchoutreach .org/articles/co-learning-translanguaging-english-language-acquisition/

Strauss, V. (2017). 34 problems with standardized tests. *Washington Post.* https:// www.washingtonpost.com/news/answer-sheet/wp/2017/04/19/34-problems-with -standardized-tests/

Style, E. (1996). "Curriculum as window & mirror": National Seeking Educational Equity & Diversity Project. The National SEED Project. https://nationalseedproject .org/Key-SEED-Texts/curriculum-as-window-and-mirror

Suárez-Orozco, C., & Osei-Twumasi, O. (Eds.). (2019). *Immigrant-origin students in community college: Navigating risk and reward in higher education.* Teachers College Press.

Suárez-Orozco, C., Pimentel, A., & Martin, M. (2009). The significance of relationships: Academic engagement and achievement among newcomer immigrant youth. *Teachers College Record, 111*(3), 712–149.

Suárez-Orozco, C., & Strom, A. (2021). *Moving stories in the classroom.* Re-Imagining Migration. https://reimaginingmigration.org/in-the-classroom/

Suárez-Orozco, C., Suárez-Orozco, M. M., & Todorova, I. (2008). *Learning a new land: Immigrant students in American society.* Belknap Press.

Suárez-Orozco, C., Yoshikawa, H., & Tseng, V. (2015). *Intersecting inequalities: Research to reduce inequality for immigrant-origin children and youth.* William T. Grant Foundation. https://wtgrantfoundation.org/library/uploads/2015 /09/Intersecting-Inequalities-Research-to-Reduce-Inequality-for-Immigrant -Origin-Children-and-Youth.pdf

Sugarman, J. (2015). *Meeting the education needs of rising numbers of newly arrived migrant students in Europe and the United States.* Migration Policy Institute. https://www.migrationpolicy.org/news/meeting-education-needs-rising-numbers -newly-arrived-migrant-students-europe-and-united-states

Sugarman, J. (2019). *The unintended consequences for English learners of using the four-year graduation rate for school accountability.* Migration Policy Institute. https://www.migrationpolicy.org/sites/default/files/publications/ELGradRates-FINALWEB.pdf

Swail, W. S., Cabrera, A., Lee, C., & Williams A. (2005). *Latino students and the educational pipeline: Pathways to the bachelor's degree for Latino students.* Educational Policy Institute.

Symons, C., & Ponzio, C. (2019). Schools cannot do it alone: A community-based approach to refugee youth's language development. *Journal of Research in Childhood Education, 33*(1), 98–118. https://doi.org/10.1080/02568543.2018.1531450

Tate, W. F. (1995). Returning to the root: A culturally relevant approach to mathematics pedagogy. *Theory Into Practice, 34*(3), 166–173. https://doi.org/10.1080/00405849509543676

Tellez, K., & Waxman, H. (2006). *Preparing quality educators for English language learners: Research, policies and practices.* Lawrence Erlbaum.

Tervalon, M., & Murray-García, J. (1998). Cultural humility versus cultural competence: A critical distinction in defining physician training outcomes in multicultural education. *Journal of Health Care for the Poor and Underserved, 9,* 117–125. https://doi.org/10.1353/hpu.2010.0233

Thomas, L. (2019). *7 Smart, fast ways to do formative assessment.* Edutopia. https://www.edutopia.org/article/7-smart-fast-ways-do-formative-assessment

Thompson, A. (1998). Not for the color purple: Black feminist lessons for educational caring. *Harvard Educational Review, 68*(4), 522–555. https://doi.org/10.17763/haer.68.4.nm436v83214n5016

Thorpe, H. (2017). *The newcomers: Finding refuge, friendship, and hope in an American classroom.* Scribner.

Tomlinson, C. A. (2016). *The differentiated classroom: Responding to the needs of all learners* (2nd ed.). Pearson.

Tomlinson, C. A., & Imbeau, M. B. (2010). *Leading and managing a differentiated classroom.* ASCD.

Turner, E. O., & Mangual Figueroa, A. (2019). Immigration policy and education in lived reality: A framework for researchers and educators. *Educational Researcher, 48*(8), 549–557. https://doi.org/10.3102/0013189X19872496

Tyack, D. (1967). *Turning points in American educational history.* Blaisdell.

Tyack, D. (1976). Ways of seeing: An essay on the history of compulsory schooling. *Harvard Educational Review, 46*(3), 355–389. https://doi.org/10.17763/haer.46.3.v73405527200106v

UCLA Law. (n.d.). *Immigrant Family Legal Clinic.* https://law.ucla.edu/academics/clinical-education/clinics/immigrant-family-legal-clinic

UC San Diego Center for Research on Educational Equity, Assessment & Teaching Excellence. (2019). *The educational value of alumni for public high schools.* Yankelovich Center for Social Science Research. https://yankelovichcenter.ucsd.edu/_files/Alumni%20Engagement%20Research%20Report%20FINAL%202019.pdf

Ulloa, J. (2017, September 16). California lawmakers approve landmark 'sanctuary state' bill to expand protections for immigrants. *Los Angeles Times.* https://www.latimes.com/politics/la-pol-ca-california-sanctuary-state-bill-20170916-story.html

Umansky, I. (2016). Leveled and exclusionary tracking: English learners' access to core content in middle school. *American Educational Research Journal, 53,* 1792–1833. https://doi.org/10.3102/0002831216675404

Umansky, I., Hopkins, M., Dabach, D. B., Porter, L., Thompson, K., & Pompa, D. (2018). *Understanding and supporting the educational needs of recently arrived immigrant English learner students: Lessons for state and local education agencies.* Council of Chief State School Officers. https://ccsso.org/sites/default/files /2018-04/Understanding%20and%20Supporing%20the%20Educational%20 Needs%20of%20RAIELs.pdf

UNHCR. (2021). *What is a refugee?* The UN Refugee Agency. https://www.unhcr.org /en-us/what-is-a-refugee.html

United Nations. (1948). *Universal Declaration of Human Rights.* https://www.un.org /en/about-us/universal-declaration-of-human-rights

U.S. News. (2019). *International Community High School.* https://www.usnews.com /education/best-high-schools/new-york/districts/new-york-city-public-schools /international-community-high-school-13168#test_scores_section

Valentino, R. A., & Reardon, S. F. (2015). Effectiveness of four instructional programs designed to serve English learners: Variation by ethnicity and initial English proficiency. *Educational Evaluation and Policy Analysis, 37,* 612–637. https://doi.org /10.3102/0162373715573310

Valenzuela, A. (1999). *Subtractive schooling: U.S.-Mexican youth and the politics of caring.* State University of New York Press.

van Nieuwerburgh, C. (Ed.). (2012). *Coaching in education: Getting better results for students, educators, and parents.* Routledge.

van Nieuwerburgh, C., & Love, D. (2019). *Advanced coaching practice: Inspiring change in others.* SAGE Publications.

Villavicencio, A., Jaffe-Walter, R., & Klevan, S. (2021). "You can't close your door here": Leveraging teacher collaboration to improve outcomes for immigrant English learners. *Teaching and Teacher Education 97.* https://doi.org/10.1016/j.tate .2020.103227

Villenas, S. (2002). Reinventing "educación" in new Latino communities: Pedagogies of change and continuity in North Carolina. In S. Wortham, E. G. Murillo, Jr., & E. T. Hamann (Eds.), *Education in the new Latino diaspora* (pp. 17–36). Ablex Press.

Vygotsky, L. S. (1978). *Mind in society: The development of higher psychological processes.* Harvard University Press.

Walia, H. (2021). *Border and rule: Global migration, capitalism, and the rise of racist nationalism.* Haymarket.

Walqui, A. (2006). Scaffolding instruction for English language learners: A conceptual framework. *International Journal of Bilingual Education and Bilingualism, 9*(2), 159–180. https://doi.org/10.1080/13670050608668639

Walqui, A., & Van Lier, L. (2010). *Scaffolding the academic success of adolescent English language learners: A pedagogy of promise.* WestEd.

Walsh, D. (2018). Youth participatory action research as culturally sustaining pedagogy. *Theory Into Practice, 57*(2), 127–136. https://doi.org/10.1080/00405841 .2018.1433939

Waters, M. C., Tran, V. C., Kasinitz, P., & Mollenkopf, J. H. (2010). Segmented assimilation revisited: Types of acculturation and socioeconomic mobility in young adulthood. *Ethnic and Racial Studies, 33*(7), 1168–1193. https://doi.org/10.1080/01419871003624076

Watzinger-Tharp, J., Tharp, D. S., & Rubio, F. (2021). Sustaining dual language immersion: Partner language outcomes in a statewide program. *The Modern Language Journal, 105*(1), 194–217. https://doi.org/10.1111/modl.12694

Waxman, A. (2017a, April 6). *Immigrant students organize to create safe haven at MPS*. Milwaukee Neighborhood News Service. https://milwaukeenns.org/2017/04/06/immigrant-students-organize-to-create-safe-haven-at-mps/

Waxman, A. (2017b, April 7). *Every school a sanctuary*. Urban Milwaukee. https://urbanmilwaukee.com/2017/04/07/every-school-a-sanctuary/

Webb & Gerwin. (2014). *Early College Expansion: Propelling Students to Post-Secondary Success, at a School Near You*. Jobs for the Future. https://files.eric.ed.gov/fulltext/ED559689.pdf

Wellstone International High School Studies. (2019). *Green Card youth voices: Immigration stories from a Minneapolis high school*. Green Card Voices.

Welner, K., & Kelley, L. M. (2018, May 16). A haven for refugees, this Nebraska high school builds a web of support for its diverse student population. *Washington Post*. https://www.washingtonpost.com/news/answer-sheet/wp/2018/05/16/a-haven-for-refugees-this-nebraska-high-school-builds-a-web-of-support-for-its-diverse-student-population/

WIDA. (2020). *WIDA English language development standards framework, 2020 edition: Kindergarten–grade 12*. https://wida.wisc.edu/sites/default/files/resource/WIDA-ELD-Standards-Framework-2020.pdf

Wiley, T. G., & García, O. (2016). Language policy and planning in language education: Legacies, consequences, and possibilities. *The Modern Language Journal, 100*(S1), 48–63. https://doi.org/10.1111/modl.12303

Wong, S., Sánchez Gosnell, E., Luu, A.M.F., & Dodson, L. (Eds.). (2017). *Teachers as allies: Transformative practices for teaching DREAMers and undocumented students*. Teachers College Press.

Woods, P. (2021). Democratic leadership. In R. Papa (Ed.), *Oxford encyclopedia of educational administration*. Oxford University Press. https://oxfordre.com/education/view/10.1093/acrefore/9780190264093.001.0001/acrefore-9780190264093-e-609

Woods, T., & Hanson, D. (2016). *Demographic trends of children of immigrants*. Urban Institute.

Wright, W. E., & Ricento, T. (2016). Language policy and education in the USA. *Language Policy and Political Issues in Education*, 1–18. https://doi.org/10.1007/978-3-319-02320-5_29-1

York-Barr, J., & Duke, K. (2004). What do we know about teacher leadership? Findings from two decades of scholarship. *Review of Educational Research, 74*(3), 255–316. https://doi.org/10.3102/00346543074003255

Yosso, T. J. (2005). Whose culture has capital? A critical race theory discussion of community cultural wealth. *Race, Ethnicity and Education, 8*(1), 69–91. https://doi.org/10.1080/1361332052000341006

Zaldivar, G. (2020, December 24). Soccer Without Borders is using the beautiful game to build a more inclusive world. *En Fuego*. https://www.enfuegonow.com/news/soccer-without-borders-is-building-a-more-inclusive-world

Zhou, M. (1997). Segmented assimilation: Issues, controversies, and recent research on the new second generation. *International Migration Review, 31*(4), 975–1008. https://doi.org/10.1177/019791839703100408

Zhou, M., & Gonzalez, R. (2019). Divergent destinies: Children of immigrants growing up in the United States. *Annual Review of Sociology, 45*(1), 383–399. https://doi.org/10.1146/annurev-soc-073018-022424

Index

Abrego, L. J., 185
Abu El-Haj, T., 6, 8, 112
Acevedo, N., 155
ACTE (Association for Career & Technical
    Education), 167
Action Research course (CUNY), 127–130
Adamson, F., 69
Adelitas: Women and Femmes of Courage,
    162, 163
Adger, C., 109, 110, 160, 166
Advancement Project, 66
Advisory periods, 70–75
After-school programming, 141–143
Aguilar, E., 97, 100, 101
Alba, R., 5
Alim, S., 1, 5, 7, 38, 128
Alum engagement, 174–178
    alum as staff, 93–95
American Civil Liberties Union, 159
American Federation of Teachers, 159
American Immigration Council, 185
AmeriCorps program, 92, 138–139, 176
Anaissie, T., 102
Ancess, J., 89
Ansari, S., x
Anti-immigrant policy, 113–114
Antrop-González, R., 15, 16, 72
Anyon, J., 1
Apple, M. W., 86, 90
Argenal, Amy, x, 1, 6, 7, 16, 38, 63
ARISE High School (Oakland, California),
    176
Arts-based partnerships, 161–162
Ascenzi-Moreno, L., 86
"Asiatic Barred Zone Act" (1917), 5
Assessments
    holistic and continuous, 63–68
    portfolios, 30, 64, 66–68
    project-based, 66–68
Assimilation, 5–6
Asylees/asylum, 184

Atteberry, A., 143
Au, W., 66
Auslander, L., 102
Ayers, W., 2

Background information, gathering, 38
    home visits, 149–151
    student intake interview form, 39
Bahruth, R. E., 14
Bajaj, Monisha, ix, x, xi, 1, 6, 7, 8, 16, 33,
    38, 42, 46, 63, 123, 124, 151, 152, 161,
    165
Baker, B., 187
Bangura, R., 9
Barros, S., 33
Bartlett, Lesley, ix, x–xi, 1, 6, 8, 16, 32, 33,
    37, 42, 46, 105, 112, 116, 141, 142,
    165
Bartolomé, Lilia, 15, 95
Batalova, J., 185
Batten-Bowman, Emma, 137, 154, 161
Beane, J. A., 86, 90
Beeman, K., 106
Benson, T., 99
Biden, President Joe, 184
Bigelow, M., 55
Blackledge, A., 106
Blad, E., 72, 75
Blum Martínez, R., 5
Boaler, J., 44
Bond, Nathan, 90
Boston International High School (Boston,
    Massachusetts), 56
Bourdieu, P., 1, 9
Boyson, B. A., 12, 45, 48, 114
Breiseth, L., 113, 124
Bridges to Academic Success, 56–61, 62, 107
Bridging Refugee Youth and Children's
    Services, 118, 131, 146, 153, 162
Bristol, T., 91, 92
Bronx International High School, 66–67

Brooklyn College, 127
Brooklyn International High School
  (Brooklyn, New York), 46, 92, 108, 128
Brown v. Board of Education, 4
Budiman, A., 187
Buhain, V., 146
Bui, T., 42
Bundy, D., 119
Burris, C., 44
Byars-Winston, A. M., 125

Calderón, M., 35
California Department of Education, 137
California High School Exit Examination
  (CAHSEE), 63
Callahan, R. M., 44, 53, 185
Cammarota, J., 6, 7, 128
Canlas, Melissa, x, 1, 6, 7, 16, 38, 63
Canyon Valley School, 41–42
Cao, V., 34
Career development programs, 167–173
CARING school environments, 15–16, 181
Carnegie Corporation "Turning Point"
  Report, 71
Carrasquillo, A., 53
CASEL, 57
CAST (Center for Applied Special
  Technology), 49, 50, 54
Castellón, M., 47, 56, 64, 67, 68, 71, 86,
  115, 164
Castellón Palacios, M., 173
Caterall, J., 161
Celic, C. M., 35
Cenoz, J., 35
Centers for Disease Prevention and Control
  (CDC), 124
Changing Worlds Arts, Cultural, and Literacy
  Connections, 162
Cherng, H.-Y. S., 91
Cheuk, T., 173
Chinese Exclusion Act (1882), 5
Christian, D., 110
Cioè-Peña, M., 57
City University of New York (CUNY), 127
City University of New York, Initiative
  on Immigration and Education
  (CUNY-IIE), 43
Civic engagement and social support,
  160–166
Coaching, school-based, 97–102
Coalition for Community Schools, 11
Cohn, D., 154

College
  community college, 22
  dual enrollment programs, 125–131
  readiness for, 83
College Now (CN), 127
Collier, V., 91
Collins, C., 115, 156, 157, 159
Colorín Colorado, 43, 114, 126, 131, 157,
  185
Commins, N., 45
Community cultural wealth, 9–11
Community partnerships, 92–95, 138–140,
  160–166, 171–172
Community walks, 151–153
Connor, McVeigh, 143
Coordination of Student Services Team
  (COST), 123
Costello, M., 113
COVID-19 pandemic, 72–73, 139–140, 143
Creese, A., 106
Cruz, L., 125
Cultural Ambassadors (Lincoln, Nebraska),
  21
Cultural capital, 9–11
Cultural heritages and histories, honoring,
  37–43
Culturally relevant pedagogy, 7
Culturally responsive teaching, 97–102
Cunningham, G., 156
Custodio, B., 55, 62

DACA (Deferred Action for Childhood
  Arrivals), 176, 184–185
Dallman, Carol, 80
Darling-Hammond, L., 2, 48, 69
de Castro, Nedda, 26
Decker, L. E., 160
Deferred Action for Childhood Arrivals
  (DACA), 176, 184–185
De Jesús, A., 15, 16, 72
De Jong, E., 45
de Mejía, A. M., 35
Democratic school governance, 85–90
Deroo, M. R., 108
Deutsch, N. L., 141
Diarrassouba, N., 99
Differentiated instruction (DI), 29–30, 49–53
Doris Henderson Newcomers School
  (Greensboro, NC), 12
DREAM Act, 184–185
"Dreamers," 176, 184–185
Dreamers of Wisconsin (DoW), 164

Dream teams, 165, 189
"Dropout" as label, 3
Dual enrollment programs, 125–131
Dual language immersion (DLI) models, 108
Duke, K., 86
Duncan-Andrade, J., 16
Dyrness, A., 6, 8

Early college programs, 125–131
Echevarria, J., 35, 53
EdBuild, 2
Edmondson, A., 87, 99
Edmunds, J., 126
Education Alliance, 75
EdWeek, 53
Ee, J., 113
El Diario, 164–165
Elementary and Secondary Education Act,
    104–105
Ellis, E., 91
Emergent bilinguals (EBs), 20
English Language Learners (ELL), 185
ESL (English as a second language) programs,
    20, 105, 185
Experiential instruction, 170–171

Family histories, 40–43
Family involvement, 147–153
Fass, P., 5, 7
Fedestin, B., 128
Feldblum, M., 185
Fenner, D. S., 125, 126
Ferlazzo, L., 54
FERPA (Family Educational Rights and
    Privacy Act) guidelines, 155, 157
Fiarman, S., 99
Figlio, D., 44
Fine, M., 128
Fink, J., 126
Fishman, E., 2
Flores Settlement Agreement (1997), 187
Florian, L., 50
Flushing International High School (Queens,
    New York), 165
Ford, K., 52
Forte, I., 71
Fort Worth International Newcomer
    Academy, 161
Fouad, N. A., 125
Fránquiz, M., 14
Frayer model graphic organizers, 29–30
Freedom Schools (YES!), 165

Freeman Field, 109
Freire, Paulo, x, 14, 128, 181

Gándara, P., 113
García, Ofelia, x–xi, 1, 8, 15, 16, 27, 31,
    32, 33, 37, 46, 57, 104, 105, 116,
    151, 185
Gardner, T., 176, 178
Gay, G., 1
Gay-Straight Alliance (GSA) club, 143
Gershenson, S., 91, 143
Gerwin, Carol, 126
Ghaffar-Kucher, Ameena, xi
Giani, M., 126
Gibbons, P., 57
Giegerich, A., 161
Ginwright, S., 6
Giroux, H., 1
Gist, C. D., 92
Glass, G., 45
Glazer, N., 6
Global Potential, 167, 171
Goldberg, C. A., 4
Goldenberg, C., 34, 35, 108, 110
Gomez, M. N., 99
Gonzales, R. G., 125
Gonzalez, R., 6
Gorter, D., 35
Graff, C. S., 153
Green Card Voices, 118
Green Card Youth Voices, 82
Greene, R., 173
Gregorio Luperón High School (New York
    City), 32, 42, 92, 105, 115–116,
    164–165
Griffith, Caitlyn, 112, 145
Groupings, purposeful, 44–48

Hakuta, K., 173
Halpin, P. F., 91
Halverson, E. R., 161
Hamayan, E., 109
Hansen-Thomas, H., 35
Hanson, D., 104
Hantzopoulos, M., 16, 64, 66, 68
Harvard Educational Review, 129, 130
Hawkins, M., 16
Health Resources and Service Administration,
    120
Health services in schools, 119–124
Heiman, D., 152
Herrera, S., 50

Hertz, Daniel, 80, 83
Heterogeneous groupings, 28–29, 47–48
Hing, B. O., x
Hmong American Partnership (HAP), 161–162
Hmoob Teen Magazine, 161–162
Hodge, A., 126
Holland, D., x
Home and community language questionnaires, 106–107, 110
Home languages, 8
  interaction in, 35
  as resources, 27–28
Homeroom periods (advisory periods), 70–75
Home visits, 149–151
Honigsfeld, A., 108
Hos, R., 55
Hossaini, S., 178
Howard, J., 7
Hudson, T., 69
Huerta, T. M., 15
Hull Sypnieski, K., 54
Hutzel, K., 161

Imbeau, M. B., 49, 51
Immigrant and Refugee Community Organization (IRCO) (Portland, Oregon), 161
Immigrant and refugee students, statistics and trends, 2–3, 185–186
Immigrant Legal Resource Center, 187
Immigrants Rising, 173, 187
Immigration and Customs Enforcement (ICE), 154–155, 156
Immigration and Nationality Act (1965), 5
Individuals With Disabilities in Education Act (IDEA), 113
Interdisciplinary projects, 38–40
International Center for Accelerated Language Learning (ICALL), 80–84
International Community High School (South Bronx, New York), 57
International High School (Queens, New York), 163–164
International High School at Prospect Heights (Brooklyn, New York), 47, 85, 167, 168–172
International Newcomer Academy (Fort Worth, Texas), 112, 115
International Rescue Committee (IRC), 120, 141, 144–145, 160–161
  Leaders-in-Training, 163

Internationals Network for Public Schools (INPS), ix, 27, 32–33, 46, 67, 72, 81, 103, 176, 188
Irujo, S., 49, 52

Jacobson, L., 143
Jaffe-Walter, R., ix, xi, 113, 126
Jiménez, Rosa, 10, 11, 35
Johnson, A., 144
Johnson, President Lyndon B., 5
Jordan, A., 50
Joyce, B. R., 97

Kamat, Anjali, 52
Kangas, S. E., 144
Kanno, Y., 144
Katzenmeyer, M. H., 86
Kegan, R., 99, 102
Kelley, R. D., 1, 117, 142
Kessler, J., 45, 46, 48
Kimsey-House, K., 102
Kirksey, J. J., 113, 154, 155
Kleyn, T. (Tatyana), 8, 27, 31, 57, 164, 166, 185
Knight, J., 99, 100, 101, 102
Know Your Rights workshops, 40, 41, 113, 145, 155–157
Kofiro, Ali, 80, 92
Korematsu v. U.S. (1994), 47
Kraft, M. A., 97, 98

Ladson-Billings, Gloria, 1, 7
La Follette High School (Madison, Wisconsin), 33, 34, 42, 108
Lafond, S., 62
LaGuardia Community College (Queens, New York), 163–164
Lahey, L., 99, 102
Lampert, M., 99, 102
Language Lizard, 118
Language policies, 104–110
Lave, J., 128
Leadership and democratic school governance, 85–90
Learning for Justice, 43, 113, 156
Lee, E., x
Lee, S., xi, 6, 7, 16, 38, 128
Lee, S. J., 126
Legal services, 154–159
Leung, C., 69
Lincoln High School (Lincoln, Nebraska), 117, 142

Linklater, H., 50
Locke, J., 160, 166
Loewus, L., 3
Lomawaima, K. T., 5
Love, D., 99
Lucas, T., 102
Luce-Celler Act (1946), 5
Luft, Joe, 176
Lukes, M., 3

Macleod, C., 6
Mam (Indigenous) language, 176–178
Mangual Figueroa, A., 6
Manhattan Bridges High School (New York
    City), 47, 164
Manhattan International High School
    (New York City), 66–67
Manning, Mandy, 150
Marble Hill School for International Studies
    (Bronx, New York), 67–68, 71
Markham, L., 2
Martínez, Gabriela "Gaby," ix–x, 175
Martin-Fernandez, J., 91
McCarty, T. L., 5
McDonald, M., 99
McEachin, A., 143
McKnight, K., 150
Mehl, G., 126
Mendenhall, Mary, ix, xi, 141, 142
Mendez v. Westminster, 4
Menken, K., 33, 63, 69, 104, 109, 116,
    151
Mental health services, 119–122
Mercado-Garcia, D., 173
Metalinguistic awareness, 35
Migration Policy Institute, 2, 155
Miller, T., 126
Milwaukee Public Schools, 165
Minero, E., 173
Mirror/window metaphor, 37–38
Mitchell, C., 91, 113
Moll, L., 7, 19
Moller, G. V., 86
Monreal, T., 7
Moquino, T., 5
Morris, M., 3
Mosselson, J., 111
Moynihan, D., 6
Multilingual texts, 33–34
Munter, J., 41, 42
Murillo E. G., Jr., x
Murray-García, J., 16, 152

Napolitano, J., 5
National Academies of Sciences,
    Engineering, & Medicine, 1, 2, 34
National Association of Secondary School
    Principals, 155
National Center for Education Statistics, 3,
    5, 50
National Early College Initiative, 126
National Education Association, 90
National School Climate Center, 111
National School Reform Faculty, 102
Nebraska Department of Education, 19
Nee, V., 5
Negrón-Gonzales, G., 185
Newcomer Academy (Boston,
    Massachusetts), 56
Newcomer programs, 44–45
    and advisory periods, 72–75
    pathways to learning, 51–53
    students, 186
    types of, 12
Newcomer Summer Schools, 143, 144
Newcomer Youth Summer Academy (NYSA),
    144–146
New Roots Garden Project, 120
New Teacher Center, 99, 100–101
New World High School (Bronx, New York),
    55–56, 97, 115
New York Performance Standards
    Consortium, 66–67
New York State Education Department
    (NYSED), 107, 186
New York State Home Language
    Questionnaire, 110
New York State Youth Leadership Council,
    165
Nguyen, C., 6
No Child Left Behind Act, 66, 80, 104
Noddings, N., 15
Noguera, P., 16
Nordmeyer, J., 108
Novak, K., 52

Oakes, Jeannie, 44
Oakland International High School
    (Oakland, California), 38–40, 43, 46,
    70, 71, 92, 117, 120, 122, 127, 132,
    143, 147, 149, 151–152, 175–177, 188
Oakland Unified School District, 156
Obama, President Barack, 184
Office of English Language Acquisition, 118,
    142, 149, 164, 184

Oliveira, G., 6, 8
Olmstead, Leigh, 80, 81
O'Loughlin, J., 55, 62
Oral History Nights (Canyon Valley School),
    41–42
Osei-Twumasi, O., 130
Osofsky, D., 72
Otero, L., 7

Page, M., 44
Panero, N., 99
Paris, D., 1, 5, 7, 38, 128
Passel, J. S., 154
Passeron, J., 1
Patel, L., 7
Payne, C., 1
PBATs (project-based assessment tasks),
    66–67
Peer observation, 89–90
Peers as resources, 28–29
Peer tutoring, 142
Penna, A., 1
Plessy v. Ferguson, 4
Plyler v. Doe, 155, 187
Ponzio, C., 108, 143
Portes, A., 6
Portfolios, in assessment process, 30, 64,
    66–68
Positive culture, 111–118
Prasad, G. L., 35, 106
Predictable pedagogical routines, 29–30
Prism, curricular materials as, 38, 42
Problem We All Live With, The (Fedestin), 128
Profiles, school
    International High School at Prospect
        Heights (Brooklyn, New York),
        26–30
    Lincoln High School, Nebraska, 19–22
    Rudsdale Newcomer High School,
        136–140
    Wellstone International High School,
        80–84
Profiles, student
    Ana, 17–18
    Asmaa, 76–77
    Ko, 23–24
    Miguel, 132–133
    Shaheen, 179–180
Project-based learning and assessment, 66–68
Public education for immigrant families
    history of, 4–7
    inequalities and challenges, 1–2

Quinn, R., 6
Quintero, D., 103

Rabin, Nina, 157–158
Radio B'alam, 177–178
Rancaño, V., 137
Reardon, S. F., 143
Refugee Educator Academy, 96
Refugee students, 6, 186. See also Immigrant
    and refugee students
Rehabilitation Act (1973), 113
Re-imagining Migration, 96
Relational engagement, 9
Relevance of student backgrounds, 38–40
Restorative justice, 115–116
Reyes, Rocio, 74
Ricento, T., 104
Richmond High School Internationals
        Academy (Richmond, California), 72, 74
Robertson, K., 62, 124
Roc, M., 67
Rodriguez, A., 15
Rodriguez, D., 53
Rodriguez, G. M., 125
Rodriguez, S., 6, 7
Rooks, N., 5
Rosales, J., 63
Rosario, V. P., 34
Rubin, B., 6
Rudsdale Newcomer High School (Oakland,
        California), 92, 97, 108, 116, 120,
        136–140, 154, 161
Rumbaut, Rubén G., 186
Russell, S. G., 142

Sadowski, Michael, 2, 3–4
Saenz, R., 6
Safe zones (sanctuary districts), 113–114,
        155–156, 165
Safir, S., 153
Salazar, M., 14, 15, 37, 38
Sales, Henry, 176–177
Samuels, B., 184
Samway, K. D., ix, 5, 12, 50, 150, 151
Sánchez, M. T., 105
Sanctuary districts (safe zones), 113–114,
        155–156, 165
Sanders, M., 160
San Juan Unified School District (Sacramento,
        California), 144
Santos, M., 2, 173
Sarr, K. G., 111

Sattin-Bajaj, Carolyn, 113, 155
School environments, positive, 15–16,
    111–118
Schools of Opportunity, 19
Schurr, S. L., 71
Schurz High School, 162, 163
Schweisfurth, M., 46
Segmented assimilation theory, 6
Seilstad, B., 2, 63
Shapiro, S., 8, 10
Short, D. J., 12, 45, 48, 114
Showers, B., 97
SIFE (Students With Interrupted Formal
    Education), 22, 55–62, 186–187
Sims Bishop, R., 38
Sin Nombre (film), 151
Skarin, R., 173
Sleeter, Christine, 37
SLIFE (Students With Limited or Interrupted
    Formal Education), 22, 55–62, 186–187
Snell, T., 57
Snow, S., 110
Soccer Without Borders (SWB), 123–124,
    142–143, 176
Social support and civic engagement,
    160–166
Socioemotional support, 169–170
Solís, Diana, 162
South Division High School (Milwaukee,
    Wisconsin), 117
Southern Poverty Law Center, 159
South High School (Denver, Colorado), 49,
    120, 160
Spanish for Heritage Learners (SHL), 20
Special Immigrant Juvenile Status (SIJS), 158,
    187
Special needs, modifications for, 49–50
Staffing, intentional, 91–96
Staples, M., 44
Stewart, M. A., 35
Strauss, V., 15
Strom, A., 42
Style, E., 37
Suárez-Orozco, Carola, 9, 15, 37, 42, 72,
    130, 186
Suárez-Orozco, Marcelo, 9
"Success," definitions of, 3–4
Sugarman, J., 3, 186
Sullivan High School (Chicago, Illinois), 146
Summer programming, 143–146
Supporting Newcomer Students (Samway
    et al.), 12

Suresh, Sailaja, ix, x, 66, 123, 124, 151, 152,
    174
Swail, W. S., 44
Sylvan, C., 46
Symons, C., 143

Talbert, J., 99
Tate, W. F., 1
Teacher development. See Coaching,
    school-based
Teaching Tolerance (Learning for Justice), 43,
    113, 156
Tellez, K., 50
Tervalon, M., 16, 152
Theory Into Practice (journal), ix
Thomas, L., 65, 91
Thompson, A., 15
Thorpe, H., 2, 49, 120, 160
Todorova, Irina, 9
Tomlinson, C. A., 49, 51
Tow, D., x, 161
Tracking, 44
Transitional bilingual education (TBE), 105
Translanguaging, 8, 27, 31–36, 105
Transnational connections, 7–9
Trump, President Donald, 184
Turner, E. O., 6
Tyack, D., 5
Tyner-Mullings, A. R., 66

UCLA Immigrant Family Legal Clinic,
    157–158
UC San Diego Center for Research, 175
Ulloa, J., 156
Umansky, I., 2, 55, 144
Unaccompanied minors, 187
Undocumented immigrants, 187
United Nations, 184
United Nations Convention on the Status of
    Refugees, 186
United Nations High Commission for
    Refugees (UNHCR), 23, 186
Universal design for learning (UDL),
    49–53
Urow, C., 106
USCIS (United States Citizenship and
    Immigration Services), 186
U. S. News, 57

Valentino, R. A., 143
Valenzuela, A., 15
Valverde, Lisa, 33, 42

Van Lier, L., 27, 50
van Nieuwerburgh, C., 97, 98, 99
Villavicencio, A., 86
Villenas, S., x
Voces de la Frontera, 165
Vygotsky, L. S., 29

Walia, H., 6
Walker, T., 63
Walqui, A., 27, 28, 50, 58
Walsh, Daniel "Danny," xi, 6, 7, 38, 76, 127, 128–129
Waters, M. C., 6
Watson, J., 55
Watzinger-Tharp, J., 105
Waxman, A., 114, 165
Waxman, H., 50
Webb, Michael, 126
Wei, L., 27, 31, 185
Welcoming environments, 111–118
Wellstone, Paul, 81
Wellstone International High School (Minneapolis, Minnesota), 80–84, 92, 108, 115, 117, 127

Welner, K., 117, 142
Wenger, E., 128
Wentworth, L., 48
WIDA, 34, 56, 105
WIDA Screener, 107
Wiley, T. G., 104
Willemsen, Laura Wangsness, 80
Window/mirror metaphor, 37–38
Wong, S., 155
Woods, P., 86
Woods, T., 104
Wright, W. E., 104

Yip, J., 102
York-Barr, J., 86
Yosso, Tara (T. J.), 1, 7, 10, 11, 152
Youth Empowered in the Struggle (YES!), 165
Youth participatory action research (YPAR), 128, 129

Zaldivar, G., 143
Zerkel, L., 173
Zhou, M., 6

About the Authors and the Contributors

Monisha Bajaj is a professor in the Department of International and Multicultural Education at the University of San Francisco and a visiting professor at the Nelson Mandela University in South Africa.

Daniel Walsh has worked at all levels of education from K–5 to secondary to undergraduate and graduate teacher education, in both the United States and abroad. He currently teaches undergraduate courses in the Education Policy Studies Department at the University of Wisconsin–Madison.

Lesley Bartlett is professor and chair of the Department of Educational Policy Studies at the University of Wisconsin–Madison and currently serves as the co-editor of *Anthropology and Education Quarterly*.

Gabriela Martínez is a recent graduate of the Master's in Migration Studies Program at the University of San Francisco, where she also currently works as a program assistant in the Department of International & Multicultural Education.

Orubba Almansouri is a doctoral candidate in urban education at the Graduate Center of the City University of New York and an educator at the Brooklyn International High School for immigrant youth.

Asmaa Amadou is a fashion designer and fiber artist born in Lomé, Togo, and based in Brooklyn. She received her bachelor of arts degree at SUNY–New Paltz in anthropology and French.

Alexandra Anormaliza served as teacher, principal, and district-level leader for over 29 years with the NYC Department of Education. Most recently, she was the senior advisor for education in the New York City mayor's office.

Lisa Auslander, Ph.D., is the principal investigator and senior project director for Bridges to Academic Success, a City University of New York (CUNY) project specializing in curriculum and professional learning for students with limited or interrupted formal education (SLIFE) and newcomer multilingual learners in New York state and districts nationally.

Emma Batten-Bowman serves as the school leader for Rudsdale Newcomer High School—an innovative school she helped develop—in Oakland Unified School District (OUSD). Rudsdale primarily serves recently arrived unaccompanied minors from Central America.

Esther Bettney, Ph.D., is adjunct assistant professor in the Faculty of Education at Queen's University in Canada.

Ariel Borns is a Ph.D. student at the University of Wisconsin–Madison in the Department of Educational Policy Studies.

Dariana Castro is a partner at Transcend, where she leads the organization's partnership strategy. She has previously served as director of school development at the Internationals Network for Public Schools and director of school design at the NYC Department of Education.

Nedda de Castro, a native New Yorker and child of immigrants, is a founder and current principal of the International High School at Prospect Heights, a public high school for new immigrants and member of the Internationals Network for Public Schools.

David Etienne is a school social work intern, with a master's in fine arts, and a candidate for a master's in social work at CUNY Hunter College.

Edmund T. Hamann is a professor in the Department of Teaching, Learning, and Teacher Education at the University of Nebraska–Lincoln and an equity fellow for the Midwest and Plains Equity Assistance Center.

Mary Mendenhall is an associate professor of international and comparative education at Teachers College, Columbia University.

Yvonne Ndiaye graduated from Brooklyn International High School and has an associate's degree in small business entrepreneurship from the Borough of Manhattan Community College and a bachelor's in business administration with a concentration in marketing from Brooklyn College.

Kathleen Rucker is the principal of the Brooklyn International High School, a public high school for new immigrants and member of the Internationals Network for Public Schools and the New York Performance Standards Consortium.

Sailaja Suresh is the senior director of strategic projects at Oakland Unified School District and previously was a founding teacher, instructional coach, coprincipal, and founder of the Learning Lab at Oakland International High School.

Claudia M. Triana is a Ph.D. student in the Department of Education Policy Studies at the University of Wisconsin–Madison.

Laura Wangsness Willemsen helped found Wellstone International High School in Minneapolis in 2001. She is now an associate professor of education at Concordia University, St. Paul.

Joanna Yip, Ph.D., has worked in education as a teacher, college counselor, instructional coach, and curriculum specialist with a focus on multilingual learners. She has also served as an instructor in teacher education programs.